HEAVEN'S BANKERS

Heaven's Bankers

HARRIS IRFAN

THE OVERLOOK PRESS
NEW YORK, NY

This edition first published in hardcover in the United States in
2015 by The Overlook Press, Peter Mayer Publishers, Inc.

141 Wooster Street
New York, NY 10012
www.overlookpress.com

For bulk and special sales, please contact sales@overlookny.com,
or write us at the address above.

Cataloging-in-Publication Data is available from the Library of Congress

Manufactured in the United States of America

ISBN 978-1-4683-1047-4

2 4 6 8 10 9 7 5 3 1

For my parents

and

for Sadia

Contents

Prologue

The Square Mile in the City of London. It's ten o'clock in the evening and in the still buzzing hive of Deutsche Bank's corporate finance division my glazed eyes are staring at now meaningless numbers on the screen. I need to put this bid to bed and get out of this dungeon. When I sleep tonight, my exhausted mind will not be capable of dreaming of anything except numbers appearing in random sequences across rows and columns. Some nights, if I'm lucky, my brain will be a little more active and my dreams will feature death-match grapples with clients or desperate attempts to courier a bid document before an impossible deadline. A few days ago I dreamt that I stepped into the lift with my colleagues and we plummeted twenty floors to our doom.

I have not ordered a late meal at the office: even if I eat at midnight, it will be in the comfort of my home instead of in this corporate slave ship. A bitter November wind is funnelling down Old Broad Street bringing near horizontal drizzle with it. Down below, I can make out the sound of umbrellas snapping out of shape against the onslaught. At least when I'm done tonight it will be late enough for me to charge a cab to the expense account, and travel in relative luxury the twenty-five miles to my home in a sleepy village in commuter-belt Surrey.

The investment bank's head of oil and gas is striding towards me with an enormous cigar jammed in an enormous grin. Despite his brash American accent – and even louder braces – his Southern-style courtesy and folksy manner make him a rarity among his peers. If he wants to chitchat about life and the universe I'm happy to oblige him, even though nothing would be more welcome to me right now than if he volunteered to finish off my bid document.

'Kinda late for ya, huh?' Something about his mannerisms and speech suggests his career was inspired by J. R. Ewing in the well-known TV series *Dallas*. It is perfectly normal for those at my modest pay grade to be here at this time, and he knows it. I am tired and irritable, but he warms to my less than warm response.

'Sheesh, you know, maybe you need to be working for a real team making real money. See, these bastard PPP guys have got you picking up scraps from the lowly table of third tier clients.' He chews on the end of his cigar thoughtfully. 'You need to reassess, buddy.' A dig at my boss, who advises companies on the financing of government-sponsored 'public–private partner-ship' infrastructure projects.

It's clear he hasn't come over to chew the breeze with me. Despite the grin, he seems to have a more purposeful air about him than is usual for our occasional chats at the water cooler. Feigning small talk with a random audience, J. R. casually turns to address the small gathering of late-night devotees huddled around computer terminals, most of them junior financial modellers whose thankless job it is to crunch numbers for people like me to interpret, repackage and convert into bid documents and financial contracts.

'Yeah, well, I would kinda like to save one of you guys from your bondage and have you shipped off to the sunny Middle East. You could be out there building up our investment bank-ing franchise, covering yourself in greed and glory, tax free bonuses, soaking up the sun on the beach, pool parties, Russian hookers in hot tubs, ya know, that kinda thing.'

One of the junior analysts perks up, keyboard clickery tempo-rarily paused, but J. R. has turned towards me, raising an unlit Partágas (Series D No. 4, natch) to his lips. I'm looking at my screen again, pretending I didn't hear him. I have work to do and I want to go home.

The analyst is keen to know more. Is the bank opening a new office? Where? Do you need a financial modeller? J. R.'s answers are vague and do little to satisfy the youngster's obvious interest. He is told that the bank is looking at the broad corporate finance picture in the Middle East and that the main board has decided the time is right to ramp up its activities out there.

'I think project finance skills will be the critical element in our new business model', continues J. R., thoughtfully rolling the well-chewed end of his cigar between his fingers. I'm still looking at the screen but I can sense he is waiting for me to respond. A pause, followed by, 'Yeah, I'm looking at taking on a guy senior enough to build up the franchise, but young enough to be close to the transacting side of the business, ya know, someone who can sell a deal internally within the bank and externally. It'll be all about greed and glory.'

I'm still looking at my screen, although I'm listening. 'Does he get a company Porsche?' I ask.

He lets out a short, high-pitched laugh (now he knows he has piqued my interest) then says, 'Bankers out there are kinda more Mercedes men.'

'Well, I wouldn't be interested then.' Another short laugh and J. R. turns to the other database drones, orders them good-naturedly to beat it and get a life, and walks away. But the bait has been cast.

Nine months later, I am installed in a serviced apartment in the heart of Dubai's rapidly expanding metropolis. The phone rings – it is my wife telling me to switch on the television. It is the afternoon of 11 September 2001 and, several time zones away, New York and Washington are waking up to a day that will define a new geopolitical era. What will follow is an extraordinary growth story in the Middle East region, catalysed by the sudden injection of repatriated Arabian Gulf money (though that story itself is not the purpose of this book). But it is this growth story that has led to the explosion of interest in Islamic finance.

The consequential rapid increase in Islamic assets seems to have been comparatively less affected by the economic crisis of 2007–8 onwards. The global Muslim population of 1.6 billion remains heavily underbanked, and though growth slowed a little, it did not plumb the depths of the conventional banking industry. One industry source believes that whilst the first trillion dollars of Sharia-compliant financial assets took forty years to build, the next trillion will be created within the next two to five years.[1] Others are even more hopeful.[2]

***

In France, Muslim women are banned from wearing the headscarf in schools and the full-face veil – the *niqab* – in public. Ironically, verbal and physical abuse of Muslim women increased after the *niqab* ban.[3] The Netherlands, too, flirts with a ban on Muslim face veils, and one prominent politician campaigns to have the Quran banned, comparing it with Hitler's *Mein Kampf*.[4] In Switzerland, the birthplace of the International Red Cross and the Geneva Conventions, 57 per cent of voters in a referendum approved a ban on the construction of minarets over Muslim places of worship, legislation that prompted even the Vatican to denounce it as an infringement of religious freedom.[5] And the United States, too, is starting to succumb to hysterical Islamophobia. Right-wing conservatives applaud as Oklahoma voters approve a constitutional amendment banning the use of Islamic law, or Sharia, in court.[6]

Their narrative is unequivocal: one neo-conservative group contends that immigrants to the United States sought 'freedom from the discriminatory and cruel laws of Sharia'.[7] For such groups, allowing for an alternative frame of reference when considering marriage, divorce, inheritance or personal finance represents the thin end of the wedge – a perversion of the freedoms that their forefathers fought for. In their world view, covert jihadis – holy warriors – work to bring down the

US Constitution, with violence being their most obvious and unsophisticated tool.

'I believe Sharia is a mortal threat to the survival of freedom in the United States and in the world as we know it', said US Republican politician Newt Gingrich in a 2010 speech. 'Stealth jihadis use political, cultural, societal, religious, intellectual tools; violent jihadis use violence. But in fact they're both engaged in jihad, and they're both seeking to impose the same end state, which is to replace Western civilization with a radical imposition of Sharia'.[8]

To neo-conservatives, Sharia is a monolithic system of medieval oppression: unless it is crushed at source, one day Americans will be forced to pray in mosques and watch public beheadings.

But there is another, more nuanced, view. Reflective observers might discover that Sharia is perhaps far removed from notions of cruelty and punishment. In fact, for the vast majority of Muslim history, a body of Islamic law has developed to accommodate the progression of human civilization, favouring tolerance over intolerance and forgiveness over punishment.

That same research might show Sharia to be more than a collection of archaic and irrelevant laws. It might show that higher moral principles and universally accepted notions of justice are the defining characteristics of Sharia. And nowhere are these notions of justice more apparent than in the body of Islamic jurisprudence related to social and economic interactions. This body of law, crafted from holy scripture and classical scholarly works, has now found its way into the sophisticated modern-day transactions that some of the world's largest banking institutions conduct.

***

I did not set out to become an Islamic banker, though as a Muslim it had always been foremost in my mind that understanding and practising conventional finance would be a means to an end. Back in the early 1990s, at the start of my career in the financial services industry, Islamic finance presented itself to the layman as a curiosity, an alternative method of financing, ethical financing dictated by a cultural need, and very much on the fringes of the mainstream financial system.

How was it that Islamic banks were able to offer products and services that conformed with the prohibition against usury, or *riba* in Arabic (literally an excess or increment)? And is that what Islamic finance was about? No *riba*? Or was there more to it than that?

Indeed there was. My journey to becoming an Islamic financier was a result of being in the right place at the right time, as are many things in life. Around the same time that I arrived in Dubai, the ruler of this tiny emirate in the Arabian Gulf decreed the formation of the Dubai International Financial Centre (DIFC), a square mile of real estate on a patch of desert with little surrounding infrastructure, and no clearly discernible means of earning a solid revenue stream.

The development of a thriving international Islamic finance market would be a cornerstone of the DIFC, building on Dubai's existing reputation as a port city and a regional hub for trading. Deutsche Bank, as one of the very first investment bank licensees in the DIFC freezone, won the mandate to provide strategic and financial advice to the government on the creation of this freezone. Despite my junior standing in the firm, as the sole investment banking representative for the bank in the region I unexpectedly had the opportunity to help shape the future of this emirate as a regional financial centre, in the same vein as Singapore or Hong Kong.

When the news spread of our appointment as DIFC's investment bank, we were approached by a large Saudi building contracting company on the creation of a *sukuk*, or Islamic bond, to finance the development of a series of towers in the Holy City of Makkah, Islam's holiest city, and one into which no non-Muslim (let alone a Western investment bank) had ever been allowed. A remarkable coup.

As we began to cement our reputation in the region, clients started knocking at our door asking us how to transact deals – the kind of deals that they had been doing all along but this time in a manner compliant with Sharia.

My colleagues and I learnt at the feet of the leading scholars of Sharia, those sufficiently versed in both Islamic law and modern finance and economics that they are able to advise and opine on complex commercial and financial transactions, and ultimately to declare them to be in compliance with Sharia (or not, as the case may be). As a result, I was privileged to be present at the birth of a number of innovations in the Islamic finance space, including that *bête noire* of the financial press – both conventional and Islamic – the derivative, those exotic financial instruments that were the catalysts for the financial earthquakes that took place at the height of the global financial crisis. If a derivative is an ethereal, intangible contract, a financial instrument whose value is derived from a 'real' asset but is not actually a 'real' asset itself, then the need for Islamic finance transactions to invest in and refer directly to real, tangible assets makes 'Islamic derivatives' sound like an oxymoron. Perhaps it is, though I will leave it to the reader to judge.

Working across many different types of financial instruments, known in the industry as 'asset classes' – such as bonds, equities, exchange traded funds, real estate or private equity funds – Deutsche Bank made a name for itself as a cutting-edge creator of the most complex financial instruments in a Sharia-compliant format. After a gestation period of two to three years, the Islamic structuring team finally cracked the creation of products whose complexity in the conventional banking industry had hitherto made them apparently impossible to replicate in the Islamic industry – products that could hedge a financial institution's exposure to macroeconomic risks, such as currency movements, or products that could give high net worth investors access to sophisticated trading activities, such as hedge funds. The market was now waking up to asset classes that had previously been closed to Islamic investors and institutions, though not without controversy along the way.

The experience had been thought provoking: was it possible to build an economically viable firm that could offer Islamic financial services on a truly ethical (or should that be Sharia compliant?) basis? Were ethics and profit mutually exclusive?

As I helped to establish Islamic finance in firms such as Deutsche and Barclays, I also delivered training courses on the principles of Islamic finance to my colleagues, from Geneva to Jakarta, some of them private bankers serving high net worth individuals, others investment bankers playing the capital markets. Much of this book was born of the questions I was asked on those training courses and my personal experiences on the real life deals that radically changed the face of the industry. In some cases, commercial sensitivities have required me to avoid naming companies or individuals, though in all cases I have been careful to select transactions that are either particularly groundbreaking in some way, or that represent a classic study of the subject matter in hand.

As this book is not intended to be an academic reference work for practitioners in the field, I have avoided a technical analysis of the products themselves. Instead, the interested reader is directed to the Glossary and will find more detail on my blog: www.heavensbankers.com. Bankers, auditors, lawyers and regulators may find more to get their teeth into there.

I have a deliberately paradoxical intent in publicizing these somewhat arcane mechanisms: to encourage healthy debate among practitioners and observers alike as to whether this industry that I work in is truly 'Islamic', and whether there is a better standard that we can collectively work towards.

Until the industry realizes that Islamic finance is predicated on a different set of rules to mainstream Western finance, a social awareness that underpins the practice of commercial and financial transactions, then an aggressive sales-led investment banking culture that ignores this fundamental ethos will always be viewed with suspicion by the end user of Islamic financial services.

Islamic finance is a discipline that is highly technical in nature, has long lead times to execution, and is poorly understood by senior management at conventional banking institutions. As a result, the inefficiencies of corporate culture, particularly at the biggest firms, have resulted in an industry dominated by those who don't care enough about doing it right.

There are countless examples of investment banks and other financial institutions with no previous history of Islamic financial services hiring individuals who may not be able to marry the complex structural aspects of Sharia-compliant products with the commercial know-how needed to execute deals. The biggest brand names in investment banking have wasted years in incubating a business that was badly designed from the start, an attempt to jump on the bandwagon opportunistically rather than cultivate a long-term business strategically. As a result, these influential institutions have in some cases concluded that there is no future in Islamic banking, though whether the Islamic finance industry should be influenced by 'a great vampire squid wrapped around the face of humanity, relentlessly jamming its blood funnel into anything that smells like money'[9] is perhaps a moot point.

And yet, despite the opportunism and cynical exploitation of an industry geared around people's values and beliefs, in the Islamic world an extraordinary growth is taking place. Islamic finance has become the poster child for that story, with some proclaiming Sharia as a panacea for global economic woes. Is it? In an increasingly polarized environment, can the Islamic world bring something of benefit to the Western world, and vice versa? And are ethics and morality relevant to the pursuit of profit?

Note on Transliteration

Where possible, I have tried to use the conventionally accepted English translations of Arabic words to avoid distracting the reader. Sometimes use of Arabic words is unavoidable, although many of the more frequently used words have already found their way into the English language (words like Sharia or jihad, for example).

The keen student of Arabic will note my transliteration of Arabic words into the Latin script follows convention in some but not all cases.

Most obviously, I have avoided using the reverse apostrophe to denote the guttural vowel 'ayn' since to do so may risk confusion with the glottal stop (conventionally denoted by a normal apostrophe). As a result, words like Shari'a and 'Umar containing 'ayn' are spelt Sharia and Umar instead. Similarly, Qur'an (containing the glottal stop) is spelt Quran. The lack of diacritical marks may also make things easier for the reader unfamiliar with Arabic words. The observant reader will also note that I have made an exception for the word *wa'd* (meaning a promise or undertaking) since it simply looked awkward without the apostrophe, and might encourage English speakers to pronounce it like the English word 'wad', which would mangle it beyond recognition.

I have made no attempt to differentiate between the two types of h, s and t sounds in the transliteration. However, the difference between the q and k sounds is represented (for example in Quran and Kaaba respectively). I have also allowed for the softer 'd' sound by transliterating it as 'dh'.

Some readers may also notice that the transliteration of proper nouns is not always consistent, particularly people's names. I have tended to use the English spellings of individuals' names as used by them: Hussein and Hussain is a good example of the same name transliterated in two different ways.

1

The Quiet Revolutionaries
of Masjid Al-Samad

When the dinar and the dirham were first minted in the form of metal coins, Iblis the accursed held them happily. He then placed them over his eyes and said to them, 'You are the fruit of my heart and the delight of my eyes; through you, I will drive people to become tyrants. I will cause them to become disbelievers and lead them to Hell. I accept from the son of Adam if he would only become attached to you, and worship you, and that's even if he would become indifferent to the remainder of pleasures of this world.

Ibn Abbas

Shortly after the sun rises over the desert dunes in the barren east, Dubai's neon-lined highways and space-age skyscrapers are bathed in colour – the gold, green and silver prisms splaying a spectrum into the Arabian Gulf beyond. All the way to the horizon the Sheikh Zayed Road, a gargantuan roaring river of multi-laned asphalt, begins feeding the city's office towers with workers.

On a January morning in 2011, Bilal parks his car in the underground car park of the Dubai International Financial Centre, takes the lift up to the marble foyer and swipes his security card at the turnstile.[1] Through the glass door of his investment bank's trading floor is an open-plan office, laid out as a miniaturized version of its big brother in London. The room is dominated by two plasma screens: one permanently tuned to the digitized ticker tape of Bloomberg Television, the other directly facing the open-plan office and displaying a live webcam feed from their colleagues' desks in London. This morning Bilal has arrived earlier than his Dubai co-workers – the salesmen and -women of the bank's emerging markets team – and so the chaotic hubbub of simultaneous conversations on a bank of trader-phones is yet to begin.

In the quiet moments before they arrive, Bilal fills his coffee mug and collects his thoughts in preparation for the day ahead. The past few weeks have been difficult. The bank's financial position remains precarious in the middle of the worst economic downturn in living memory. Rumours have been circulating of mass redundancies.

'A rainmaker in the Islamic finance market': that's what they dubbed Bilal when his bosses hired him two years ago. But like the wider banking industry, tumbleweeds have been blowing through the Islamic finance industry for the past couple of years and capricious bosses in London have blown hot and cold on the need for the bank to invest in this frontier market. Can we afford this luxury? Should we devote resources to understanding it? Or should we retrench to what we know best?

Bilal logs in and, almost as if in answer to his concerns, an email pops up. It's good news. An Islamic deal that the bank closed last year has just been awarded one of the industry's leading accolades. It is the first time that an independent body has recognized the bank's contribution to the Islamic finance industry and, as such, is a vindication of the effort of his team.

If the Islamic finance market is about to turn the corner, then this bank will be at the forefront. Perhaps today is going to be a good day.

Bilal settles into the day's work. His firm is in the process of setting up a vast platform, a factory of financial products that conform with Islamic law. The output from this factory will be sold to high net worth individuals and financial institutions in the Middle East, all looking for investments that conform to their religious beliefs. At the same time, Bilal's team is working with banks throughout the Middle East and South-East Asia to establish itself as their preferred banking counterparty on large transactions: currency trades, commodity investments, and 'swap' contracts to lubricate the cogs of the fastest growing segment of the world's finance industry. It is an enormous undertaking and one that he hopes will propel his firm up the industry league tables. But does the bank's senior management team in London believe that?

Bilal's BlackBerry rings from a number he doesn't recognize. It is the head of HR asking him to step into the conference room. He sighs and silently shakes his head – this morning's email arrived too late to make a difference. He knows what this call means and resigns himself to the conversation that is about to take place. Ironically his last act as an employee is to send an email to his colleagues congratulating them on the award. He collects a few personal items and picks up his briefcase.

As Bilal enters the conference room his London-based boss is displayed on a giant television screen on one wall, seated in a glass-fronted corner office at the edge of a vast trading floor in Canary Wharf. In the conference room itself are the head of HR and the bank's chief executive officer for the Middle East. In front of all three are identical pieces of paper. Their manner is impeccably professional, though they manage to look both grim and kindly at the same time. Yep, this looks pretty final.

The woman from HR begins reading a script, 'We regret to

inform you that your position is being made redundant as of today.' As she reads on, Bilal cannot help the flicker of a smile curling from his lips. Somewhat perversely he finds his mind detaching itself from the situation and begins to enjoy the faux sympathy of his co-workers, as if he were watching this practised ritual in a television drama. Even as she reads on, Bilal is reminded of the contempt he has for the corporate world, for the way in which it dehumanizes every protocol, every inter-action between employer and employee, between boss and subordinate, rationalizing its behaviour in the pursuit of short-term profit over long-term stability.

Bilal's last interaction with his colleagues reinforces his nat-ural cynicism of Big Corporate. He has long held the view that large corporations are incapable of feeling or of acting in their employees' and their customers' long-term interests. Modern corporations create social arrangements that force employees to reduce the world to a collection of potential threats, opportun-ities and the accumulation of wealth. This enforced morality renders all other considerations inconsequential. Corporate social responsibility, ethics, integrity: they are just words used by the press office. Perhaps it is this outlook that steered Bilal towards Islamic finance in the first place.

Bilal snaps back to the conference room. Who will take up the Islamic mantle after he leaves? His boss doesn't feel it is neces-sary to be in the market. 'You're a good guy and it's nothing personal. We just don't need someone of your ability or experi-ence – the products aren't complex enough.' The regional CEO squirms uncomfortably in the seat next to Bilal. He has spent the past year telling his clients and colleagues in the Middle East how strategically important it was to offer Islamic finance in this market and now he will be forced to backtrack. But he plays the party line and nods his head as his London colleague explains why the bank will not continue to pursue Islamic finance.

'I'm afraid I have to ask you to hand in your BlackBerry

and security card,' says the woman from HR apologetically. Phlegmatically, Bilal blinks slowly, reaches into his pocket and hands them over, still with a half-smile on his face. 'Is there anything we can get from your desk? A personal mobile? Your wallet?' Bilal shakes his head.

'In order for you to receive your redundancy payment, there is an agreement we will require you to sign.' She hands over the compromise agreement, a catch-all designed to ensure that the terminated employee does not rat on the firm, defame it in public, or solicit any of its employees or clients. Bilal takes the paper, shakes hands with his colleagues and is escorted out of the building.

And that's it. In an economic downturn precipitated by unethical practices the bank has decided that a system of finance based on ethics and morality was an unnecessary luxury, and Bilal's two years of work are wiped clean. And although the bank's senior management do not yet realize it, their number is up: the bank will shortly be indicted by authorities around the globe in a massive financial scandal.

A short walk away, over at Goldman Sachs's Dubai offices, the Islamic finance specialist is also having a bad day. His firm has just tried to raise $2 billion of finance from Islamic investors and is struggling. For some reason, Islamic investors are staying away from Goldman Sachs, and ethics and morality may be the reason.

And in eighteen months' time, the world's largest provider of Islamic banking products to retail customers, HSBC, will be investigated by the US authorities for alleged links to drug money and terrorist financing. Despite the healthy commercial returns from HSBC's subsidiary, Amanah, HSBC will shut down Amanah's Islamic retail banking operations in key markets. Officially, its excuse for the withdrawal is that '[HSBC] allocate[s] capital to markets and businesses with clear growth potential. . .we [therefore] no longer offer Shari'ah compliant products in some markets.'[2] Only a few months earlier, HSBC Amanah's own chief executive claimed that these markets were growing at an incredible rate of 23.5 per cent year on year.[3] But something has changed internally and, according to bitter insiders, Amanah finds itself an unwilling political football.

* * *

The House of Wisdom

Every Friday, in the first three or four rows of the congregation at the Masjid Al-Samad – an avant-garde cubically proportioned mosque serving the Emirates Hills area of Dubai – one will find the epicentre of today's Islamic finance revolution. As the imam begins his weekly sermon, in those front rows will be silently sitting two CEOs of Islamic financial institutions, and five of the world's leading Islamic finance bankers and lawyers, all of them global heads of Islamic finance at gigantic investment banks and English law firms. Many of their staff will also be at this gathering.

This is New Dubai. Twenty kilometres south of the old creek dredged by the first ruler of Dubai, this previously virgin desert stretches south towards the emirate of Abu Dhabi, the area redeveloped so that expatriates can buy their own freehold properties and establish themselves in the United Arab Emirates as more than merely transient economic migrants. Not many in this Friday congregation of some thousand worshippers are aware that a quiet revolution – one that may have a far-reaching impact on the global banking system – is being orchestrated by a handful of men (for the instigators of this revolution are almost exclusively men), many of whom sit among them at this moment.

A neatly turbaned Australian-Egyptian with a trim beard stands at the pulpit. His speech is thumpingly cadenced and impassioned, his audience rapt. Today's sermon is about knowledge.

'Centuries ago, Muslims built a civilization of excellence based on beneficial knowledge', he says. The English-speaking congregation sit cross-legged on the floor of the mosque and look up in silence at this charismatic lay preacher, a forty-something university lecturer who translates the official Arabic sermon:

Allah tells us in the Quran:

Behold what is in the heavens and the earth!

He says 'behold'. What does this mean? It means we are instructed to seek knowledge, to contemplate the secrets behind creation, and our status is raised if we seek knowledge and education. And this is what we were doing while Europe was in its Dark Ages. Between twelve hundred and seven hundred years ago, Baghdad was the world's intellectual capital, and *Bayt al-Hikma*, the House of Wisdom, was its heart. How many of us know this? How many of our kids are taught this at school?

He looks around at his congregation. It's pretty clear that their Western-centric education has taught them that Galileo was the father of astronomy; that Thales, Socrates and Descartes gave birth to modern notions of philosophy; and that almost nothing happened in the medical world between Hippocrates and the development of vaccines in the nineteenth century.

Little is taught in the Western world of Islamic history, but it is difficult to fathom why, given the geopolitical importance of the Islamic world today. So influential is Western learning in all its facets that, even in the Arab world, few today know much about the House of Wisdom, an institute of learning from the heyday of Baghdad, which collected the cream of intellectuals and culture into one powerhouse of arts, science and letters.

The Australian preacher's eyes twinkle as he peppers his speech with glorification of his Lord. He tells his congregation that Muslim scholars translated works from every scientific and philosophical discipline across the world into Arabic, an undertaking so productive that, without it, today's Europe would not be reconnected with its own ancient scholarly history. A spiritual quest to derive the secrets of the heavens and the earth – as their Lord had instructed them in the Quran – would lead the Islamic scholars of the Middle Ages to reinvent the sciences, to rationalize the seemingly magical world around them. No matter what the source of the knowledge they absorbed, if it were of benefit it would be incorporated into their own works. From the ninth century of the Christian era onwards, with a population of over one million and second in size to Constantinople, Baghdad boasted a reputation for intellectual prowess and riches second to none. Under the reigns of the caliphs Al-Rashid, Al-Mamun, Al-Mutadhid and Al-Muktafi, its denizens existed on the cutting edge of science and technology, arts and literature, of civilization itself. The Caliph Al-Mamun is reported to have had a dream in which Aristotle appeared to him saying: 'Knowledge has no borders, wisdom has no race or nationality. To block out ideas is to block out the kingdom of God.' Al-Mamun is then reported to have instructed men to travel to Byzantium and Persia, to bring back the greatest books from their libraries, and establish a centre for scholarship and learning in Baghdad, the House of Wisdom.

Four generations of caliphs took a personal interest in the development of this centre of learning: the collation of manuscripts, the building of a library and its wings for each branch of science, the procurement of works from all over the world, sometimes brought in by 100 laden camels, all instigated and overseen by the rulers.[4]

As the sermon and congregational prayer are concluded, the preacher reminds his audience of a traditional saying of the Prophet Muhammad (peace be upon him):[5] *Who took a path asking in it for knowledge, Allah enhances a path for him to Heaven.* Then the congregation rises. They greet each other and plan the weekend's football matches and family picnics. Their families are part of one community, sharing dinner parties, births and deaths, an old-fashioned connectedness that they didn't find in their home countries – for most of them the United Kingdom – where each has typically spent the first thirty years of his life before migrating in search of fortune. That fortune lies in Islamic finance.

Quite how Dubai, and this area of Dubai in particular, has managed to attract so many singularly qualified individuals is difficult to fathom. Perhaps there was a design at work, man-made or otherwise. Perhaps it is the serendipitous confluence of many factors: the creation of an international financial centre; the repatriation of Gulf money from overseas following 9/11; the increasing perception of Islamophobia in Britain, prompting an exodus of the best and brightest minds; the 'East meets West' tolerance of this emirate, the creation of its freehold property zones and subsequent real estate boom.

Traditionally the Islamic finance industry was once populated by bookish experts in Sharia law, often graduates of Indo-Pakistani universities, typically sincere and ideologically led, but more often than not lacking a commercial background, or the hard-nosed business sense to rise to the top of a commercial organization. Their specialism was understanding canonical law derived from the word of God, recorded in the Quran, and the actions of their Prophet – the *Sunnah* – that provide them with a precedent. They know what God wants from us: to be good to our fellow man. They know that God wants us to be fair and just in our dealings with one another. That we should be transparent and equitable. That social harmony is an over-riding objective in any of our day-to-day human interactions. But can they help us to translate these simple principles into a system that ensures profit may be pursued, and men may become wealthy as a result, but that wealth is also equitably distributed, and the vulnerable are protected? In other words, a just or caring form of capitalism.

Before Masjid Al-Samad, the industry attracted conventional bankers alongside the bookish Sharia experts. Sometimes these bankers were the ones who couldn't quite make it in conventional institutions and saw Islamic banks as a soft alternative, and sometimes they were the opportunists who saw it as a chance to make a quick buck.

But that is changing, and Masjid Al-Samad may find itself a precursor to a modern-day House of Wisdom and a reclamation of past glory, emerging from the confluence of individuals within Masjid Al-Samad and their part in the global banking system. The bankers and lawyers of Masjid Al-Samad are forging their own path, 'asking in it for knowledge'. Their idealism has the backing of technical competence, and they look to apply the techniques they've picked up from the conventional (Western) banking industry to expand Islamic finance far beyond its ancient principles of justness and transparency in commercial dealings.

Perhaps it may be a fantasy too far to suggest that this is what is happening today in Dubai – a cosmopolitan melting pot and a forum for discourse in Islamic finance. Perhaps, with the patronage of Dubai's ruler, the Islamic finance industry may find its own Muhammad Al-Khwarizmi, the father of algebra, or its own Al-Kindi, the most accomplished of Arab philosophers.

Or perhaps in the mad scrambling race to accumulate wealth and celebrate growth, this is but a fanciful romanticism. Time will tell. Regardless, in the fight for the spoils in a trillion-dollar industry, Dubai remains a key protagonist, and its access (within a short flight) to a large share of the global Muslim population may hold the key to its dominance of the industry.

According to a number of analysts, the total dollar value of assets of Islamic financial institutions is over one trillion dollars,[6] dwarfed of course by its equivalent in the conventional banking industry, but nevertheless a gigantic leap from its near zero value in the early 1970s. Although Islamic banking growth has declined in recent years in line with the wider economy, it has continued to outpace overall banking assets and gross domestic product (GDP) growth. In the depths of the global financial crisis in 2009, for example, Islamic assets grew at 15 per cent whilst total banking assets remained static and GDP growth was negative.[7]

The Islamic banking market has consequently increased its share across the Islamic world, with particularly notable gains in the markets of the Gulf Cooperation Council (the GCC, comprising Saudi Arabia, the UAE, Bahrain, Kuwait, Qatar and Oman), South-East Asia (mainly Malaysia and Indonesia) and Turkey. Not surprisingly, conventional banks have been desperate to tap into this lucrative customer base, though their so-called 'Islamic windows' have met with variable success, as we shall discover throughout this book.

What are the origins of modern Islamic finance?

To consider this question one must first separate the activities of merchants in early Islamic history whose business was conducted according to the tenets of Sharia, and the activities of modern financial institutions who purport to conduct financial transactions according to Sharia. It is the latter that I focus on throughout this book, though in examining the extent to which such institutions have met both the letter and spirit of Sharia, we will benchmark against the fundamental precepts that have applied to Muslims throughout the ages.

The birth of modern Islamic finance occurred sometime in the 1950s or perhaps the 1960s, depending on what we choose to be the catalyst for the growth of the industry as we know it today. European mutual banking institutions and cooperatives may have been the inspiration for social banking experiments in the early 1950s in Pakistan, as well as for the formation of the Malaysian Tabung Haji (a fund set up by the Malaysian government to assist pilgrims travelling to Makkah) in the 1960s. However, typically many observers tend to credit the Mit Ghamr experiment in Egypt in 1963 as the forerunner of today's Islamic banks.

Eighty kilometres north of Cairo, Mit Ghamr is a town on a branch of the Nile, today producing around 70 per cent of Egypt's total aluminium output. In 1963, the economist Dr Ahmed Elnaggar devised and implemented a remarkable experiment in this otherwise unremarkable town. He founded the Mit Ghamr Savings Bank, a profit-sharing institution that neither charged nor paid interest, and engaged in what today would be referred to as 'real economy' transactions. Thus, it engaged in trade and industry, sharing its profits with depositors, functioning less as a commercial bank and more as a vehicle for savings and investments.

The experiment lasted four years, during which time eight other similar institutions sprang up in Egypt. In time, the Mit Ghamr Savings Bank would become part of Nasser Social Bank, which would be declared an interest-free commercial bank. Interestingly, to avoid the impression that the experiment and its consequential creation of a commercial institution were driven by an overtly Islamist agenda, the charter of Nasser Social Bank made no reference to Islam or the Sharia, a dilemma that some apparently Sharia-compliant institutions are facing today.

The baton of the Islamic finance industry quickly passed to pioneers in Saudi Arabia, Kuwait and Dubai. The first Islamic banks in the GCC were capitalized in the mid-1970s, including the largest bank in the UAE, Dubai Islamic Bank. At first, the experimental phase of the modern Islamic finance industry produced institutions that were true to the principles of risk sharing, building on concepts of investor/manager relationships in which a provider of capital entrusts that capital to a specialist for the purpose of investment, and both parties share in the ensuing profits or losses: the essence of Islamic finance, rather than the borrower/lender relationship typical of conventional banks.

The experiment continued in Pakistan following General Muhammad Zia ul-Haq's military coup in 1977, after which he installed himself as the country's president and merged Sharia laws into Pakistan's existing penal code. In 1979, Zia introduced a programme intended to Islamize the economy and, on 1 January 1980, around 7,000 interest-free counters were opened at the nationalized commercial banks. Pakistan had become the first nation to establish a fully fledged Islamic banking system.

But Pakistan's courting of Islamic economics was overly simplistic, focusing on basic issues related to interest-free banking, the abolition of *riba* (interest), the laws of inheritance and *zakat* (the annual wealth tax that all Muslims are obliged to pay). Some questioned why Islamic imperatives of equality and social justice had not been addressed by the imposition of an Islamic economy, and surmised that it was another attempt to assert an Islamic identity based more on a political agenda in parallel with Zia's support for the resistance against the Soviet invasion of Afghanistan, and the development of a nuclear capability.

The programme was crudely implemented. A cousin of mine recalls being ordered by family elders in the port city of Karachi to (literally) get on his bike and collect the family savings from the bank (in this case Habib Bank and United Bank Limited). The hapless youngster cycled furiously from branch to branch, one of many who were sent out that week by families desperate to withdraw their savings before the deadline for a compulsory tax payable on each bank account. This, the 2.5 per cent compulsory *zakat* stipulated in Islam to be payable by all on one's wealth, had become the reason for a run on the banks.

The minority Shia community had argued that it should be exempt from the compulsory deduction, since it operated its own community *zakat* system. Indeed, my cousin heard heated debates amongst uncles arguing that perhaps it was time to use the family Shia connection. After Zia's death in 1988, the programme was terminated and the economy reverted to a conventionally Western basis.

As the business model of GCC-based Islamic financial institutions matured, early pioneers such as Dr Elnaggar and Sheikh Saleh Kamel, the founder of the Dallah Al-Baraka Group, began to observe that such institutions operated by mimicking the practices, operations and customer products of conventional banks, and were failing to deliver economic and social development to the Muslim demographic. It is certainly the case that conventional international banks did not fail to recognize the potentially enormous demographic they had hitherto failed to tap. It was clear that their recognizable brands, economies of scale, access to talented product designers – known in the industry as structurers – and pushy international sales staff had the capability of ousting established Islamic institutions as the bank of choice for the Muslim customer. In time, their 'Islamic windows' would be regarded as the engine rooms of growth for the Islamic finance industry.

At first, international banks merely oiled the wheels of motion in the industry by providing money-market lines to Islamic banks desperate for liquidity. As they cottoned on to the potential for growth, their bankers approached Sharia scholars directly to learn more about the structuring of products on a Sharia-compliant basis, and established their own departments to do just that. The scholars were flattered by the attention – the world's largest financial institutions were willing to lavish unimaginable remuneration on these clerics for their knowledge of Islamic commercial law.

By the early 2000s, the Islamic windows of conventional banks were employing conventional experts in the various disciplines of international finance – specialists in mergers and acquisitions, infrastructure finance, real estate finance, derivatives, equity share markets and corporate loans – all of whom had studied the basics of Sharia contracts, and all of whom had started to establish direct relationships with key departments in Islamic institutions. These key departments included treasury operations that manage exposure to market rates, currencies and other volatile macroeconomic variables; proprietary trading desks who invest the bank's own money; private wealth management teams who sell funds and sophisticated personal investment products to high net worth customers. Now the conventional banker was deeply connected to an entirely new customer base.

Most significantly, the biggest international institutions, known as the 'bulge bracket', were able to call upon their abundant global resources to sell Sharia-compliant bonds, or *sukuk*, to investors around the world, just as they would for corporates and sovereigns raising conventional bonds in the international capital markets. Just as companies could raise money on international exchanges by issuing bonds – a loan divided into tiny pieces to be traded like a stock – so, too, could they raise an Islamic bond to be sold to Islamic investors. *Sukuk* would change the face of the Islamic finance industry: a publicly traded debt of a corporation or a sovereign nation, owned by and traded amongst thousands of investors, looking and feeling like its conventional equivalent: the bond. Until recently, those Islamic investors looking to own 'fixed income' instruments – that is, those which pay out a fixed running yield for the maturity of the debt – had few alternatives to the conventional, interest-bearing bond. Perhaps they could buy a property and rent it out to earn a fixed income yield. They could do the same with other large assets, like ships and aircraft, but these were not 'liquid' instruments – ones that could be converted into cash quickly and easily with a relatively stable price on an open market. Now the bond had become Sharia-compliant and Islamic investors were able to step into a more sophisticated trading arena.

The infrastructure for these tradeable debt instruments was

already there: technology from the world of conventional bonds to price and trade *sukuk* on exchanges, offices around the world populated by hungry young salesmen and -women with clients desperate to diversify their investment holdings away from the stodgy world of conventional corporate bonds.

The bulge bracket firms, aptly described as 'flow monsters', immediately sensed that the key to raising money for their clients in the form of *sukuk* was their superior firepower, their industrial ability to create giant 'financial factories' to make product 'flow' out of the door. Local and regional Islamic institutions in the Middle East, and to a lesser extent in Malaysia, simply could not compete with the likes of Deutsche Bank, HSBC, Citibank and Goldman Sachs. And as governments and large corporations looked to fuel their aggressive infrastructure and expansion pro-grammes in the post 9/11 boom, diversifying their traditional investor base was foremost on their mind. Who better to target than the under-served Islamic investor – and how better than to harness the financial muscle of the biggest global players?

In the public mind, *sukuk* became the Islamic finance industry. Often touted in the press as 'bonds which circumvent Islam's ban on interest', by the mid 2000s they had become the tool of choice in the GCC and Malaysia to raise capital on an enormous scale. Global investment banks built their Islamic finance prac-tices on the back of selling billions of dollars of *sukuk* for their multinational clients. Ironically, more than half of the notional value of *sukuk* was sold to conventional investors looking for alternative places to park their money or looking for exposure to new geographies or asset classes. In the language of finance, these conventional investors were seeking 'alternative risk/ reward relationships'.

This was understandable. At first, yields – that is the rate of profit on the bond, typically paid to the bond investor in the form of a periodic coupon – were particularly attractive for investors as the risks inherent in the Sharia-compliant contracts that governed the bond and the bond's underlying assets were not clearly understood. When investors cannot clearly quantify the risk inherent in a given financial instrument, they attach a risk premium to its price – they expect to be paid more because they perceive it to be more risky. Although the contracts governing a *sukuk* transaction are typically drafted under English law, they are also drafted in adherence to the principles of Sharia, and this creates a potential for dislocation between a court's view of English law and Sharia. Not surprisingly, many perceive this as an additional risk.

In theory, the coupon on a *sukuk* instrument (economically the equivalent of interest on a bond) is supposed to be generated as a result of the income or profit resulting from the financing of an underlying asset. So, for example, a company may issue a $200 million *sukuk* to finance its ongoing activities, typically by selling real estate assets that it owns to the *sukuk* holders. These *sukuk* holders are often represented by a 'ring-fenced' shell company known as a special purpose vehicle or SPV, specifically set up for the purpose. Having paid the $200 million purchase price to own the real estate, the *sukuk* holders (represented by the SPV) then lease those assets back to the company, and the ensuing periodic rental income becomes the equivalent of a periodic coupon on a bond. Once the *sukuk* mature – in other words when the 'loan' terminates – the real estate assets owned by the SPV are sold back to the company typically for a consideration equal to the original issuance value of the *sukuk*.

The net economic effect is that the company has 'borrowed' $200 million and paid a rate of return to the creditor for the duration of the borrowing, then repaid the $200 million on maturity. During this time, a real asset passed from the borrower to the lender and back again.

When a real asset passes between the parties, the *sukuk* is described as 'asset-backed'. In other words, the lender has recourse to that specific asset in the event the borrower can't repay. And that's good, because there is a tangible link between the financial paper trade and the real commercial one.

In practice, most *sukuk* end up being 'asset-based' rather than truly 'asset-backed'. In such a case, although there is some contractual link between the financing and the underlying asset, the originator of the *sukuk* – in other words the company raising the financing – is the ultimate guarantor of the bond. The company guarantees the repayment of this bond through a 'buy-back' mechanism at maturity, a commitment to repay. As a result, the credit rating of the *sukuk* is in fact the credit of the originator (the company raising money), and not that of the specific assets that underpin the *sukuk* (such as real estate owned by the company).

No wonder conventional investors were so keen to add these exotic new instruments to their portfolios, and no wonder so many asked the question 'what is Islamic about Islamic finance?' *Sukuk* looked and acted like conventional bonds, and conventional investors could now diversify their exposure to new geographies and assets, earning significantly more than they would for conventional issuers of equivalent credit quality.

In time, as investors became more familiar with Islamic issuers and Islamic finance in general, *sukuk* yields began converging towards their conventional equivalents and for a while all seemed well in the world.

And then came the global financial crisis, precipitated by the bursting of the US housing bubble in 2007 and the subsequent institutional failures of September 2008. Within a year, a number of high-profile *sukuk* had defaulted. Suddenly, Sharia risk loomed large on the radar of financial institutions, both Islamic and conventional. The Islamic finance industry began experiencing an existential crisis and the 'Samadiites', the young bankers and lawyers of Masjid Al-Samad in Dubai, found themselves at the centre of it.

2

The Nature of Money

What is condemned is the greed of wealth that is unable to
see beyond one's selfish desires. . .

Justice Mufti Muhammad Taqi Usmani

In January 2010, at the World Economic Forum Annual Meeting
in Davos, the erudite and prolific Sharia scholar, Justice Mufti
Muhammad Taqi Usmani, was invited to present a paper with a
somewhat radical theme: reforming the world's post-crisis financial landscape through the lens of religion.[1] The paper generated
little interest from the world's media, who preferred instead to
focus on the lack of plans for reform or 'real achievement', and
the predictably defensive stance taken by bankers.[2] Had they
taken the time to read the thirty-seven-page document, they
might have concluded that 'caring capitalism' had the potential
to be perhaps more than a mere romantic notion.

Yet Mufti Taqi Usmani's paper proved inspirational for
introspective Islamic bankers searching for direction, in that
it questioned the very nature of money, thus inviting a radical
philosophical shake-up of their ordered universe. Perhaps few in

the audience (if any) were moved that day to tweak their banking practices as a result of the paper's suggestions for reformation of the world's financial system, but they nonetheless came away with the counsel that social awareness ought to be the underpinning of finance.

When you read in the newspapers about the launch of another new Sharia-compliant product, or the establishment of a financial institution that conforms to the principles of Sharia, it is often the case that journalists refer to Islamic products as ones that 'conform with the religion's ban on interest', as if that were the only relevant criterion. It is as if every time we read about the conventional banking industry we are reminded parenthetically that the business of banks is to make loans with interest, ignoring the diversity of activity that retail bankers, private bankers, investment bankers and fund managers engage in. Accordingly, in the minds of the public, Islamic finance seems to stand for one thing – no interest.

Perhaps as a direct consequence, there are Muslims who find the modern practice of Islamic banks abhorrent, and little different to the practice of conventional banks. Their reasoning is that if Islam prohibits the receipt or payment of interest, then the only business that Islamic banks should be engaging in is interest-free lending, conveniently ignoring the fact that an interest-free loan is construed as an act of charity in Islamic law, and no enterprise driven by the profit motive can be predicated on charity.

The profit motive is an emotive subject for Muslims, particularly when set in the context of a world economy creaking ominously under the weight of capitalism as we know it. To what extent is the pursuit of profit acceptable in Islam, if at all? How is one allowed to make profit in a *halal*, or permissible, manner? How are Islamic financial institutions allowed to deploy and invest capital to be profitable in a manner that is compliant with Islamic law?

In order to begin to answer these questions, let's consider the value system inherent in Islam. To understand how and why Muslims behave as they do – or perhaps, more accurately, how they are instructed to behave – we note that Islamic thinking revolves around the fundamental belief that there is one God, Allah, and that the universe is created and controlled by Him.

A brief examination of the word 'Islam' will provide us with a clue to understanding why Islam governs every aspect of a Muslim's life, even those aspects that a non-Muslim would deem to be outside the domain of religion. Islam literally means submission – submission to the will of Allah. In a world dominated today by Western cultural practice, freedom has come to signify that most precious attribute of a civilized society: freedom to think what we want, say what we want and do what we want, within the bounds of the (man-made) law. And yet the very word Islam implies that we are dependent upon, and submissive to, God, the ultimate arbiter. And so freedom is contained within the bounds of sacred law.

The 'Muslim' is one who has submitted, and the ethical value system that governs his or her everyday thoughts and actions are derived from two sources. First, from the word of Allah (documented in the Quran), as revealed through His final messenger, Muhammad. Second, from the *Sunnah*, the actions and sayings of Muhammad as recorded in the Hadith, the books that document the *Sunnah* through a chain of scholarly authority.

These two sources lead the Muslim to believe that every thought, intention and action is an act of submission to the sovereignty of Allah. The way of life espoused through the Quran and *Sunnah* is intended to promote a healthy and balanced society, in equilibrium with itself. How Muslims conduct their daily business dealings is one aspect of ensuring this harmonious balance, and hence why a system of commerce that adheres to Islamic law has become such an essential consideration for Muslims today. So when we talk about Islamic finance, what we really mean is a framework for commercial and financial transactions in accordance with the principles of Sharia, as derived from the Quran and *Sunnah*.

In order to establish what are the guiding principles – the principles that will lead to a just distribution of wealth, to accommodate the economic needs of all segments of society on a fair basis – we need to begin just after the beginning.

Codifying the Sharia

In the year 632, or the tenth year after the Prophet Muhammad had fled persecution in his home town and migrated with his followers to the agricultural oasis of Yathrib, he led his people on the first Muslim pilgrimage – the Hajj – back to his birthplace, the holy city of Makkah. From the pulpit of a dusty valley near the bleakness of Mount Arafat, the 63-year-old Prophet delivered what would become his final sermon. For three months later he would fall ill with fever and die with his head resting in the lap of his wife, Aisha.

During that final sermon, God revealed a verse to the Prophet that would turn out to be suitably timely: 'This day have I perfected your religion, and completed My favours upon you and approved Islam as a religion for you.'[3] And in those words God would be putting His seal of approval on a lifetime of the Prophet's actions. The Prophet had been the messenger whose mission it was to leave behind the word of God, setting out the principles to govern people's daily lives. His actions – the *Sunnah* – had been duly recorded and orally transmitted by his many companions, as an example to his followers, and his final sermon was the culmination of that lifetime's work.

The final sermon was succinct and yet at the same time widely encompassing. In it, the Prophet began by reminding his followers that life and property are a sacred trust, that they should hurt no one by their actions, and that they would one day meet their Lord who would reckon their deeds. He continued: 'Allah has forbidden you to take *riba* [interest], therefore all interest obligation shall henceforth be waived. Your capital, however, is yours to keep. You will neither inflict nor suffer any inequity.'⁴

Muhammad realized he was entering his final days and perhaps took what he saw as his last opportunity to raise once again issues of the utmost importance, issues that he didn't want his *ummah* – his nation – to let lapse. His final sermon covered women's rights, the need to perform the daily prayers, to fast during the month of Ramadan, and to give to charity. He emphasized that no Arab had superiority over a non-Arab, no white over black nor vice versa, except by piety and good action. And he ended by reminding his followers that he was the last of the messengers of God, and that no other would follow him, and therefore that the Quran and *Sunnah* would be the definitive legal precedents for all time.⁵

It was a farewell remarkable for its timeliness and impact, one that would be felt for centuries to come. To the Prophet's followers, the finality of this last speech at the Mount was palpable: 'I know not whether after this year, I shall ever be amongst you again. Therefore listen to what I am saying to you very carefully and take these words to those who could not be present here today',⁶ he told them. In the space of a few minutes, the Prophet had reminded his followers for the last time that human rights and property rights were paramount. That justice and fairness should be a driving force in their daily lives. And that they now had a complete framework from which to build a new world, irrespective of whatever the curiosity and ingenuity of the human mind would discover or create.

With the death of the Prophet, the link with divine revelation was abruptly severed and the Prophet's nation would be forced to think for itself. For some, the death of the beloved Prophet was inconceivable. One of the Prophet's closest companions, Umar ibn al-Khattab, almost fainted at the news but regained his composure to stand before the gathered crowd. He swore fiercely that the Prophet would return just as Moses had communed with his Lord in secret for forty days and forty nights, and condemned those who said he was dead as hypocrites. Few would risk the considerable wrath of Umar except the Prophet's closest companion, Abu Bakr as-Siddiq.

'Umar, be seated,' he told him calmly and Umar refused. Abu Bakr continued. 'Whoever worshipped Muhammad, prayers and peace be upon him, let them know Muhammad is dead now. But whoever worshipped Allah, let them know He is Ever Living and He never dies.' As Abu Bakr recited a verse of the Quran reminding the people that Messengers were mortal but the message was eternal, Umar fell to his knees and grieved. Where would divine law come from now?

In the frighteningly infinite possibilities to come, the nation of Islam would discover new ideas, push the frontiers of knowledge, and grapple with the critical question of whether such new concepts were permissible according to God's law. Astronomy, mathematics, chemistry, medicine, architecture, commerce – all of these disciplines and more would be subject to the scrutiny of the clerics. The Prophet's companions, and the men who would come a generation after them, would turn out to be the codifiers of God's law, particularly in the field of commercial transactions, and their legal analysis would prove to be the lubricant for the advancement of human knowledge, rather than an insurmountable barrier of dogma and intolerance that many today have come to regard as the attributes of religion.

Though the Prophet had advocated charity to the poor and needy – and had himself lived an austere life – he had certainly not decreed *haram*, or impermissible, the accumulation of wealth. The Prophet himself had been a competent *mudarib* – that is, a trader or manager of other people's capital – and there was no indication that a man may not be both rich and pious at the same time. Nor had he discouraged a market economy, though he had consistently advocated an equitable distribution of wealth within that economy.

Though an outwardly inflexible and strict man, Umar ibn al-Khattab – the grief-stricken companion who threatened to kill anyone who said the Prophet had died – was driven by the idea of the protection of the weak, and it was he who carried forward the idea of a compassionate society on the Prophet's death. As the second caliph of the new Islamic era, Umar instituted the *Bayt al-Maal*, the 'House of Wealth', a state-run financial institution responsible for the administration of taxes, including the distribution of *zakat*, the charitable wealth tax. He established the Central Treasury in the city of Madinah, and introduced welfare programmes to ensure equality and a basic standard of living was extended to all citizens. In Umar's quest to ensure systematic provision for widows, orphans, invalids, the unemployed and the elderly, limitations were placed even on governors and officials, with the most manifest example of this being Umar himself whose personal wealth was meagre despite his status as the leader of what quickly became an empire.

He introduced the concept of public trusteeship and public ownership through the charitable trust system, the *Waqf*, a legal form of social collective ownership that allowed public property to generate an income stream for the benefit of the needy and contributed to the building and maintenance of schools and hospitals – and that has survived and evolved to this very day in, for example, the English trust law.

The basic principles of social advancement through charity and commerce were thus in place at the time of the Prophet's death and through the subsequent institutional creations of his closest companions. By acting as conduits for the redistribution of wealth, rather than by using their positions to accumulate wealth (as pre-Islamic rulers had done), they were building an egalitarian society rather than an aristocratic one. But the Islamic world still needed the right person to turn these principles and social institutions into practical commercial tools, tools that might lead to a type of caring, or just, capitalism. With a little insight, the principles could be codified to place constraints on greed, speculation and opaqueness. They reprioritized the very nature of money itself.

Abu Hanifa – the founding father of Islamic economics

One man in particular would come to be regarded as one of the greatest scholars of Sharia that the world would ever see. Born at the turn of the eighth century in the town of Kufa in what is now Iraq, sixty-seven years after the death of the Prophet, Al-Numan bin Thabit at first demonstrated little inclination to a scholarly life, though his was certainly a pious one. His family lineage has been lost in the mists of history, but some suspect his grandfather was a former slave of a conquering Arab tribe, and likely to have been of Persian descent.[7] As a merchant in the garrison town, Al-Numan's textile business flourished and he established a reputation for scrupulous honesty and fairness. In time he would come to be known as Abu Hanifa, a nickname meaning 'the Father of Orthodoxy', and the parallels between the Prophet's reputation as a merchant – who himself had earned the nickname Al-Amin, meaning the Trustworthy One – as well as the Prophet's closest companion, Abu Bakr as-Siddiq – who had been a textile merchant – did not go unnoticed.

Subsequent generations would relate many stories about Abu Hanifa, but perhaps one of the most famous – and most indicative of the man himself – was the purchase of a silk garment from a woman who came to his store. The lady offered to sell the garment to Abu Hanifa for 100 dirhams but Abu Hanifa would not buy it. 'It is worth more than a hundred', he told the surprised woman. 'How much?' he asked her again. She offered to sell it for 200 dirhams and he turned her down. Then she asked for 300, then 400, at which point the exasperated woman scolded him. 'You are mocking me', she declared, and prepared to walk away from the deal to try her luck elsewhere. So they summoned another merchant and he solemnly valued the garment at 500 dirhams. Rather than profit from the woman's ignorance, Abu Hanifa had opted to settle for a fair trade, a principle he would abide by all his life – that the greedy should be regulated from taking advantage of the vulnerable.

It was not until a providential encounter with one of Kufa's leading jurists that the young Abu Hanifa finally embarked upon his calling. Whilst walking to the market one day, the merchant was spotted by a locally famous scholar named Ash-Shabi. The scholar called out to the young man and scolded him for passing by while wrapped up in his temporal thoughts of making money and without an apparent care for the spiritual. 'Do not be heedless', he said. 'You must look into knowledge and sit with the scholars. I discern alertness and energy in you.'[8] And indeed Ash-Shabi had been right. There was something about Abu Hanifa, an indefinable presence, a greatness even. Or perhaps, more prosaically, it had just been the older scholar's way of making small talk with a passerby. Whatever the case, Abu Hanifa decided not to go to market that day, and instead sat with Ash-Shabi's students.

It was immediately clear that Abu Hanifa had a preternatural scholastic aptitude. Before long, he had immersed himself in and mastered theology, literature, grammar and poetry. He systematically analysed and codified the application of Islamic law. His predisposition towards fairness in dealings with one's fellow man inspired him to develop a legislative framework for commercial and social interactions based on the life and actions of the Prophet. He and his students and followers, the Hanafites, would develop his ideas, enshrining the works of ancient Greek philosophers, themselves the subject of much research in Persia. The foundation stones of Islamic economics would be laid on a bedrock of a systematic development of Sharia.

To Abu Hanifa, God was supremely rational. Instead of shunning alternative philosophies and schools of thought, and providing they did not conflict with fundamental principles encapsulated in the Quran and *Sunnah*, Abu Hanifa embraced them. Here on the banks of the Euphrates River, the town of Kufa was part of the cradle of Western civilization, a nodal hub of knowledge and an ideal birthplace for a man who was liberally inclined and inquisitive, as he himself observed.

'I was situated in a lode of knowledge and jurisprudence, so I learned the jurisprudence of Umar, of Ali, of Abdulla ibn Masud, and of Ibn Abbas,' he said, referring to the scholarly companions of the Prophet who had preceded him. 'The most knowledge-able of people is the one with the most knowledge of people's differences.'[9] He proposed that Muslims should seek to deter-mine from the Quran and *Sunnah* the purpose underpinning God's laws. Logic and analogy were the key tools to codifying the law and soon the Hanafites would clarify the Quran's prohi-bitions on commercial speculation and unjust transactions. They critically analysed each and every recorded action of the Prophet to determine its authenticity and authority. Where they found no direct Quranic or prophetic guidance on a matter, or where the actions of the Prophet's close companions unearthed little new information, they exercised their minds to derive additional rules. First, by logical deduction, then by analogous deduction, then finally by relying on the social customs of the time. These were the roots of jurisprudence and the evolution of the Sharia itself.

Abu Hanifa's work – and those of others like him – on the fundamentals of jurisprudence, followed by the codifying of commercial law, would eventually lead to the development of a widespread money economy, with gold and silver giving way to paper notes. At first, traders relied on prophetic injunctions against usury or uncertainty in transactions or manifest exam-ples of immoral behaviour (avoiding selling goods suspected as being stolen, for example). As scholars like Abu Hanifa built upon prophetic traditions, cheques and letters of credit followed naturally, and before long a market-oriented capitalistic economy – underpinned by an ethical code – was thriving in the Islamic world. Arab and Persian merchants forged trade links to India and the Far East, becoming indispensable in the chain of trade between East and West. An Arab merchant from Baghdad might travel to Cordoba in Spain, taking with him a letter of credit – a *suftaja* – to be encashed on arrival by an agent, part of a network of money transfer that came to be known as *hawala*. Indeed the *hawala* would go on to influence the development of the agency concept in common and civil laws throughout Europe. The *sakk* – the forerunner of our modern-day cheque, and the singular of the word *sukuk* – allowed the early banker to become indispensable to every trader as a guarantor of paper money at markets in cities throughout the Islamic world.

Sugar cane, cotton, rice and silk were not the only commodities that the merchants brought with them. Like early management consultants, they disseminated knowledge along their trade routes, advancing fundamental human development on the way: the production of silk and paper from China, the use of the compass and numerals from India, the development of financial tools to oil the wheels of trade from the Arabian peninsula. An agricultural revolution was taking place, with Muslim traders introducing crops and plants along their trade route and spreading advanced farming and industrial techniques, such as water turbines and gears in mills. In boosting agricultural yields through the mechanization of production, Muslim traders – and the later Crusaders who carried ideas back home with them – laid the foundations for Europe's Industrial Revolution some centuries later.

These Muslim traders would share the profits of their ventures with their sponsors in a pre-defined manner that would come to be the hallmark of Islamic economic activity, an investment partnership that modern Islamic banks now refer to as *musharaka* and *mudaraba*. An exchange economy became the framework for Islamic merchant capitalism.

The main cities of the Islamic world became the centres of Islamic capitalism. Islamic commerce shifted from Baghdad to Cairo, strengthening trade links into the Mediterranean. Whilst Europeans were venturing little further south and east than the islands of Greece, Arab and Persian traders were ranging across continents. By the tenth and eleventh centuries, ultra high net worth merchant families – the Rockefellers and Rothschilds of their day – began to dominate commercial activities between the two cultures. In the major cities along the East/West trade route, the *funduq* was born: a trading exchange, like a large shopping mall, often the centre of trading activity for a leading merchant family in the region. The *funduqs* developed into commodity exchanges and warehouses, and the great wealth accumulated by the families who controlled these exchanges enabled them to finance state projects and operate an early form of banking institution, taking in deposits and advancing credit to customers.

Within a few centuries the Crusaders would encounter Arabian merchants and carry their new-fangled ideas – such as the trust law encapsulated in the *Waqf* and the agency concept intrinsic to the *hawala* – back to the Mediterranean. Not only would the techniques of commerce and finance filter through to medieval Europe, but also an entrepreneurial spirit of enterprise that had, to date, been less widespread in Europe. Ironically, given the negative connotation that 'capitalism' has today – with all its implications of greed and selfishness – it was the Islamic world that institutionalized capitalism and brought it to the West in the form that we might be familiar with today. Somewhere along the way, 'Islamic' capitalism – of the type that Abu Hanifa legislated in favour of, and that afforded protection to the weak and the needy – became diluted.

At a time when Islamic ideas of commerce were starting to

filter through to Europe, the Islamic world began to lose many
of the essential characteristics of 'Islamic' finance. Inheriting the
mantle of defenders of the faith from their Arabian brethren,
the Ottomans rose to become the pre-eminent Muslim power
by the end of the fifteenth century, and their approach to
financial and monetary institutions was pragmatic and flexible.
Dispensing with customs, traditions and religious guidance
became a characteristic of the early Ottoman Empire, aided
no doubt by the heterogeneity of a region populated by both
Christians and Muslims speaking in Greek and Turkish.[10]

Although earlier banking systems such as the *hawala* method
of money transfer were still widely in use, and the 100,000
pilgrims travelling annually to Makkah continued to make
use of the *suftaja* bill of exchange in order to draw money at
their journey's end, court records of Anatolian cities show that
interest-based lending was a frequent and apparently tolerated
practice. Most disputes were in relation to small-scale transactions from person to person, with interest rates ranging from
10 to 20 per cent.[11] There appeared to be no attempt to con-
ceal the interest-bearing nature of the transaction, and indeed
the local pious endowments became important providers of
credit in major urban centres. Though some clerics denounced
the practice of charging interest as incompatible with Sharia, the
majority adopted the pragmatic view that disallowing the practice might harm the community.

Ottoman merchants continued to make use of the business
partnership models developed by the earlier classical scholars,
models such as the *mudaraba*, or investment partnership, which
typically financed long-distance trading ventures without resorting to a fixed interest charge. These risk-and-reward sharing
models had certainly not been killed off by the reversion to conventional banking practices, nor was the need lessened for earlier
innovations such as the letter of credit. However, little development of an Islamic system of economics and finance took place

during the 600 years of Ottoman power. As European money-lenders gained in prominence, eventually Ottoman practices fell into line, and it would not be until the middle of the twentieth century that Islamic finance would reassert its identity.

The legacy of Abu Hanifa

And so today, several decades into the modern post-colonial era and shortly after the Mit Ghamr experiment, we meet one of the men who has taken up the legacy of the classical scholars such as Abu Hanifa. Mufti Taqi Usmani – our incongruous speaker among the pinstriped suits at Davos in 2010 – is no stranger to controversy. A retired judge on the Sharia Appellate Bench of the Supreme Court of Pakistan, he has established himself as one of the world's leading contemporary scholars of Islamic jurisprudence, and is a recognized authority on Islamic finance, economics and the books of Hadith.

Wearing a long straggly beard often traditionally dyed with henna, his moustache trimmed in accordance with prophetic tradition, and uncorrected dentures hinting at his humble origins, he speaks with a heavy subcontinental accent. At first, the urbane Western sophisticate will struggle to identify with and be captivated by the words of this outwardly unremarkable and slightly built man. Born in the city of Deoband in northern India in 1943, he studied at the Grand Mufti of Deoband school in Pakistan, and went on to further study at Darul Uloom in Karachi. Armed with degrees in law and Arabic literature, he taught Hadith whilst authoring books in Arabic, English and Urdu on subjects ranging from Hadith and jurisprudence to comparative religion and Islamic finance.

He was a key driver in the creation of Pakistan's Meezan Bank and now chairs the Sharia board of the quasi-regulatory body, the Bahrain-based Accounting and Auditing Organization of Islamic Financial Institutions (AAOIFI). AAOIFI's stated aim is to prepare accounting, auditing, governance, ethics and Sharia standards for Islamic financial institutions and the industry. Although an independent international organization supported by 200 institutional members, it is widely viewed as an authoritative body whose pronouncements on the acceptability or otherwise of contractual structures in relation to Islamic financial instruments are to be viewed in the same vein as regulatory edicts.

In November 2007, Mufti Taqi Usmani courted controversy through his remarks made to a Reuters journalist at the annual AAOIFI conference in Bahrain, an event attracting the heavyweights of the industry, including the eighteen Sharia scholars who sit on its Sharia board, and who provide guidance to the Islamic finance industry on matters of Sharia compliance. At that conference, I completed my own presentation and stepped off the stage to make my way to the heaving buffet tables with my fellow Samadiite bankers and lawyers. Mufti Taqi had been part of the same panel, politely observing the slick executives alongside him making thinly disguised pitches for their products. Their brash presentations were filled with structure diagrams so complex that they looked like electrical wiring circuits, peppered with the impressive argot of their industry. By contrast, the modest scholar had no PowerPoint slides and quietly reiterated a mantra familiar to those who knew him: if the Islamic finance industry was about bringing the spirit of the Sharia to our daily business interactions, then the industry needed to focus on profit-and-loss-sharing principles that contrasted with the rapacious debt culture of the conventional banking industry. He was approached by a young Reuters journalist looking for a scoop. There was nothing unusual in this post-conference interview ritual, but on this occasion perhaps the eminent scholar was caught a little off guard. The journalist was intrigued to learn more about the contractual structure of *sukuk*, the tradeable debt instruments issued by borrowers looking to raise Islamic funds from investors. These Islamic bonds evidently seemed to be guaranteeing repayment of the bond, somewhat at odds with the Islamic concept of sharing in risk when funding a business venture. The journalist wanted to know where the risk was if the borrower undertakes to repay the bond in full, and how this distinguished the *sukuk* from a conventional interest-bearing bond.

'For current *sukuk*,' responded Mufti Taqi, 'risk is not shared and reward is not shared according to the actual venture proceeds. About 85 per cent of *sukuk* are structured this way.' The man from Reuters thought for a moment, pondering Mufti Taqi's words, which suggested that *sukuk* have the same structure and risk as conventional bonds and that most *sukuk* in the markets today are not in compliance with Sharia.

The comments were published the next day under the headline 'Most *sukuk* not Islamic'[12] and a cold sweat broke out across the Islamic finance industry. Investors began to ask themselves whether the Islamic financial instruments that they held in their portfolios were truly Islamic. Suddenly the proprietary trading desks of Islamic institutions – those who manage an institution's own investments – as well as Sharia-compliant fund managers and high net worth individuals were faced with the very real prospect of being forced to dump their assets. If the investment parameters of a given fund stipulated Sharia compliance of its holdings, then it would have no option but to divest. Had the vast majority of buyers of *sukuk* been only conventional institutions, this would be no issue, but given the substantial investment by Sharia-compliant investors and institutions, the nightmare scenario had come to pass.

Fortunately, the anticipated crash in *sukuk* valuations never took place, at least not as a result of this pronouncement. For two or three months, investors held on, seeking clarity from their own Sharia boards, and clarity came in the form of a directive drafted by the Mufti himself, and issued by AAOIFI in February 2008. Crisis averted, the industry mopped its brow and went back to work.

Money – a commodity to be traded?

Rather than taking at face value the notion that the world's leading Islamic finance scholar believes the Islamic finance industry is substantially a fake, it is necessary to consider this in more detail. I have already hinted that social awareness is the underpinning of Islamic finance, that human beings should do good to one another, that whatever contractual and social relationships they have with each other should be just and equitable, and to their long-term mutual benefit. But there is something almost as fundamental to consider, a concept that endows Sharia-compliant finance with its sturdy endoskeleton. It is the question of money: is money a commodity to be traded?

According to the Sharia, money is merely a means to achieve an objective and not the objective itself. In itself, money has no intrinsic utility or usufruct. It cannot be processed to build a house or be woven into clothes. It cannot be eaten and it does not provide heat or shelter. It cannot be created out of itself. It cannot be created from thin air. It is merely a store of value.

At a stroke, we immediately come into conflict with the modern notion of money as a commodity. Today, central banks are printing money in a process that economists term quantitative easing. They *create* money. Financial institutions enter into phantasmagoric trades with one another, with corporations and with individuals, to lend money and receive more in return; to enter into 'contracts for differences', or swaps, where one party swaps one cash flow for another (for example, in interest rate swaps or forward currency transactions); to sell highly complex intangible instruments whose values are derived from other assets and to which they may not themselves have legal title; to take speculative positions on the outcome of events over which the buyer of the instrument may not have an intrinsic interest.

In all of these transactions, value has apparently been created even where a real economy transaction has not taken place. Recall the Mit Ghamr experiment: an institution whose primary role was to enter into trades in the real economy, to invest and develop businesses so that investors' money was put to work in a tangible way. And when those investments came to fruition, investors would share in the spoils alongside the manager of their money, the 'bank'. This was an institution where money was a store of value, a medium of exchange, a means to achieve an objective, and not a commodity to be traded between borrower and lender, the objective itself.

If individuals cannot earn money from money by depositing it into an interest-bearing bank account, they will be forced to put it to work. Hoarding money would defeat its purpose.

So now we come to what conventional observers understand to be the definition of Sharia-compliant banking: banking without interest. Interest on money becomes an injustice because money is required to exist for another purpose, a purpose that the modern financial system appears to have bypassed, injecting into it anabolic steroids and juicing it up on 12,000 volts.

The celebrated twelfth-century Islamic theologian and thinker Abu Hamid Muhammad ibn Muhammad Ghazali, more commonly known as Ghazali, analysed the nature of money, stating that Allah had created dirhams and dinars 'so that they may be circulated between hands and act as a fair judge between different commodities and work as a medium to acquire other things'. He concluded that 'whoever effects the transactions of money is, in fact, discarding the blessings of Allah, and is committing injustice, because money is created for some other things, not for itself. So the one who has started trading in money itself has made it an objective, contrary to the original wisdom behind its creation, because it is an injustice to use money other than what it was created for.'[13]

Ghazali had not reached this view in isolation. Indeed Aristotle had argued over a millennium earlier that gold and silver had no intrinsic value, an argument that Ghazali would uphold and build upon many centuries later.

If we are prohibited from trading money, then we cannot create money out of money, and we cannot lend at interest. And this religious injunction was not unique to Islam alone. Some anthropologists argue that before money, there was debt.[14] Five thousand years ago, elaborate systems arose to enable early agrarian societies to buy and sell goods and services on credit, since coinage had not been invented. So a farmer buying clothes from a merchant might pay with an IOU. If the merchant then decides he needs to fix the door on his house, he gives the IOU to a carpenter. The carpenter accepts, on the basis that the farmer's standing in the community is good and he'll make good his debts. Eventually, after a series of transactions within the community, the farmer buys goods or services from a party who holds his IOU and pays it back with some crop from his harvest. The IOU doesn't even need to come full circle. It can stay in circulation for ever, acting in the same manner as modern money. Money originates as debt.

When the community becomes large and powerful it gains the ability, as anthropologist David Graeber argues, to conquer and enslave neighbouring peoples. Now human beings are reduced to mere inventory, material commodities to be traded.

Early civilizations held surplus commodities in temples – essentially large commercial and industrial concerns – and these commodities were lent out to merchants to transport for trade. Auditing the profits and losses made by merchants would have been impossible for the temples, so instead of taking a stake in the merchants' trading activities, the temples would have demanded a fixed rate of return. In other words, interest. In turn, merchants would also lend to others at interest. As these loan contracts became more prevalent, they became more elaborate: now merchants demanded collateral against the debt. Typically collateral started with grain, livestock and household goods, but if the debtor was still unable to pay, and the collateral was insufficient to redeem the outstanding principal, then there would be one option remaining: offer up oneself or one's children or wife as a debt peon[15] – as bonded labour, until the debt was repaid. Owning a human being became debt's most egregious manifestation. Slaves were no longer just war booty. Now they could be anyone. The debt could be passed from generation to generation and violent coercion became the primary enforcement mechanism. In years of bad harvests in Mesopotamia, the poor became increasingly indebted to rich neighbours and would start losing title to their fields, becoming at first tenants, then sending their children to become bonded servants to creditors' households, then finally enslaved and sold abroad.

In several early civilizations, those slaves who escaped their bonds would join nomadic pastoralist tribes. Once these tribes had grown large and powerful enough, they might return to overrun the cities and conquer their existing rulers, and the cycle would repeat itself: the wealthy lend to the poor, the poor are enslaved, some poor break free, become powerful and enslave their former masters. It is not hard to see why, for example, Nehemiah, the governor of Judaea in the fifth century BC, issued a Babylonian-style clean slate, the Law of Jubilee, ruling that all debts would be automatically cancelled in the Sabbath year (in other words, every seventh year), and debt peons would be returned to their families.[16] Nehemiah's Mesopotamian ancestors had done just the same to preserve economic order and avoid being overrun by the desperate poor.

In fact, this practice still exists in some form today: in January 2013, a parliamentary committee in Kuwait took a step closer to avoiding an Arab Spring-style unrest by proposing to pay off interest on loans incurred by citizens over a six-year period. Two years earlier, the ruler had granted 1,000 dinars (around US$3,500) to each citizen and free food rations for thirteen months.

Religion and capitalism

Throughout the ages, intellectual movements questioned the morality of materialism, and the necessity of violence and conquest to uphold the economic system. Religion came to play an important role in galvanizing opinion against materialism, debt and usury. Jesus visited Herod's Temple in Jerusalem at the time of the Passover, when hundreds of thousands of pilgrims would have been in the city. He would thus have had quite a crowd witness him furiously expelling money changers from the Temple: 'And making a whip of cords, he drove them all out of the Temple, with the sheep and oxen. And he poured out the coins of the money changers and overturned their tables, and the seats of them that sold doves. And he told those that sold the pigeons, "Take these things away, and do not make my Father's house a house of trade."'[17] 'My house shall be called a house of prayer, but you make it a den of robbers.'[18]

Throughout the Bible, numerous injunctions can be found against usury, and early Christian universities debated as to why it was sinful: it was theft of material possessions, or a theft of time, or an embodiment of the sin of Sloth. Yet in time the Church found itself looking the other way as moneylenders found they might exploit semantic differences between 'interest' and 'usury', the latter being considered a severe and oppressive form of mere interest.[19] Islamic law, meanwhile, remained unwavering on the issue of usury, treating money as a means to an end, not the end itself.

Medieval Christian financiers had a neat solution to the problem of usury. In a passionate treatise advocating the reform of the modern economic system, *The Problem With Interest*, the former derivatives dealer turned Islamic finance consultant, Tarek El Diwany, describes an elaborate medieval ruse known as *contractum trinius*. This legal device allowed moneylenders to circumvent the Church's ban on usury and some analogies may be drawn between this and some practices evident in modern

Islamic finance: 'The investor would simultaneously enter into three contracts with an entrepreneur: to invest money as a sleeping partner; to insure himself against any loss; and to sell any profits over and above a given level back to the entrepreneur in return for a fixed amount of money per year.'[20]

In isolation, each of the three contracts remained compliant with the Church's injunction against usury, though in combination a loan with interest had quite evidently been created. *Contractum trinius* allowed financiers to meet the letter of the law but not the spirit. In time, even this combination of smoke and mirrors would disappear, as the substance of the transaction became acceptable and the form was dispensed with in favour of simple bilateral agreements. Centuries later, those moneylenders would find even more abstract methods to conjure trade from a unit of value.

El Diwany goes on to note that the acceptability of interest-based finance throughout the world makes the objections of today's Muslims appear conspicuously old-fashioned:

'Nowadays, injunctions against usury from religious quarters are frequently seen as little more than an embarrassing appendage of backwardness, motivated perhaps by simple-minded distaste for the money-lenders of old. Often, the religious arguments seem unscientific and weak when placed before the articulate economists of the pro-interest camp.'[21]

And indeed within modern investment banks, Sharia-compliant financing techniques are wearily viewed as a necessary additional service for a demographic of unsophisticated and anachronistic clients. The cadre of young and ambitious structurers and sales staff touting these products may have little empathy with the philosophical framework within which their clients live. To many of these bankers, Islamic finance is merely the provision of modern sophisticated instruments, whether interest bearing or not, within an alternative legal jurisdiction. The key is to find the appropriate legal devices to circumvent the restrictions under which Islamic finance may operate. It is a common complaint of the lay observer that much of Islamic finance has merely mimicked its conventional counterpart, and added little in the way of ethical or moral guidance, or a participation in the real economy.

As Ghazali had presciently noted about the financier, 'it becomes easy for him to earn more money on the basis of interest without bothering himself to take pains in real economic activities. This leads to hampering the real interests of humanity, because the interests of humanity cannot be safeguarded without real trade skills, industry and construction.'[22]

Was Ghazali predicting the rise of the modern financial services industry? Had he, eight centuries ago, foreseen the rise of the modern banker, predisposed to seeking 'value creation' in increasingly arcane manipulations of global cash flows? The same generation of bankers who have presided over the creation of a derivatives market worth more than ten times the world's total gross domestic product? Or had he perhaps failed to conceptualize a future in which the world has been miniaturized, where commodities and cash could be beamed from continent to continent in the click of a button, and where corporations and governments would look to hedge their exposures to macroeconomic risks on a global scale through complex instruments that we call derivatives?

Let us briefly consider what Ghazali might have meant by real trade. Typically, a trade involves the transfer of ownership from one party to another for a consideration. It is generally understood that the seller has ownership of the subject of the trade, and indeed this is a precondition of a trade in Islamic jurisprudence: that the seller must not sell what he does not own.[23] In addition, the seller must also have the goods in his possession,[24] which is closely related to the injunction that the seller may not earn profit from a commodity the risk of which he does not assume.[25]

These are the rules of engagement for trade in the real economy – they are simple rules and designed to ensure apportionment of risk in appropriate measures, and transparency in risk assessment. So far, so good. What does this mean for modern commercial and financial transactions? So much of modern commerce involves profiting from movements in markets in which one does not have tangible involvement. 'Short' selling, that is selling what one does not own, is a common trading technique often used by hedge funds – typically funds that invest in a manner that generates an 'absolute return', in other words a return that is uncorrelated with the wider market, and able to extract profit perhaps even when markets may generally be in decline. They are so called because they tend to hedge their positions to movements in markets, for example by 'going long' (or buying) certain stocks, whilst simultaneously 'going short' (or selling) others. This natural balancing act means that they may find positive returns in markets whether those markets are bullish or bearish.

Modern economists and observers of financial markets tend to have a strong fundamental belief that the ability to short a market ensures free and efficient markets. In contrast, scholars such as Mufti Taqi Usmani believe that short selling is a characteristic of speculative markets, and that actual delivery of sold goods is often not a characteristic. To Mufti Taqi, the end result of a series of such ghost transactions is the payment or receipt of a difference in prices, such a system resembling gambling rather than commercial business.

The requirement for certainty and transparency in any commercial transaction leads us to another characteristic of Sharia-compliant transactions: that one may not sell a debt or cash flow. Without full control on the goods being sold, the seller is entering into a trade that creates uncertainty for both parties. If a seller owns debts that are payable to him from his obligors, it is not a certainty that those debts will in fact be repaid. By selling such debts to another party, the risk of default is also being transferred to that buyer. The buyer will lose a portion of the money paid to the original seller should one or more obligors fail to repay their obligations. In Islamic jurisprudence this uncertainty is considered a fundamentally unjust transaction.

But what if both parties have mutually agreed the terms of that sale of debt? What does it matter? After all, both have accepted the uncertainty inherent in the transaction and take their own (presumably calculated) risks. Not so, says the branch of Islamic jurisprudence concerned with commercial transactions. Mutual consent does not necessarily justify a transaction. The sale of narcotics may be by mutual consent but that does not make it permissible. Bribery may be by mutual consent, but does not benefit the interests of society at large. If a transaction either fails to meet the interests of both parties, or has harmful social implications, that is, it is *unethical* in the secular vernacular, it may not be consummated. And in Islamic law, interest is considered harmful to society, whether we choose to label it interest or usury to denote an 'excessive' rate of interest, as the Church eventually did.[26]

To Ghazali and his present-day successors, capital must be deployed in other ways to generate a permissible profit. According to the scholars, the equitable way of utilizing the savings of depositors is to deliver to them a proportionate share in the profits – and losses – in investments undertaken on their behalf. Can today's depositors, accustomed as they are to unexciting and secure returns on their deposits, be persuaded to share their profits with the bank, or indeed to contemplate the possibility of losses on their principal? Are businesses seeking to raise capital from financial institutions prepared to relinquish some of their profits to the bank? Or perhaps will only the more risky ventures find this profit-and-loss-sharing model an attractive proposition on the basis that the bank is prepared to share the downside with them as well?

In the context of the modern banking system, depositors might need to make a giant leap of faith in order to consider placing their principal in an institution whose business model seems primarily equity based rather than debt based. But that is just the point. That an economic system should be based on the concept of risk sharing, of equity. And with sufficient diversification and tranching of deposits so that depositors can specify the level of risk they are prepared to accept, according to explicit investment parameters, perhaps the Islamic banking model need not be at an economic disadvantage to the conventional model, provided that a critical mass of depositors and business enterprises participate. This is exactly what the Egyptian, Pakistani and Malaysian experiments of the last few decades have tried to achieve with varying degrees of success. Their challenge was to deliver lasting success within the framework of the fractional reserve banking system.

Fractional reserve banking

We're nearing the end of this examination of the nature of money, and yet I've only just mentioned the elephant in the room. If we fail to address the suitability of fractional reserve banking as an appropriate modern economic system, then we cannot have a discussion on Islamic banking and economics. The world economy functions according to this model.

Briefly, it is the practice of all modern commercial banks, who keep a fraction of a bank's deposits as reserves for withdrawal by depositors. These reserves are cash and other highly liquid assets. Money deposited by depositors at the bank is partially retained as reserves, with the majority being loaned out to borrowers or spent on securities. Any money loaned out or spent is deposited with other banks, thus increasing the reserves of those other banks. In turn, they are able to keep a fraction of the new deposit, and lend or spend the remainder. New deposits are continually created as cash travels through the system from bank to bank. The total amount of money available in an economy at any given point in time, known as the money supply (calculated as the currency in circulation plus demand deposits), is expanded by this practice to a large multiple of the cash reserves held by banks.

We can trace the root of this modern commercial banking practice to sixteenth-century Europe. Four centuries ago, state money was denominated in gold, and the goldsmith was the banker, his vault being the bank account. Savers would deposit their gold coins and other precious metals with the goldsmith, in return receiving a 'running cash note' as it was then known, what we would call a certificate of deposit, or a bearer receipt. Anyone bearing this receipt in future and presenting it to the goldsmith would claim back the sum deposited, hence why we still see 'I promise to pay the bearer on demand the sum of five pounds' on a British five-pound note, meaning that the Bank of England's cashier would hand over a 5 lb weight of gold coins on demand (in the days when the notes from the Bank of England still had a link with gold).

In time, depositors came to realize that the receipts from goldsmith bankers could be accepted elsewhere as payment for goods and services. Indeed, why bother returning to the goldsmith to redeem one's running cash note, when one could simply present it to a merchant in exchange for goods? The merchant could simply redeem the note at the goldsmith's or, better still, reuse the note to purchase goods and services for himself. Bank money had been born, and the bearer receipts circulated in the economy.

At this point, the goldsmith realizes that he has a hefty cache of gold locked up in his vaults, sitting idle, whilst the bearer notes they are linked to are gainfully employed and changing hands. It would seem perfectly good business sense for the goldsmith to lend gold to reliable and prudent borrowers, ensuring of course that he did not lend too much in case other depositors demanded their gold back. The fraction of gold held for depositor redemptions is the reserve ratio, and would have been a suitably small enough number (since only a limited number of depositors would redeem at any given time) now that the goldsmith is running a bank in the modern sense of the word, rather than a storage facility for precious metals. The goldsmith has become a banker.

Clearly, the smaller the reserve ratio, the greater the potential for profits from loans, but the greater the risk of being forced to close the bank doors in the event of a 'run on the bank' (depositors simultaneously demanding their deposits back). And why indeed should the bankers lend physical gold to borrowers? After all, if the wider economy found bearer notes to be an acceptable currency, then why not simply lend out their own receipts instead of gold coins? In the event of heavy withdrawals, the bank would simply enter into arrangements with other banks to borrow additional gold.

Bankers made their profits from the interest on lending, on money that they had themselves created. However, the interest had to be repaid with money that had not yet been created. If the total money supply was £10, of which £1 was the total amount of money created by the state, and the other £9 was lent by banks, and the interest outstanding on the total amount of bank loans was a further £2, where will this additional £2 come from? It needs to be created, and there are only two methods to do so: either the state increases the supply of money or the banks lend even more. If neither takes place, borrowers would be forced to default.

And that is fractional reserve banking in a nutshell. A business idea without compare in any industry – a licence to print money – but with significant implications for society.

The world practises it; it is supported by almost all of the world's economists and no practical alternatives are actively considered by any government in the developed world. Capitalist democracies are generally considered the most free and success-ful societies in the world, and their economic model is therefore held up as an ideal. Those who criticized the model were once viewed as lunatics on the fringe of economics, dismissed as long-haired ranting anti-globalization protestors. But in the light of recent economic turmoil, fractional reserve banking has increasingly become a topic for discussion among established economists and scholars. Tarek El Diwany echoes the views of a small group of Western academics and politicians, Muslim thinkers and scholars, and is convinced that fractional reserve banking is the main economic issue of our time. Although those like him might be dismissed by the establishment as misguided and raging lone voices, he believes that the 'mainstream' in Islamic banking and finance has 'studiously ignored [it] for over three decades with fundamental implications for the structure and product range of the industry'.[27]

Are the young bankers and lawyers in Masjid Al-Samad part of the system, ignoring the implications of the methods they use to replicate conventional financial instruments with Sharia-compliant contracts, operating as they do within the mainstream banking system? Are they going through the motions to pay the rent and the kids' school fees? Or are they actively work-ing to create a new economic paradigm, one that they believe could and should change the world for the better? Is their active involvement in the mainstream a work in progress, a means to an end, the only way for Islamic banking and finance to survive, break through and succeed?

If fractional reserve banking was an invention born out of the cunning of the goldsmith banker, and his desire to grow and accumulate wealth, then perhaps the concept of growth itself – that indicator of success in the capitalist system – is at fault. The modern world's emphasis on corporate and GDP growth rates has been known to come at the expense of both the tangible and the intangible: the environment, societal values, marriage, family life, health, safety, mortality. In an Islamic framework, these factors are a fundamental consideration in every business transaction that one undertakes. One is not only to refrain from what is wrong, but to enjoin what is right and good.

I leave you with the story of the American tourist and the Mexican fisherman. Although originally a short story by the German writer Heinrich Böll,[28] this anecdote often gets retold with different protagonists in different settings. Here's the version that I know:

An American businessman stood at the pier of a picturesque coastal Mexican village when a small boat docked. The lone fisherman stepped out with his catch for the day, several large yellowfin tuna. The American complimented the Mexican fisherman on the quality of his fish.

'How long did it take you to catch them?' asked the American tourist.

'Only a short while', replied the fisherman.

'Why not stay out and catch more?' asked the American.

'I have enough to support my family's needs', said the fisherman.

'But what will you do with the rest of your time?'

'I sleep late, fish a little, play with my children, take a siesta with my wife. In the evening, I stroll into the village, sip wine and sing songs with my friends.'

The American scoffed. 'I have a Harvard MBA and work as a management consultant for McKinsey. I can help you.'

'How, señor?' said the fisherman, taken aback.

'Spend more time fishing. With the proceeds, you can buy a bigger boat, and with the catch from the bigger boat, you could buy several boats. Eventually you would have a fleet. Instead of selling your catch to a middleman, you would have the power to sell directly to the customer, eventually opening your own canning factory. You would control the product, the processing and the distribution. You could leave this small coastal village, and move to Mexico City. After that, Los Angeles and then eventually New York where you would run your expanding enterprise.'

'How long would that take?' asked the fisherman.

'Oh, fifteen, maybe twenty years.'

'And after that?'

'Ah, now this is where it gets really interesting', replied the management consultant with the MBA from Harvard. 'When the time is right, you announce an initial public offering, and sell the company's shares to the public. You would be rich, make millions.'

'Millions, señor? Then what?'

'You retire! You can move to a beautiful coastal village where you would sleep late, catch a little fish, play with your children, take a siesta, then in the evening you could stroll into the village and enjoy drinks and songs with your friends.'

3

The Gentler Face of
Londonistan

Deal not unjustly and you shall not be dealt with unjustly.

Quran, 2:279

In the winter of 1996 I was invited to a seminar for Muslim city
workers in HSBC's group headquarters next to London Bridge.
The City of London's famous Square Mile was cosier in those
days: the big banks had yet to move across to the soulless steel-
and-glass campus of Canary Wharf and the clubbier atmosphere
of the City seemed to offer room for diversity and niches.

A handful of curious junior bankers were ushered into a modest conference room to be introduced to a managing director of
Indian origin by the name of Iqbal Khan. Billed as a networking
event, I wasn't quite sure what to expect – a friend had suggested attending, mostly for the canapés, I think, and a chance
to get away from the tedium of our daily grind – but this MD
was something of a curiosity. In an environment where the old
boys' network was still very much alive, and the 'olde worlde'

British merchant bank – all oak panelling and the faint whiff of Monte Cristos – remained pre-eminent in the City, Khan's pencil-thin moustache and Aligarh University education were an anomaly. That such an individual had made it to the lofty grade of MD before the City was invaded by the more meritocratic global investment banks was all the more remarkable.

He greeted us warmly and introduced us to a robed gentleman sitting silently in the corner, his Arab headdress pulled so far forward that for a moment you imagined that seated in the shadow underneath was Sir Alec Guinness in the role of Obi-Wan Kenobi. There was no light-sabre under the robes, though there was an extraordinarily sharp intellect and a ready wit.

I was meeting Sheikh Nizam Yaquby for the first time, and I imagine it was probably the first time the scholar was introduced to a wider audience than a select few bankers at HSBC. Perhaps he really had mastered Jedi mind tricks, as the impression he left on us was indelible and his softly spoken but carefully delivered words would inspire more than one person in the room to pursue Islamic finance as a career.

For Iqbal Khan, the event was more than simply a meet and greet. He was trawling the market, seeking out bright young things, Western educated but with an Islamic outlook. His creation would be the first of its kind: Islamic finance offered to the masses by a conventional bank with branches all over the world. Though Sheikh Nizam would be his spiritual guide, without the right lieutenants installed in key posts Khan's efforts at hacking the jungle to a new frontier would be in vain. If HSBC was to become a world leader in Islamic finance, he needed bankers who could be leaders in conventional finance. Today's gathering was the start of a talent search.

Sheikh Nizam introduced the gathering to the jurisprudence of Islamic commerce: the dos and don'ts of ethical and moral – of Islamic – transactions, and the use of these rules by modern banks to create a new industry. Most in the room were already familiar with the sources of jurisprudence in Islam, and had a passing familiarity with the relevant rulings from the Quran and the Hadith – the books documenting the sayings and actions of the Prophet – though few really understood what it meant for a commercial transaction to be compliant with Sharia.

Fewer still understood the recent history of the modern Islamic finance industry, and knew little of the Islamic finance experiments in Pakistan and Malaysia under Islamist governments. But this was different. This was not a social experiment, or an apparently insidious attempt to introduce Sharia into the daily lives of ordinary Britons.

It had not been many years since Salman Rushdie's *The Satanic Verses* had disgorged thousands of protesting British Muslims on to the streets of London, Birmingham and England's northern mill towns. Britain was fast gaining a reputation for a ghettoized Muslim minority with a tendency towards radicalization. Parts of London had been dubbed Londonistan, a place where women exited the house in full black *burqa* and men assembled at their community mosques dressed in long white Arabic *thawbs* or the baggy-trousered South Asian *shalwar kameez*.

But the urbane Iqbal Khan's soiree was not an attempt to change legislation or evangelize a way of life. This was about a commercial attempt to offer an ethical system of finance for everyone, Muslim and non-Muslim. HSBC was here to make money, and if non-Muslims found something beneficial in its product offering, so much the better.

There would be, and had been, attempts to introduce Sharia into legislation in other parts of the world, of course. Only three years later, the Supreme Court of Pakistan would look to ban interest on deposits and loans, and in an historic judgement would put forward arguments for and against the eradication of interest. Not surprisingly, it would be a colleague of Sheikh Nizam, the eminent Mufti Taqi Usmani, who would lead that effort. But today's gathering was not about a campaign against centuries-old English law, it was about kick-starting a practical initiative at the coal face of banking within the existing legislative environment. It was about convincing young bankers that there was a future in ethics and social responsibility.

Sheikh Nizam spent the evening explaining the basic rules of the Islamic finance industry. Although by 1996 the industry had barely progressed beyond simple commodity-based transactions, within a short space of time firms such as HSBC and Deutsche Bank would begin to operate at the cutting edge of product development, giving birth to new markets in complex Sharia-compliant financial instruments: *sukuk* to raise capital for corporations and governments in increasingly innovative ways; hedging instruments to manage the exposures of financial institutions to movements in currency fluctuations, commodities prices and borrowing rates; and investment products for the trading desks of institutions or for sophisticated high net worth investors to invest in different asset classes in markets around the world. In time, these investment products would attain the sophistication of their conventional counterparts, with (for example) the ability to protect investors against market losses, or 'gearing' financial instruments to accelerate their profits.

Sheikh Nizam explained that the guiding principles of Islamic finance were based on the principles of human interaction in the Sharia: fairness, justice, equality, transparency and the pursuit of social harmony, all such principles derived from the primary sources of Islamic law. But how does one engage in commercial and financial transactions in such a way as to remain compliant with the Sharia, so that ultimately wealth is equitably distributed, and so that a just and equitable form of capitalism is established?

In the absence of explicit legislation laid out in the two primary sources of Islamic knowledge, Muslims rely on qualified jurists to undertake *ijtihad*, literally an 'exertion', or the act of a scholar to expend effort in examining textual evidences. If performed according to the correct methodology, this intellectual exertion will lead to a ruling on a given matter and these rulings constitute the body of knowledge known as *fiqh*, or jurisprudence.

Jurisprudence and the role of scholars

Finance in its modern form with its many sophisticated applications did not exist at the time of the Prophet. Yet today scholars opine on the manner in which individuals may invest in a venture, or engage in commercial transactions with one another, on the basis of the moral principles laid out in the Quran, the actions of the Prophet and his companions, and the body of jurisprudence arrived at by a process of intellectual study. In addition, rulings in Sharia that contribute to the body of jurisprudence may be arrived at through consensus achieved among a community of scholars. This scholarly consensus is a key component of Islamic jurisprudence and is often employed by jurists as an evidence of a particular ruling.

The next two sources of jurisprudence are a little more complex and subjective, and perhaps the manner in which they are explored may lead to a difference in opinion amongst scholars, even though they may agree on the basic guiding principles. They are the assignment of a ruling by analogy to a prior ruling, and the accepted and established customs of a community. The application of analogy in particular is a carefully considered process, requiring the jurist to examine the original case on which a ruling was made, refer to the new case requiring a ruling, find the attribute or effective cause of the prohibition present in both cases, and then ruling on the second case by analogy with the first. A scholar's view on modern financial instruments will require this methodology to a large extent. The established customs of a community, on the other hand, would appear at face value to be more straightforward. If a custom of a community does not contradict explicit injunctions in the primary sources of jurisprudence, then the custom may be considered acceptable.

The sheikh ran through these sources of jurisprudence at breakneck speed, aware that his audience would quickly tire of a law lecture. He didn't touch on the collection of principles that jurists employ to derive the body of law. He didn't spell out in detail the legal maxims identified by jurists over several centuries, and often used as guidance in the application of Sharia. Nor indeed did he suggest the process by which Sharia scholars are appointed or approved by their communities.

With our limited understanding of the nascent Islamic finance industry, we hadn't thought to ask perhaps the most pertinent question of this softly spoken and enigmatic man. Who are you? What makes you and others like you qualified to opine on Sharia, those attributes that make you a rare and precious commodity?

This single man was able to wield power and influence within some of the world's largest financial institutions, with far-reaching economic consequences. Scholars are the lifeblood of the industry, and it is often said there are not enough of them to go around. According to traditional sources, the list of attributes that scholars are required to possess is long, and underpinned by an individual's personal qualities. Classical scholars from Islamic history were known to toil for years to reach sound legal conclusions. The burden on them was considered greater than the burden on the layman – their unenviable task was to interpret the law of Allah, and should they be negligent in their analysis, their punishment in the Afterlife would be all the more severe. For perhaps this reason, Abu Hanifa had repeatedly turned down the governor of Kufa's order for him to be appointed *qadi*, or judge, a refusal that led to his imprisonment and torture. With seditions rife in the region, the governor swore to flog the scholar if he refused.

'If he wanted me to restore the doors of the Wasit Mosque for him I would not undertake to do it,' Abu Hanifa told his fellow scholars. 'What should I do when he wants me to write that a man should have his head cut off and seal the document? By Allah, I will never become involved in that!'[1]

Abu Hanifa was severely beaten and fled Kufa to the safety of the Grand Mosque in Makkah, where he immersed himself in the study of Hadith and jurisprudence. When the Caliph Al-Mansur came to power some years later, Abu Hanifa returned to Kufa but was again tested with the offer of a judgeship. The Caliph demanded that Abu Hanifa accept the post of Chief Judge of Baghdad and plied him with gifts – in one case, 10,000 dirhams and a slave girl – which were consistently turned down.[2] Instead of accepting the post, Abu Hanifa continued to make statements and *fatwas* for the good of common people and frequently clashed with the officially appointed judges.[3] Floggings and imprisonment again followed, and he died of his injuries. Some say poisoning by the Caliph may have hastened his end.

I don't dare to equate the lives of the modern jet-setting Islamic finance scholar with the trials of one of the great classical jurists, and though today's scholar may not be subject to the same threat to life that men like Abu Hanifa endured, their burden is not wholly dissimilar. After all, as standard bearers for Islamic jurisprudence, the consequence of getting it wrong is still an eternity in Hellfire. Today, modern scholars have access to modern tools, increasing their efficiency and output. But although libraries of information are now available at their fingertips, integrity, piety and independence remain personal attributes as important as they have ever been. The prevalence of Islamic websites has led many to deride online knowledge seekers as 'Sheikh Google' and 'Mufti Facebook'. Whilst modern information technology is undoubtedly a powerful tool in its own right, it is no substitute for a holistic understanding of Islamic knowledge, often derived through a lifetime of study, although in this respect Islamic jurisprudence is no different from any other academically rigorous discipline.

To be qualified to engage in a process of exertion (*ijtihad*) to reach religious rulings, even the modern scholar must have a classical training. A detailed understanding of theology, law and classical Arabic (to be able to understand the primary texts); a comprehensive grasp of Quran and Hadith, including the context in which each Quranic verse was revealed (and abrogations of such verses as appropriate) or the context in which each legal rite and pronouncement of the Prophet was applied; a sound understanding of the derivation of Islamic legal theory, general legal maxims, and the objectives of the Sharia. Finally, and perhaps the most rare and subjective of all attributes, they must have a keen intellect and be of sufficient wisdom of judgement to be trusted.

And what of these apparent differences of opinion? Are these the same differences that account for why Saudi legislation deems women unfit to drive a car, while in Pakistan, Bangladesh and Indonesia, women have led government? Why some scholars allow their flock to take on a conventional – interest-bearing – home mortgage as an act of necessity, while others shun modern finance of any description?

Most Muslims belong to one of four schools of jurisprudence, all generally acknowledged to be of equal orthodoxy and ranking. On the Prophet's deathbed, he appointed his closest companion, Abu Bakr as-Siddiq, to lead the prayers. After the Prophet's death, a committee of prominent members of the Muslim community decided to appoint Abu Bakr as the *khalifa*, the caliph or deputy of the Prophet, to rule as the first leader of the Muslims. Two more caliphs would follow before the Prophet's son-in-law, Ali ibn Abi Talib, was appointed as the fourth of what are known (by the majority of Muslims) as the *Rashidun*, the Rightly Guided Caliphs. On Ali's appointment there followed a period of political and theological differences in the Muslim community. Since some of the early Muslims felt that Ali should have been the rightful successor of the Prophet as his deputy on his death, they came to be known as the *Shia*, or partisans, of Ali. Thus the Muslim community became split into the majority Sunni and the minority Shia sects, and this split has given rise to some theological differences between the two.

In time, the companions of the Prophet and their followers would transmit knowledge orally, and their students recorded such knowledge, and applied the tools of jurisprudence to undertake intellectual study. For several hundred years after the death of the Prophet, Islamic jurisprudence would experience a golden age of analysis and expansion.

Among the Sunni majority there are generally considered to be four eminent jurists of Islam (imams), each of whom is responsible for an eponymous school of jurisprudence: Imam Abu Hanifa (whom we have already met), Imam Malik ibn Anas, Imam Muhammad ibn Idris al-Shafii and Imam Ahmad ibn Hanbal who respectively give us the Hanafi, Maliki, Shafii and Hanbali schools. In addition, the juristic works of Imam Jafar as-Sadiq represent the school for the vast majority of the Shia community. Not surprisingly, there is some contention in the Sunni community as to whether his juristic views have been correctly represented by the Shia community. In summary, whilst each school tends to hold identical views on the principal tenets of Islam, they may hold differing views on the periphery. Islamic finance, as a relatively new playground for modern scholars, represents a frontier of Islamic knowledge that is bound to give rise to differing juristic opinions, and hence is why some confusion continues to exist as to the Sharia compliance of certain products.

Prohibitions: *riba* and *gharar*

That evening in the HSBC conference room, our modern-day scholar, Sheikh Nizam Yaquby, turned his attention to the basic types of contract allowable in Islamic commercial law.

Contracts are categorized according to their purpose: contracts of exchange such as a simple sale and purchase agreement, or a lease contract; contracts of investment to permit profit for partners in a venture, which may involve the investment of either capital or labour; contracts of charity such as donations or interest-free loans, such contracts entered into for the sake of pleasing Allah, and which have no conditions attached, being a unilateral transfer of wealth; contracts of security that create rights over an asset, such as a mortgage over a property or a guarantee of a debt; and agency and trust contracts that fall into a miscellaneous category.

And finally the scholar turned to what was probably the most significant point he would make that evening: the prohibitions. These are the fundamental things you cannot do in Islamic commercial and financial transactions.

Of course, these prohibitions are a component of the full body of knowledge and, in and of themselves, do not adequately complete the study of jurisprudence related to transactions without a reading of the conditions for the legal existence of a contract to make it valid, executed, concluded and binding.

With regard to these restrictions the sheikh referred us to the Quran:

> Those who take usury will not stand on the Day of Judgement except as he who has been driven mad by the touch of the Devil. That is because they have said 'trading is like *riba*', but Allah has permitted trading and prohibited *riba*. Whosoever receives an advice from his Lord and stops, he is allowed what has passed, and his matter is up to Allah. And the ones who revert back are the people of the Hellfire. There they remain forever. Oh you who believe, fear Allah and give up what remains due to you from *riba* if you are truly believers. And if you do not, then take notice of war from Allah and His Messenger, but if you repent you

shall have your capital sums. Deal not unjustly and you shall
not be dealt with unjustly.[4]

We discussed earlier that Islam considered the earning of money
upon money, or *riba* – commonly translated as usury or interest
– as being unjust. The Quranic verses above, revealed at a time
when a tribe pledging allegiance to the Prophet proposed to
retain their rights to pre-existing usurious contracts as a condition to accepting Islam, state a clear prohibition against the
practice. However, it is to the practice of the Prophet, and the
study performed by scholars, that we must turn in order to
understand the practical implications of this prohibition.

It is interesting that given such a severe injunction against
riba both at this point in the Quran, and elsewhere in the Quran
and Hadith, that Muslims today persist in the giving and taking of *riba*. Indeed, in many Muslim communities throughout
the world, the banking profession is accorded the same respect
and prestige, perhaps more so, than in the non-Muslim West.
Pakistan, for example, has produced many exceptional bankers who have excelled in the world's leading financial services
institutions, and yet within Pakistan itself the Shariah Appellate
Bench of the Supreme Court – presided over by none other than
Mufti Taqi Usmani – issued an historic judgement on interest
in 1999 declaring interest in all its forms as being equivalent
to *riba* as outlawed in the Quran, and setting forth a legislative
approach to eradicate interest in the country.[5]

So entrenched are many Muslims in the modern economic
system that they either do not recognize the severity of the
transgression in their religion, or assume that necessity dictates
its use since there is no viable alternative. To the non-Muslim
observer, this dichotomy is perplexing given the severity of
punishment accorded to the one who participates in *riba*. It is
considered one of the seven most heinous crimes, a group that
includes the crimes of murder or believing in gods other than

Allah. At least six collections of books from the Hadith state that Muhammad has cursed the receiver and payer of *riba*, the one who records it, and the two witnesses to the transaction, saying: 'They are all alike [in guilt].'[6] So even the accountant and the lawyer documenting the transaction are guilty, and considered to be at war with Allah.

So why do Muslims do it? What justification do they find for taking conventional mortgages on their residential properties? Or corporate loans to grow their businesses? For working in the banking industry or as accountants or finance lawyers, auditing and documenting interest-bearing loans?

In the famous 1999 judgement at the Supreme Court of Pakistan, the four judges of the Shariah Appellate Bench analysed some common misconceptions about *riba*. The most common defence for the use of interest is the doctrine of necessity. How else can I buy a home or a car? How does a nation fund itself within a global economy? Some appellants (many being representatives of domestic financial institutions) argued that the interest-based economy has become a universal necessity and that no country could live without it.[7] To outlaw its usage would be a suicidal act for Pakistan, shattering its economy, and therefore should not be declared as repugnant to Islam. They argued that once the prohibition of interest is enforced, development projects would breathe their last and the economy would face sudden collapse.

Mufti Taqi's response was measured. He conceded that Sharia was pragmatic enough not to bind an individual or a state to something beyond its control, and indeed the doctrine of necessity is a doctrine enshrined in the Quran and the *Sunnah* of the Prophet. A case in which the doctrine may be called upon is the concession that one may eat pork – prohibited for consumption in Islam – in case of extreme hunger to save one's life, and indeed this was an example cited by one of the appellants to the case. However, the magnitude of necessity is a key determinant in the allowable usage of this doctrine. As Mufti Taqi wrote, before deciding on the basis of necessity, 'one must make sure the necessity is real and not exaggerated by imaginary apprehensions and that the necessity cannot be met by any other means than committing an impermissible act'.[8] In other words, if you have a *halal* – or permissible – alternative, take it. So do we have a *halal* alternative?

According to the eminent scholar and his fellow judges, they believed the threat of economic collapse was exaggerated. For domestic transactions, they proposed a banking system based on the concept of profit-and-loss sharing, and other Islamic modes of financing, though they recognized the immaturity of the Islamic finance industry and therefore the effort that would be required to implement this alternative banking system. They also recognized the necessary role that the government must take in ensuring a level playing field for Islamic financial institutions, perhaps tacitly acknowledging the failure of President Zia ul-Haq's crude attempt to Islamize the economy two decades earlier (recall my cousin cycling through the streets of Karachi to withdraw the family savings). Without the appropriate legislative framework in place, such institutions would always be at a disadvantage to their conventional counterparts, unless of course the domestic government outlawed conventional banking in its entirety.

Beyond the argument defending the doctrine of necessity, other champions of conventional financial services have posited alternative arguments in favour of the acceptability of interest in Islam, though these too were refuted by the scholars of the Supreme Court. One argument in favour of interest contended that the verses of the Quran that prohibit *riba* were revealed in the last days of the life of the Prophet. Consequently, he did not have an opportunity to interpret and implement them properly, and that therefore the term *riba* remains ambiguous in nature. The scholars responded by pointing out that the earliest revelation relating to the express prohibition on *riba* took place in the second year following the Prophet's migration to the city of Yathrib, subsequently known as Madinah. Earlier verses had been revealed in the Makkan period of Islam condemning the practice though without explicit injunctions. In short, there was ample time in which to digest the impermissibility of *riba*.[9] Subsequent verses and Hadith backed up the earliest recorded evidence of a ban.

Another argument put forward was that the word *riba* refers only to the usurious loans on which an *excessive* rate of interest was charged by lenders, such a rate deemed exploitative. Christians over the centuries had engaged in similar discussions, with the Church gradually relenting until, by 1917, even the Catholic Church allowed itself to invest in interest-bearing securities.[10]

According to this argument, modern banking does not charge an excessive or exploitative rate, and bank interest cannot fall within the definition of *riba*. Proponents of this argument contended that the first Quranic verse to ban *riba* is qualified by a specific amount of usury: 'Oh you who believe, devour not usury, doubled and multiplied; but fear Allah that you may (really) prosper.'[11] Does this mean that interest is classified as *riba* if the principal repayable is double the original amount? Not so, said the scholars.[12] An examination of the different verses should readily reveal that the reference to 'doubled and multiplied' is an idiom that is not meant to be taken as a restrictive qualification, but applies to all loans where an increase of money against principal takes place.

The Quran bans *riba* on consumption loans and not commercial loans, said the bankers. They contended: surely *riba* refers to the increased amount charged on consumption loans as taken by the poor of the Prophet's time for their day-to-day needs? Surely the ban is intended as humanitarian support for the oppressed, to avoid exploitation of the weak by the strong? Commercial loans were not prevalent 1,400 years ago, and the Quran has not explicitly addressed them. Today the debtors of these commercial loans are not the poor, they are well-funded and healthy corporations requiring little in the way of humanitarian protection. The scholars responded that the ban is an absolute ban, without distinction on the type of borrower.[13] Furthermore, the contention that interest cannot be an injustice against the rich or against powerful corporations assumes firstly that money can be treated as a commodity (which it cannot, as noted earlier), and that it has no adverse effects on production and distribution in an economy. Today, even conventional commentators might suggest that leverage is harmful to individuals, corporations and countries alike, and so this argument was refuted by the scholars.

Finally, the advocates of an interest-based economy argued that only a specific category of *riba*, known as *riba al-jahiliyyah*, was banned, a practice of the pre-Islamic period whereby a loan was advanced for a given period of time with no interest charged. If at maturity the capital was not repaid, then the loan would roll over and interest would be charged to it. According to the defenders of modern interest, if an increased amount is stipulated in the initial agreement of the loan, then it does not meet the Quranic definition of *riba*. It would, however, meet the definition of another category of *riba*, *riba al-fadl*, prohibited by the *Sunnah*, and thus a prohibition of a lesser degree and considered harmful rather than impermissible. Once again, the scholars argued against this on the basis that the definition of *riba al-fadl* covers the transactions of sale only (and not loans), and the ban on *riba* does not specify any such exception anywhere in the Quran or *Sunnah*.[14]

The Supreme Court judgement was radical, though its implementation over the years has remained sketchy at best. Despite this, the text of the judgement is a case study for Muslim governments around the world.

On that London winter evening in 1996 Sheikh Nizam, his

Arabic headdress pulled tight over his slight features, turned his attention to the second important prohibition: *gharar*, or uncertainty. Uncertainty in sales and other transactions is considered to void or invalidate a contract, and may indicate that the party practising it is deceiving or defrauding his counterparty, and indeed cheating and fraud are generally considered to be special cases of *gharar*. However, uncertainty does not have to be deliberately deceptive in nature. It arises when there is a lack of knowledge of the subject matter, such as the failure to identify the subject matter of the contract or the failure to determine the contract; lack of knowledge of the price of the subject matter, or the quantity, or the deferred period of delivery if there is one; lack of knowledge of the existence or the impossibility of its acquisition, including hindrances to its delivery; and lack of knowledge of its sound or continued existence.[15]

Some examples might include agreeing to sell my house if Manchester United beats Liverpool (uncertainty due to conditionality); agreeing to sell my car that has been stolen (uncertainty due to existence or availability); selling one out of a herd of cows without specifying which cow (uncertainty due to quality or the nature of the object). Uncertainty does not apply to charitable contracts or gifts, so there is no prohibition in offering a gift that is not yet in one's possession, or in making a charitable donation without specifying when delivery will take place.

Abu Hanifa deemed *gharar* to be so serious a matter that on one occasion when he heard that a sheep had been stolen in the town of Kufa, he enquired as to the lifespan of a sheep and was told it was seven years. Fearing to such an extent the purchase or consumption of stolen goods, he abstained from eating mutton for seven years.

Since no contract can be entirely free of uncertainty, minor *gharar* would not render a sales contract defective. For example, the sale of a pregnant cow would be deemed valid, despite the unknown status of the calf, and the higher price for a pregnant

cow compared to one that is not would be considered acceptable. However, the sale of the unborn calf by itself would not be
valid since it may be stillborn. In the case of the pregnant cow,
the cow itself is the primary subject of the sale and therefore the
uncertainty is deemed to be minor.[16] Uncertainty must be excessive in order to invalidate a contract. It is this quantification of
excess that, ironically, leads to some uncertainty in the analysis
of *gharar* in contracts.

Many classical jurists recognized the legitimacy of the seller's
ability to deliver at the point of contracting as the overriding
factor in a valid sales contract, almost irrespective of existence,
ownership, availability and possession. It is a necessary condition
of a sale contract that the seller must own the subject of the sale
prior to selling, and that the seller has no right to sell something
he does not own. As a result, almost all short selling as conventionally practised in the financial markets (that is, selling shares
or other securities that one borrows but does not own) would
not be valid in Sharia. However, the matter is less clear cut on
whether the subject matter of the sale must exist at the time of
contract conclusion.

Thus, whilst a farmer cannot enter into a contract to sell
whatever crop is harvested in his fields without knowing the
quantity or quality of the future harvest (since there is excessive
uncertainty in such a contract), the farmer may instead sell a
fixed quantity of a crop with specified quality to be delivered
at a specified point in the future. This contract is quite simply
a forward sale, as practised in the conventional financial world
today, and does not demonstrate the characteristics of *gharar*.
The analysis of some scholars leads them to conclude that the
existence of the subject matter of the sale is not necessary at
the time of entering into the sale agreement, but that the seller
must have the ability to deliver the goods on the pre-specified
delivery date. One condition sometimes applied by such scholars to ensuring uncertainty is minimized may include that the

commodity being sold under such a contract should be readily available in the market throughout the term of the contract.

It is worth noting that the characteristic of risk itself is not necessarily so inherently uncertain that it invalidates a contract. After all, an investment partnership takes risk in deploying capital to a venture in the hope of making profit.

At what point does one reach the conclusion that a contract might have major and not minor *gharar*, and is therefore invalid? Some jurists would suggest that excessive uncertainty is a dominant feature of such a contract, overwhelming its potential outcome, whereas minor *gharar* outweighs a greater benefit, as in the case of the sale of a pregnant cow. Mahmoud El-Gamal, Professor of Economics and Statistics at Rice University, suggests that *gharar* is 'trading in risk', using the language of the modern financier.[17] He summarizes *gharar* as incorporating uncertainty regarding future events and qualities of goods, perhaps as the result of 'one-sided or two-sided and intentional or unintentional incompleteness of information'.

The key attribute that El-Gamal is seeking is significant (possibly unquantifiable) risk and uncertainty. If there is the possibility of unanticipated loss to at least one party, then the contract may be a form of gambling, and therefore invalid without any ambiguity. If the contract may lead to disputation between contracting parties, then there is also major uncertainty present. Interestingly, Professor El-Gamal likens the prohibition of uncertainty as equivalent to the prohibition of the 'unbundled and unnecessary sale of risk', which in its most extreme form is gambling. He suggests that since modern finance – both conventional and Islamic – is primarily concerned with the allocation of credit or risk, particularly through advances in securitization and financial derivatives, that the two main prohibitions in Islamic commercial transactions, that is *riba* and *gharar*, are best characterized as trading in unbundled credit and trading in unbundled risk respectively.

I find the analogy to trading of unbundled credit and risk as an excellent pointer in applying a sense check to the degree of excess and uncertainty in a contract, and at a stroke, it renders a large swathe of the modern financial services industry to be in conflict with the basic principles of Sharia. Unbundled risk is where the risk that attaches to the ownership of an object is detached from that ownership and is sold in a separate contract. Some might argue that the modern insurance industry is riddled with uncertainty, since the risk of an accident that damages or writes off a car should belong to the owner of the car, and when he transfers that risk to an insurance company for a fee he has allowed the detachment of risk from his ownership. This does not, however, preclude the possibility of Islamic insurance contracts based on the principles of voluntary contribution and mutual cooperation.

Perhaps a more topical example in the investment banking industry is a credit default swap, or a CDS as it is more commonly known. This is a type of insurance contract bought by a party ostensibly to protect itself from the risk that a particular company or nation state might default on its debt obligations. For example, a financial institution may have lent significantly to the public sector in Greece and may be concerned with the deteriorating credit situation in the country, and therefore the increased risk of default by its debtors. It may therefore decide to partially 'hedge' itself by buying protection against the risk of default in the form of a contract – a 'derivative' contract – known as a CDS, usually issued by a large financial institution. If this insurance policy, the CDS, is linked to Greek sovereign debt, then in the event the sovereign defaults on its debt obligations, the 'writer' of the CDS (the large financial institution acting as an underwriter) will pay out a sum to compensate the holder for defaults that presumably will now trickle down through the rest of the Greek economy. Thus the buyer of the CDS has been paid out in a manner similar to an insurance policy, and the risk of the subject matter is not attached to its ownership – a perfect example of the disintermediation of risk and reward.

Imagine now that the buyer of the CDS has no intrinsic interest in the subject matter, in other words has no exposure to loans in Greece. He is taking out an insurance contract on something he doesn't own. Is he merely seeking to take a speculative punt on Greek debt default? Is this therefore a form of gambling? We will come back to this point in Chapter 7 when we discuss derivatives in more detail.

***

Doing God's work: HSBC takes Islamic finance to the masses

That evening in 1996 may not have been the actual birth of HSBC Amanah, but it certainly felt like a precursor. The Islamic finance subsidiary of a high-street behemoth was the creation of a master salesman who had not only found his talismanic spiritual leader in Sheikh Nizam, but had also persuaded the senior management of one of the world's largest financial institutions to back him. In a world increasingly suspicious of Muslims and their alien and insatiable demands, Iqbal Khan's personal jihad – from the Arabic, a 'striving' or 'effort' – demonstrated political savvy, diplomacy and clever PR as a sophisticated way to market a gentler face of Islam to the wider world.

The introduction of Islamic finance to the masses hinged on Khan finding areas of commonality with the men who could make it happen: Stephen Green, then Group Treasurer of HSBC Holdings plc, and John Bond, its then CEO. Both would come to one day hold the positions of chief executive and chairman of the bank. Green in particular had a common spirituality with Khan: while Khan dreamt of serving the *ummah* – the global community of Muslims – Green was an ordained priest in the

Church of England. For both men, ethical finance was not an oxymoron. It could be real, and it *would* be real through HSBC Amanah. Even the name they chose for the new entity would reflect its mission: *amanah* meant trust, and HSBC's customers could be reassured that their money was in a safe place, deployed prudently and responsibly.

Khan was on a mission, a financial evangelist. According to one staff member, 'he united [Amanah's] members with fiery speeches full of hope, principle, and the wider values that would serve the *ummah* and would eventually transform the infidel world'.[18] Another said that 'he could sell coal to Newcastle, ice to the Eskimos'.[19] He didn't talk details, just the big picture. He read human nature well and understood that his employees were looking for meaning in their lives, not just a pay cheque. In the banking industry, when end-of-year compensation discussions are typically carefully choreographed to manage staff expectations, Khan's approach was to ask his staff whether they wanted their reward now or in the hereafter.

It proved an effective approach for many years. His troops were fiercely loyal and, more than anything, Khan looked for loyalty. At such an early stage in the growth of the modern Islamic finance industry, being intellectually cutting edge was not important. Certainly not at the expense of faith. And so he surrounded himself with strategy consultants looking to do good in their lives, rather than bankers and deal execution specialists who valued the profit motive above all else. He ignored the potential for complex derivative products, all fancy structures and slick sales operations. HSBC Amanah was a solid high-street brand, its customers looking for dull but worthy products such as savings accounts and home financing, not credit default swaps on Greek sovereign debt.

Was Khan missing a trick, perhaps? Was there a more lucrative complex Sharia-compliant product out there on which there was money to be made? It didn't matter. Whatever he was doing was good enough for the ordained minister Green, who would go on to become HSBC's chief executive. Khan and Green were getting down to the soul of banking, doing God's work. And in doing so, the high streets of London and elsewhere were offering Islam to the masses in a friendly package. Ethical finance. Socially responsible investing. Put your trust in HSBC.

It wasn't to last. Khan's strategy of surrounding himself with loyalists meant that HSBC's conventional product desks viewed their Amanah colleagues with suspicion: over the years, they observed the Amanah cult working together, eating together, and – most insidiously – praying together. Whilst CEO Stephen Green enjoyed the thought of an elite cadre of HSBC executives putting God ahead of mammon, Amanah's lack of diversity meant that when Michael Geoghegan was appointed chief executive of the bank, Khan fell out of favour, and many of those he had made in his own image felt similarly exposed.

'These holier than thou consultants wanted real business responsibility', said one former HSBC executive. 'People resented that.' On his arrival into the post, the thrusting new CEO demanded a strategic review of each business within the bank, and Amanah's Khan prepared his case. Rumours abounded of HSBC Amanah being spun off from the group – one insider fantasized about 'billions of dollars and holding companies and IPO exits and shareholder value'[20] – but it was not to be. The plans were too grand, the vision too ambitious for Geoghegan, and he opted instead to make the Amanah brand disappear by integrating its Islamic products into the wider conventional business of the bank. Why have a special group of people, after all, when one can simply replicate the necessary products from conventional product desks?

'There was no place for the Sharia any more at HSBC', said one former member of staff with sadness.[21] Khan's favoured status with Green and Bond evaporated with the arrival of the new CEO, and pent-up resentment from conventional product desks accelerated his demise. Some within Amanah felt that Geoghegan was 'merely' a retail banker who viewed Saudi Arabia and other Gulf markets as retail markets rather than specifically *Islamic* retail markets.

Perhaps there was something inappropriate, distasteful even, about this apparent jihad that Khan was conducting. He had told his staff that their work was a form of worship of their Lord. Religion and finance? A holy warrior for the *ummah*? Incompatible bedfellows, thought some, and Khan was forced to tender his resignation, driven to fall on his sword by his own 'suicide brigade'.[22]

Sharia had become a hot potato in many walks of life. Shortly afterwards, the head of the Church of England, Archbishop Rowan Williams, was himself facing demands to quit his post. He had dared to suggest in a speech at London's Royal Courts of Justice that there might be room for 'supplementary jurisdictions' to that of civil law, setting out a nuanced view of the Sharia and its place in British society.[23] Despite support from the legal community, the expected knee-jerk reaction from elements of the press and his own Church forced him to deny accusations of proposing a parallel legal system within Britain. As one of the most thoughtful men to have occupied the post of Archbishop of Canterbury, Williams felt – quite rightly – that 'certain provision[s] of Sharia are already recognised in our society and under our law', though he also felt that 'sensational reporting of opinion polls' clouded the issue. Peers and politicians alike foamed at the mouth at his suggestion for 'a constructive accommodation with some aspects of Muslim law',[24] reasoning that the imposition of the Sharia could only mean barbaric beheadings and the oppression of women.

As the Amanah brand began to wane, Khan slunk away to a dark corner to plot his next paradigm-shifting venture, and for a while nothing was heard from him. Many of his former staff despaired at Geoghegan's vision of an integrated bank and themselves departed. 'The spirit of Amanah disappeared when Iqbal left', lamented one of Khan's former lieutenants.[25] The Islamic bankers mourned their charismatic leader and Amanah would never be the same again.

4

The Rocket Scientists of Deutsche Bank and the Billion-Dollar Scholar

Bankers and lawyers get huge fees. . . So should we just sit in front of the mosque door and beg. . .?

Sheikh Hussain Hamed Hassan[1]

Every year in Bahrain, the Islamic finance industry gathers at the World Islamic Banking Conference, the WIBC. In November 2010, despite the dark clouds of austerity looming over the world's economy, a group of young bankers and lawyers from Dubai battled through the heaving crowds at the Gulf Hotel. While presentations from the industry's *Who's Who* took place in the main ballroom, in the adjoining exhibition hall impromptu networking was in full flow. As the WIBC participants banged elbows around the coffee and croissant stand, catching up on the latest people moves and deals, with others jostling for space in corridors hoping to notice and be noticed, it cannot have failed to escape the casual observer that Islamic finance was very much alive and kicking.

The group from Dubai – all of whom attended the Masjid Al-Samad, a single mosque in the heart of the tiny Arabian Gulf state's expat community – were bemused and fast running out of business cards. 'What the hell is going on?' asked one of the Samadiites. 'It's insane. I can't even get a coffee around here.'

The same could not have been said of the previous year, when the industry was feeling the effects of the global economic melt-down, and high profile *sukuk* – or Islamic bond – defaults were taking place against a backdrop of allegations of corruption and mismanagement in Gulf-based family offices and financial institutions,[2] both conventional and Islamic. That year, the WIBC had been a little more subdued, a little less manic, and the annual back-slapping that was the various industry award ceremonies had not been quite so glitzy. Indeed, the 2009 keynote speaker at the WIBC had been the outspoken doom-monger and critic of the modern financial services industry, Nassim Nicholas Taleb, the ground-breaking author of *Fooled by Randomness* and the celebrated *The Black Swan*.[3] Yet in 2010, with the feel-good factor inexplicably returning to the Islamic finance industry, despite unresolved bearishness in the conventional industry, the event organizers decided to draw the crowds with a bullish emerging markets investment guru, Mark Mobius, of the global fund management company Franklin Templeton Investments.

He proved a good draw. Islamic institutions wanted reminding that they had something of distinct value to offer their customers, and the emerging markets represented the front line of their campaign. They wanted to believe they were immune from the global financial crisis. They weren't, of course, but there was no denying they hadn't suffered appreciably from exposure to the toxic waste that had infected the world's largest financial institutions such as subprime mortgages and credit derivatives, the 'weapons of mass destruction' that investor Warren Buffett had warned against.[4]

Every year, the WIBC works with a management consulting firm – in recent years McKinsey & Company or Ernst &

Young – to publish the World Islamic Banking Competitiveness Report, a 130-page collection of standard consulting fare in the form of pie charts, three-dimensional bar graphs and the ubiquitous and increasingly wacky matrices so beloved of consultants. The report has become something of an industry fixture and is presented at the annual conference at a plenary session by a partner from the consulting firm. By late 2010, a number of key themes and trends were being identified: Islamic banks continued to experience robust asset growth and outperformed their conventional counterparts; Islamic 'windows' of conventional banks – that is, a separate area within a conventional bank that offers Islamic products – continued to grow rapidly, constituting an increasing share of the overall Islamic banking landscape; and Islamic banks remained relatively unsophisticated and had limited access to Sharia-compliant instruments that hedge their macroeconomic exposures, like mismatches between their balance sheet assets and liabilities, or other 'gap' risks within their treasury operations and proprietary trading desks.

In previous years, the report had focused on the global *sukuk* market, which had grown exponentially since 2001 but which had lately been experiencing a slowdown in new issuances from governments and corporations looking to tap public markets for new debt. It had also been one of the first to champion the idea that the majority of GCC-based investors would buy Islamic products if those products demonstrated the same price, performance, liquidity and other attributes of conventional products.

However, it had not been until a slick Anglo-Saxon SWAT team from Deutsche Bank arrived on the scene in 2004, launching a range of Islamic derivatives products, that the industry finally took notice that constraints in offering new products had always been on the supply side. In other words, banks had not previously figured out how to design and engineer new Islamic products – 'structuring' as they termed it – to issue the most sophisticated products required of investment banks: those infamous weapons of mass destruction. In contrast, on the demand side, customers had been waiting patiently for instruments to hedge their exposures to foreign currencies, interest rates, commodity prices, share volatility – all in a Sharia-compliant package.

And that day had arrived.

***

Deutsche's Godfather of the Middle East

By the mid 2000s Islamic finance was entering adolescence, with none of the growing pains that this should have entailed. A uniform blandness swept through the industry: banks would fund each other by offering simple money-market lines using commodities as the underlying asset, a so-called commodity *murabaha* transaction. Depositors would place their money with banks and earn a return linked to these commodity transactions. Home financing was inflexible and expensive, perhaps because Islamic banks had not learnt how to protect themselves, or hedge, against significant macroeconomic exposures to currency fluctuations, borrowing rates and other market movements. Corporate loans would either be made using the ubiquitous commodity *murabaha* or through the equally clumsy sale and leaseback of the borrower's assets. It was dull, it was expensive and no one cared.

Yassine Bouhara sat in a glass-screened corner office in Deutsche Bank on London Wall and wondered why no one had taken the Islamic finance industry by the scruff of its neck and shaken it up. The Francophone Swiss of Algerian origin had joined Merrill Lynch in Frankfurt at the age of twenty-three to trade equity derivatives, just as the market began to take off. By 1996, Deutsche Bank was greedily eyeing up merchant banks and securities houses with the intention of joining the exclusive club of bulge-bracket investment banks. Bouhara's and Deutsche's ambitions collided, and he jumped ship to rise to the post of Global Head of Equities in London.

Here at Deutsche Bank, on a trading floor the size of a football field, he was an emperor, and he hadn't even turned forty. But it wasn't enough. He had conquered the conventional world, but not the Islamic. No one had conquered that. Why were there no simple Islamic securities traded on a stock exchange, structured investment products or treasury management and liquidity products? Where were the Sharia-compliant cross-border mergers and acquisitions? The Islamic mortgage companies?

Bouhara was a fast-talking star of the equity derivatives industry, famed for his rapid rise to the top and his single-minded pursuit of profit. His early career had been forged in the white heat of the trading floor, and he revelled in recounting his salad days as a non-English speaker overcoming the odds in an Anglo-Saxon trading environment. With his penchant for oversized watches, expensively tailored Super-180 cloth and island properties in Dubai, it was clear that the glam years of investment banking had been good to him.

But now, having achieved so much, he was searching for something more, and one day his private banking colleagues in Bahrain came calling. Knowing of his desire to create a stir in the Islamic markets, they brought a unique proposition to him: an ultra high net worth merchant family from Saudi Arabia, looking to set up a dedicated Islamic finance consulting firm, and to finance real estate in Islam's holiest city, Makkah.

That merchant family were the Binladins, half-brothers to the infamous Osama, and owners of Saudi's largest contracting firm, the Saudi Binladin Group. The Binladins had a unique proposition: having already endowed a chair at the University of Oxford to promote the Islamic finance industry, they were keen to extend their reach beyond the world of academia. And so they asked their private bankers whether they might work with them to create an entity dedicated to research and development in Islamic finance, a think tank.

At first, Deutsche's private bankers struggled with the concept. It wasn't just that the Binladins shared a name and bloodline with the world's most wanted man, and that Deutsche Bank would by association be thrust into the limelight, outside the comfort zone of the secretive world of private wealth management. It was also that these Geneva- and Bahrain-based relationship managers – hired for their ability to tell a Monet from a Manet – had no training in the technical discipline of Islamic products and thus had no idea where to start. The joint venture entity they set up with the Binladins and Oxford, named Dar Al Istithmar – the House of Investment – lacked teeth, populated as it was by academics with no experience of the commercial environment, and borrowing its intellectual property from its largest shareholder, Deutsche Bank. Its status as a think tank certainly created a halo for its shareholders, but wasn't making them much money.

When you need to make money, you turn to a man who knows how to make it. Could Yassine Bouhara, a member of the bank's Executive Committee – the body populated by the bank's most senior executives and ultimately responsible for the investment bank's activities – create one iconic deal to set the Islamic market alight? Could he, a conventional banker, establish the Islamic credentials of the Dar Al Istithmar joint venture and its benefactors?

Bouhara put into motion a plan of action for which perhaps no one in the bank was better suited. Deutsche would work with this client, he assured them, and he would put his top guys on it. His top guys meant the equity derivatives team, already known to house some of the bank's proven 'rocket scientists' and seemingly with a licence to pursue opportunities wherever they may be. Entrepreneurship was the watchword for his people.

'Do not be 'eld back by ze bondareez of your job', he would advise his rocket scientists in an impenetrable French accent. 'Mek mo-nay', he would tell us. The word 'mo-nay' would often be accompanied by a proffered hand, thumb and first finger rubbing together to emphasize the importance of all that investment bankers live for.

Two years previously, his team had launched an Islamic exchange-traded fund – a certificate typically traded on a stock exchange whose price mirrors the performance of an underlying basket of equities. As the underlying equities rose in price, the certificate would also rise in price, like a stock in its own right – a neat way of investors participating in the returns of a group of shares, or perhaps an entire market. Whilst Bouhara's structuring specialists may not have understood the Islamic finance industry profoundly, they were at least capable of devising solutions to problems within specific parameters, and their complex skill set was their ticket to 'meking mo-nay'. The exchange-traded fund had proven a success and Bouhara knew that the approach from the Binladin family was his opportunity to make a meaningful impression on the industry beyond merely an opportunistic one-off product.

The Binladins were Saudi's biggest builders, responsible for some of the most expensive real estate in the world located in the holy cities of Makkah and Madinah in the Kingdom of Saudi Arabia. The three brothers Bakr, Yahya and Shafig Binladin had, not surprisingly, distanced themselves from Osama, and played extensively on their business relationships with the family of US President Bush and other leading American politicians and businessmen. Bouhara was certain that the brothers would bring him into the fold of the region's leading ultra high net worth merchant families, princes and sheikhs. All he needed was one deal, the one that would put Deutsche on the Islamic map.

At a beachfront restaurant table at the Dubai Ritz Carlton in late 2004, I sat down with a colleague and Bouhara to wait for a representative of the Binladin Group to arrive. Bouhara outlined his vision of the future to us, his manner intense and engaging. The Binladins were about to offer him a mandate to finance the construction of a series of towers in the holy city of Makkah. Naturally, the financing would have to comply with the Sharia, but the Binladins wanted more than that. They wanted the industry to look up to this transaction and deem it worthy of replication. The assets that it would finance would be of the highest quality, in perhaps the most iconic city in the world, certainly one to which no Western investment bank had previously been invited to conduct business.

'Ze Meedle East is fool of bool-sheeters', he began, manically waving his hands, lengthening and drawing out the word 'bool-sheet'. 'I do not want you to care about ze titles, ze name-dropping, if you tell everyone "I know zees sheikh, zat sheikh, *lalala*". I. Do. Not. Care.' Bouhara was just warming up, a flash of his monstrous Audemars Piguet visible under his cuff as he gesticulated wildly each time he said '*lalala*', a Bouharaism for 'et cetera et cetera'.

'Do your job, be technee-cally excellent, ozerwise everyone zay, "Ere eez zis bool-sheeter again wiz 'iz bool-sheet, *lalala*". And zay will come banging on my door zaying "Oo eez zees guy you 'ire?"'

Bouhara's dream was to commoditize the industry so that Muslim buyers of Islamic financial services could walk into a bank, or better still go online, picking and choosing produce like fruit in a supermarket. He didn't want vacuous salespeople – *bool-sheeters* – to forge this new frontier, he needed technical experts.

'Look at ze Beeg-uh-Mac-uh,' said Bouhara. The Big Mac? My colleague and I looked at each other. Were we still talking about Islamic finance?

'It is zc perfect product. Everywhere I go in ze world, I find ze same Beeg-uh-Mac-uh, manufactured to ze same stondard. I want you to create a factory of Eeslameec product like ze Beeg-uh-Mac-uh.' He would populate the Islamic team with first-class front office specialists, with technical credibility in their chosen product disciplines. Whether you bought his product in London or the Middle East, its quality would be the same. It was a radical departure for a region predisposed to mediocrity in financial services.

In the moments before his client arrived, he emphasized how career defining this particular transaction would be. How it would put Deutsche Bank, and us, on the map. 'Do you want to be anuzzer expat wiz ze expat disease and walk around town saying pee-pul want to 'ave lunsh wiz me because I am from Deutsche Bank, *lalala*? Non. Back 'ome, you are eensig-neef-icant. Do not be like ze bool-sheeters 'oo claim zey 'ave a lot of mo-nay. Zay to zem: where eez eet? Where eez your f***ing Ferrari? I cannot protect you from ze mob back 'ome, once you 'ave lost credibility.'

His voice dropped from a high-pitched rant and he leant forward, still intense in manner, but now quieter and more deliberate. 'So be focal-ized. Mek mo-nay. Zen I mek you rich.' He leant back, eyes sparkling and teeth bared in a wide grin, satisfied that he had captured the imagination of his rapt bankers, daring them to dream of a new frontier that they would control.

His client arrived and after brief introductions Bouhara flashed his trademark smile and left us to talk business. Deutsche would be getting the mandate to finance the towers in Makkah, but the instrument we would create needed to be special. It needed to set a new trend and make its originator a pioneer. The Binladins wanted their best customers to be rewarded: if they bought the bond to finance the project, then those customers should be granted a unique preferential status to purchase the very best luxury apartments with the world's most expensive view. If Deutsche could make this happen, it would be rewarded with even bigger future mandates, with the potential to leapfrog its way to becoming the region's leading investment and private bank.

The Saudi government had awarded the Saudi Binladin Group a contract to construct the Abraj Al-Bait, a series of seven gigantic towers overlooking the holy mosque at the centre of the Islamic world, the Masjid Al-Haram. At the centre of the Haram is the Kaaba, the cubic structure draped in black cloth that Muslims claim has been in existence since the time of the Prophet Abraham, towards which 1.6 billion Muslims turn five times a day to offer their daily prayers, and to which every Muslim with means is obliged to make a pilgrimage once in his or her life.

It would be a project of immense significance, breaking a multitude of records in its vast construction, and yet – perhaps more crucially – sealing a break with Makkah's historical past. No more rundown hotels, crumbling old buildings, and low-tech low-rise anonymity. Fifty yards from the gate of the Masjid Al-Haram, Abraj Al-Bait would herald the advent of a new era in the world's holiest city – brash, high tech and progressive. A symbol of modernity for the world to marvel at. A place where the rich could entertain and be entertained, could worship from the comfort of microchip-controlled seven-star luxury, where piety and wealth were not mutually exclusive. The project would drag Islam kicking and screaming into the modern age whether it liked it or not, and in the process would destroy any symbols of its heritage. Not even the hills around Makkah would be safe, detonated into a billion pebbles, whilst old forts and other buildings of immense historical and architectural significance would be obliterated for ever.

At the centre of the towers would be the Makkah Royal Clock Hotel Tower, the tallest clock tower in the world, apparently modelled somewhat bizarrely on London's Big Ben and housing two million LED lights on each of its four faces. On completion, the towers project would house the tallest and largest hotel in the world, have the world's largest building floor area, and the second tallest tower in the world. After circumambulating the Kaaba in a millennia-old ritual believed to have been initiated by the Prophet Abraham, the devotee could stroll into an air-conditioned, marble-lined mall and sip a skinny Frappuccino® from a cardboard cup.

Deutsche Bank would be right there at the inception of this new era.

Deutsche set to work by employing the services of some of the region's leading scholars led by a Dubai-based Egyptian named Dr Hussain Hamed Hassan. Despite his advancing years, Sheikh Hussain's impressive work ethic and intellect proved to be a surprise to the bankers from Deutsche. He took on the role of chairman of the three-man Sharia panel, conveying the salient transaction details to his colleagues in an attempt to find a contractual structure that worked from a commercial and Sharia perspective.

The transaction proved troublesome: there were limited precedents for similar types of real estate financings in Saudi Arabia, and Makkah in particular was subject to specific restrictions on foreign ownership and investment in the sector. An international capital markets issue was one thing, but a tradeable security with attached rights to subscribe to underlying real estate added an additional degree of complexity. Saudi's complex tax laws proved unhelpfully vague, and the tax advisors found themselves unable to draw definitive conclusions about the treatment of this instrument by the Kingdom's Department of Zakat and Income Tax. In the end, it took two years of legal, tax and Sharia structuring to meet all the commercial parameters, and both the client and its bankers grew weary of the deal with its increasingly complex web of sub-companies and sub-agreements.

'I don't understand why you guys need to overanalyse things', complained the Binladin Group's in-house finance manager. 'Just do the deal. Draft up the docs with a structure that roughly works and print the damn thing.'

The bankers were reluctant to proceed with an approximate solution. For the head of Bouhara's structuring team, Belgian equity derivatives specialist Geert Bossuyt, who would go on to co-found Deutsche's Islamic finance team, approximate was not a word he understood. It had to be perfect or nothing. With a background in actuarial science, and a training in Luxembourg-based tax-efficient investment products, creating a financial instrument was a precise science, not an art, and there could be no compromise. This had to be an instrument worthy of selling to the international investment community, and Bossuyt's impeccable north-European logic would allow for no gaps or fault lines in the products his team would create.

After two years of back and forth between the client, legal counsel, tax advisors and the regulatory authorities in Saudi and Bahrain, Sheikh Hussain was finally able to settle on a legal structure that would also meet the requirements of the Sharia. The overall transaction structure would be governed by a type of contract known in the Sharia as a *mudaraba* – an investment partnership whereby investors place money with a manager who invests or manages that capital on their behalf to produce a return. The connection with classical Islamic commerce could not have been closer: the Prophet Muhammad himself had been a *mudarib*, a manager of other people's capital. The ensuing certificate, or *sukuk*, would be called a *sukuk al mudaraba*. To complicate matters, the holder of the *sukuk* would have additional rights to buy apartment units in the Safa Tower, the first of the seven towers to be constructed. Thus the bond financier could leapfrog the queue to buy this iconic real estate.

Whilst the investment contract would be the principal document governing the nature of the *sukuk* investment (mandating the investment manager to invest the proceeds in a real estate development project), underpinning it would be a network of companies and contracts to effect the required commercial outcome within the boundaries of oftentimes awkward jurisdictional and tax parameters.

On the issue date of the *sukuk*, investors would advance US$200 million to the issuer, a Bahrain incorporated 'special purpose vehicle' – a financial shell company specifically set up to hold legal title to the real estate asset in favour of the investors – and the issuer would enter into an investment agreement with the *sukuk* holders, appointing the issuer as their manager to invest in the development and sale of units in the Safa Tower. Each *sukuk* investor would additionally receive a subscription right attached to the *sukuk*, granting him the right to buy a long lease on certain units of real estate in the Safa Tower.

Then the legal structure gets labyrinthine. In turn, the issuer as agent for the *sukuk* holders would invest the proceeds into a sub-investment agreement with a sub-manager, since the issuer (remember, this is just a shell company to represent the *sukuk* holders) cannot actually build the tower itself. So it appoints a Saudi contracting company owned by the Binladin Group under a type of construction contract – known in the Sharia as an *istisna* – and the capital under this agreement would be disbursed according to a schedule of construction milestones over a two-year construction period. But since the whole of the $200 million construction cost is injected by investors into the issuer on day one, a large amount of capital sits around remaining undisbursed to the contractor during the construction period.

Geert Bossuyt applied his cold Belgian logic to this apparent leakage of value from the project. The problem was how to invest surplus cash into a liquid (in other words, readily tradeable) instrument or deposit account on a Sharia-compliant basis. In parallel with their ground-breaking work on the Safa Tower deal, Bossuyt's crack unit developed an overnight 'Islamic liquidity product', an equivalent to cash deposits or money-market products in conventional markets. Now institutions, individuals, corporations and large-scale projects like Safa Tower need not fear the inefficiencies of Islamic finance.

This was all getting a bit convoluted. Surely this was a simple build-operate-transfer development project, just like any other real estate deal? No wonder the Binladins' finance manager was so vexed.

But the structuring still wasn't finished. A spaghetti bowl of cross-jurisdictional issues and nebulous tax laws meant that the leasehold interest of the property had to be perfected. As the original leaseholder of the land, the government body owning the land around the Holy Mosque granted the long-term lease to the Binladin Group, who in turn would sublease units in the

tower to end customers, the holders of the *sukuk*. The subleases
would be governed by a forward lease and proceeds from these
forward leases would fund the construction costs.

Confused? That was just the simplified version of the transaction structure. It had been a herculean effort to resolve the very
many tax, jurisdictional, regulatory and Sharia issues to make
the deal happen. Millions of dollars of legal and financial fees
racked up over two years, but was it all necessary?

As it happened, no. Despite concluding the contractual structure and receiving all relevant regulatory and Sharia approvals,
the Binladins lost patience and sold the whole tower in one go
to a single buyer. Strangely, it did not matter to Deutsche – such
a wealth of goodwill had been generated in the structuring and
marketing phases of this unprecedented financial instrument that
Islamic investors and the competition were in awe of Deutsche's
boldness and capabilities. A Western investment bank had been
allowed into Makkah and imagined possibilities of which others
had dared not dream.

Ultra high net worth target clients looking to splash out up to
US$27 million on a top-floor suite overlooking the Kaaba were
proffered the slickest of marketing tools to accompany the legal
documents from their private bankers at Deutsche. Juxtaposed
with the typically dry but impressively complex documents were
wafer-thin personal computer tablets that took them on a virtual
tour of the apartments. The disbursal of these high-tech freebies
– several years before Apple's game-changing iPad – allowed the
prospective investor to view an astonishing level of detail, from
the fixtures, fittings and views of the real estate units, to the intricate construction of the financial transaction itself. Indeed, no
stone had been left unturned, as structuring head Geert Bossuyt
had promised, and these same ultra high net worth clients knew
that one day, when they had a deal that no one else could solve,
they could turn to the only rocket scientists plying their trade in
Islamic finance today.

Deutsche Bank's Islamic finance team was born, though not,

it must be said, without the tragic destruction along the way of pieces of Islamic history. Makkah was transformed, the Islamic finance industry had made a quantum leap, and not everyone felt that either change was for the better.

***

Cross-border M&A discovers Islamic finance

The Safa Tower deal had created quite a buzz about Deutsche's capabilities in the Islamic space. So much so that when Deutsche was appointed as sole advisor on another headline-making deal for the Middle East, Bossuyt's team got the call from their corporate finance colleagues upstairs in London Wall.

It was the autumn of 2005. Fuelled by a boom in commodities prices, real estate, tourism and regional trade activity, the Dubai government had audaciously announced its intention to acquire the British global ports operator, Peninsular and Oriental Steam Navigation Company, or P&O.

The government had stipulated the involvement of its flagship institution, Dubai Islamic Bank, in which it held a stake, and Deutsche's London-based mergers and acquisitions (M&A) bankers knew that they would need in-house help to make the financing happen. Some of the German bank's deal specialists thought that this could turn out to be a problem: as a much smaller regional bank, the team from Dubai Islamic Bank (DIB) had not previously worked on a cross-border acquisition of this magnitude before, and Deutsche's seasoned London-based M&A experts had never come across Sharia structures before. Two worlds were about to collide.

One man knew the immensity of the task ahead. Chairman of DIB's Sharia board, the same Sheikh Hussain Hamed Hassan who had masterminded the Sharia structure of the Safa Tower transaction, knew that this transaction was uncharted territory for any institution. As the Safa Tower deal approached its conclusion, Sheikh Hussain requested a meeting with what was now becoming internally recognized as an unofficial Islamic team at Deutsche to discuss the new transaction. 'Bring me all your cash flows, all your financial statements', he requested in what was now his trademark request. 'If the doctor is not given all the information, all the symptoms, all the patient history, he cannot find the cure.' Neither his own bankers from DIB nor the Barclays Capital team – the other investment bank chosen by the government to arrange the financing – were invited. The Sheikh was nominating his favourites for the job, perhaps doubting the ability of anyone other than Deutsche's structurers for grasping the complexities of the task ahead.

In just a few days' time, the British financial services regulator would require a statement from the financing banks. This official bid document would tell the regulator that there was a high degree of certainty of providing the financing package to acquire P&O, and Deutsche's M&A bankers were more than a little nervous. On a conference call attended by bankers in Dubai, London and New York, the talk was of creating a conventional 'bridge' financing, that is, one in which debt financing would be put in place for a short time period – to bridge a gap, typically for one to three months – and thereafter refinanced. That would allow the banks more time to work out how to refinance the deal on an Islamic basis. Why jeopardize the deal for the sake of appeasing one awkward bank? Submit a conventionally financed bid and be done with it. Let DIB worry about its portion later.

'I don't care about the Shar-eye-ah stuff! Just get me the waiver!' cried one New York-based acquisition finance banker, as if all one needed to do was sprinkle fairy dust over the loan contract and a scholar would rubber stamp it. The message was clear: just get the deal through the door and let these Dubai Islamic Bank guys worry about their piece later. For the investment bankers for whom careers could be made as a result of this deal, the Islamic element was proving to be an impediment to a year-end bonus bonanza.

But the Deutsche Islamic specialists were undeterred. They knew that if DIB were not brought on board, there would be a gaping billion-dollar hole in the transaction and the Dubai government would not be happy. Keeping their heads down so as not to alarm their conventional colleagues with the complexity of the challenge, they met discreetly with the sheikh in order to craft a financing instrument that would sell on the capital markets like a bond.

The total financing package to raise the money to acquire P&O would not merely be a loan financing involving a syndicate of banks – it would also incorporate a public *sukuk* issuance raising money from investors across the world, with the proceeds of the *sukuk* used to part finance the acquisition. It would be a mammoth issuance: the overall financing package would be US$9.6 billion in size, most of it conventional financing from the syndicate of arranging banks, but with the Islamic capital markets element alone needing to raise around $3 billion, an unprecedented size for a Sharia-compliant financing.

To complicate matters further, the cash flows generated by the underlying company would not be sufficient to repay the *sukuk* within the two-year financing time frame. As a result, the instrument needed to be structured as a 'convertible' or 'exchangeable' bond, that is one that converts into the equity shares of the underlying company, or exchanges into the equity of a related company. That way, hard cash would not need to be made available to repay investors, a common ruse in acquisitions of this nature, and a way of cheapening the quantum of ongoing repayments during the term of the bond.

The corporate finance bankers suggested to the client that the circumstances of the acquisition lent themselves well to what they termed a 'pre-IPO exchangeable bond', that is, an instrument that pays a fixed rate of return to the bond holder, with the principal value repaid when the borrowing company floats its shares, or those of an associated company, on a stock exchange at some point in the future. The shares created in this initial public

offering (IPO) would be the currency used to repay bond holders, who would become equity shareholders on maturity of the
loan. Indeed the bond could be structured as a 'zero coupon',
one that pays no interest at all during its life, but instead rolls
up the interest cost into the final repayment at maturity. So the
investors start out as holders of the company's debt, on which
they earn no cash payments, but eventually become shareholders
of a company they hope will become hugely successful.

Not surprisingly, such a sophisticated instrument had never
previously been created in Islamic format, let alone sold in such a
massive size. *A Sharia-compliant pre-IPO zero coupon exchangeable bond.* Even the very description strikes fear into the heart
of a banker looking for an easy ride to his year-end bonus. For
Deutsche's Anglo-Saxon corporate financiers, it was madness to
even try. Perhaps even if it could be structured, there would be
no market for it. Sheikh Hussain called his favoured bankers and
lawyers to his office and began the structuring process.

'The transaction is a *musharaka*', he declared emphatically,
informing us that the underlying Sharia contractual structure
would be a type of investment partnership arrangement. 'The
partners are the company performing the acquisition and the
sukuk investors. The company shall be the managing partner,
responsible for deploying the proceeds from the *sukuk* according to an agreed business plan: the purchase of P&O.' With
the building blocks of the Sharia structure established, we
set to work.

The Dubai government entity responsible for the purchase
– the Ports, Customs and Free Zone Corporation (PCFC) –
would issue a pre-IPO exchangeable *sukuk al musharaka*, which
would be placed by the three arranging banks. The *sukuk* would
require a *fatwa*, or legal opinion, in order for it to be accepted by
Islamic investors. This judicial pronouncement – typically a short
document announcing that a qualified scholar had reviewed the
legal and commercial aspects of a transaction and found them to
be in compliance with the Sharia – would have to be issued by

the Sharia board of DIB, since it was the only Islamic bank of the three, and its investor base was exclusively Sharia compliant. In contrast, Deutsche Bank and Barclays Capital would sell the instrument predominantly to a conventional client base: buyers of convertible and exchangeable bonds from pension funds and hedge funds spread across the world from California to Hong Kong. Those guys weren't looking for a *fatwa*, just a solid financial proposition worth investing in.

As the bid deadline loomed, an ebullient Sheikh Hussain was determined to prove to the banks that the Sharia need not be an impediment to the demanding pace of modern finance. 'For every door that closes in the Sharia, a hundred others open', he declared in his trademark booming voice at a meeting with the Deutsche structurers and their lawyers. 'We will find this company a SOLUTION, and we will BEAT their deadline. They will NOT need to refinance.' He thumped a clenched fist on the table, startling his colleagues as glasses full of water bounced off the table top, spilling their contents onto precious sketches of contractual diagrams and cash flow spreadsheets. The sheikh did not seem to notice. He was just getting into his stride, every critical word emphasized so that people in adjoining offices could hear. 'We will make this transaction an example for the industry. So everyone can see we [the Islamic banks] do not lack ANYTHING.' Another thump of the table.

Combative and charismatic at the same time, despite his advancing years Sheikh Hussain's energy levels were truly remarkable. His working day began at the *fajr* early morning prayer, his office overlooking the old downtown area of Dubai near the airport, a vista of concrete flyovers and traffic jams. His status as chairman of many Sharia boards, and the outward manifestations of corporate seniority, seemed not to be of huge concern to him. Almost always dressed in a half-sleeved shirt, baggy corduroy trousers and comfortable old shoes, the casual observer might be forgiven for overlooking him in a room full of bespoke-suited corporate drones. Yet the casual observer would soon be put right the moment the scholar opened his mouth, his voice a resonant powerhouse and punctuated with the banging of a pugilist's fists.

Getting a word in edgeways was a fine art, mastered only by a select few in whom he put his trust. His closest aides seemed to fear and respect him in equal measure, both deferential and submissive, never challenging his authority, and always referring to him as 'the Doctor'. Their stock response to structuring questions posed to them as gatekeepers to the scholar seemed to be 'Doctor says no' as if they had been too timid to ask him the right question or explore possible solutions. In contrast, the small coterie of international bankers and lawyers the scholar seemed to enjoy working with – Samidiites, many of them – were more willing to investigate and robustly debate their commercial position, whilst maintaining a respectful courtesy. Perhaps the charismatic Doctor had simply been waiting to put his keen intellect and knowledge of comparative legal systems to the test, and this new breed of Islamic finance specialist was the conduit. These cross-border, multi-tranche, time sensitive, big ticket deals were finally his chance to show what Islamic finance was truly capable of.

Deutsche's M&A bankers, unaware of Sheikh Hussain's efforts behind the scenes and still nervous of the Islamic component to the deal, advised their Islamic colleagues to back off the structuring process. With only a few days remaining until the regulatory deadline, they preferred to leave DIB to its own devices.

It was a large and complex financing, and wherever such transactions involve both conventional and Islamic institutions it is almost always the conventional banks that tend to have the upper hand. Often more sophisticated than their Islamic counterparts, with bigger balance sheets, and usually with stronger and more recognizable brands, they are natural leaders on the biggest deals. But they also tend not to understand Islamic finance well, and naturally fear what they don't understand. The

first instinct of Deutsche's M&A bankers was to seek waivers so
that either the Islamic portion was no longer required or was
somehow magically certified so that it would look and feel like
the conventional portion. Since the former would have increased
the two conventional banks' exposure to the deal and failed to
meet one of the client's commercial objectives (that of involving
one of its flagship financial institutions in the acquisition), and
the latter would not have been acceptable to one of the most
conservative scholars in the field, the Deutsche Islamic structuring team and their fellow Samadiite lawyers found themselves in
a race against time.

As the weekend before the bid deadline approached, I boarded
a late-night flight to Jeddah with a colleague and we made our
way to the Holy Mosque, the Masjid Al-Haram, in Makkah.
Dressed in the traditional pilgrims' garb known as the *ihram*,
the two pieces of white cloth worn by attendees of the annual
Hajj pilgrimage, we circumambulated the Kaaba seven times
and travelled between the hills of Safa and Marwa seven times,
thus completing our pilgrimage rituals. But we had not come
for the sole purpose of making a pilgrimage. At three o'clock
in the morning, in the lobby of a small hotel on the fringes of
the Holy Mosque, we sat with Sheikh Hussain, still dressed in
ihram like the disciples of a Greek philosopher in the Agora.
Our return flight to our Dubai base was only four hours away
but we were determined to nail this transaction and have the
Sharia-compliant transaction documents ready in the hands of
our doubting colleagues before they returned to their desks in
London on Monday morning. If there was one man who could
solve the deadlock, to plug a billion-dollar hole, it was this man,
the billion-dollar scholar.

And so in that singular setting, with the commercial terms of
the deal set by our conventional colleagues, we worked into the
dawn hours to set the seal on the Sharia structure of the PCFC
sukuk, which we would convey that same morning to our legal
counsel in order to draft up the contracts. The capital markets

issuance needed to raise at least US$2.8 billion, and would have a tenor of two years. During this time it would pay no coupon, but accrue a rate of profit. Like the interest rate on any bond being launched in the conventional markets, this accrual rate would be set at the time of launch of the *sukuk*. It would be in PCFC's interests to ensure that it floated its underlying companies and allowed *sukuk* investors access to the stock, otherwise it would have to repay a greater cash amount to *sukuk* holders.

So that conventional investors would take comfort in this instrument, the *sukuk* documentation would be drafted according to the standards of conventional eurobond issuances. This would ensure that they would be tradeable and clearable by bond market dealers and clearing houses, and investors would see an instrument on their trading systems that looked and felt like a conventional bond, even though its underlying structure was very different.

As with many *sukuk* transactions, the notes issued to investors would be 'limited recourse' obligations of the issuer. In other words, in the event of a default by PCFC, the note holders would only have recourse to those assets specified in the investment partnership agreement, the *musharaka* that Sheikh Hussain had declared earlier. The investors would also have the benefit of an undertaking offered by the 'obligor', PCFC, who promised to repurchase the units of the *musharaka* partnership on redemption of the *sukuk*. This type of undertaking is known as a purchase undertaking and is an often used contract in *sukuk* transactions in order to give comfort to investors that their bond will be repaid by the obligor at maturity.

As one of the earliest large-scale international *sukuk* transactions – and indeed the very first exchangeable *sukuk* deal – Mufti Taqi Usmani's famous views on *sukuk* redemptions had not yet been made public. That is, a *sukuk* based on an investment contract may not be redeemed at its par (or initial) value, and only at its market value at the time of redemption, otherwise it would be in breach of Sharia's requirement for risk sharing to take place between the financier and the financee. Thus the redemption of investment units in the PCFC *sukuk* would be at the initial issue value: if the investor bought the bond for $100, he would get $100 worth of shares back at maturity in two years.

No doubt this apparently guaranteed repayment helped to attract conventional bond investors to the deal, though some industry commentators such as Tarek El Diwany subsequently expressed their disappointment that an instrument based on the concept of profit-and-loss sharing was turning into 'a shallow subterfuge in violation of industry standards'.[5] To El Diwany, a supposedly Islamic instrument was guaranteeing its repayment come hell or high water, rather than allowing the investor to share in the underlying company's profits *and* losses. Park that thought for now – it is a discussion of critical importance to which we must return because it goes to the heart of what makes Islamic finance 'Islamic'.

The issuing special purpose vehicle itself was majority owned by PCFC and, at Sheikh Hussain's suggestion, partly owned by Dubai Islamic Bank. This holding by DIB enabled the bank to act as an independent party, a share agent, for and on behalf of *sukuk* holders in order to protect their interests. Each of the *sukuk* notes were in the form of trust certificates representing an undivided beneficial ownership interest in the trust assets, held on trust for the holders by the issuer in its capacity as trustee. This *sukuk* transaction was not only intended to be ground-breaking, its structure was also intended to be a replicable best practice for the Islamic finance industry.

The trust assets represented the issuer's rights and interest in the investment partnership itself, and were the crux of the real economy transaction underpinning the financial transaction. Remember, it is that real economy transaction that is of interest to Sharia. The purpose of this partnership was the generation of profit from the application of capital contributions of *sukuk* holders and PCFC's in-kind contribution.

So what was this in-kind contribution? PCFC offered to the

partnership usufruct rights – the right of 'usage and enjoyment' – of fifty-three cranes at the port facility for a period of eleven years,[6] in other words a real underlying asset with economic value. These capital contributions would be deployed in accordance with a specified business plan appended to the investment partnership agreement. PCFC's usufruct rights would generate an ongoing return to *sukuk* holders, and profits under the agreement would be split between PCFC and the investors (through the issuer). The obligations of PCFC as the managing partner to execute the business plan were set out in a separate management agreement, allowing the managing partner to earn profit over and above a stipulated cap (being the pre-specified yield on the *sukuk*) as an incentive payment, similar to that of a fund manager. In other words, perform well, and the company would be rewarded.

To complete the contractual circle, PCFC as obligor granted an undertaking – that controversial purchase undertaking we spoke about earlier – in favour of the issuer to purchase the units in the investment partnership on redemption of the *sukuk*, thus ensuring repayment of the bond in full.

Hang on a moment. We're talking about the rental of cranes as the basis of a bond instrument. So what happened to the headline purchase of P&O, the acquisition that this deal is all about? Was this not a part of the business plan? The offering circular made numerous references to the impending acquisition,[7] though it clearly had no direct link with the monies advanced by *sukuk* holders. To all intents and purposes, it seemed the *sukuk* holders were primarily taking income revenue risk on the lease of fifty-three cranes owned by PCFC, and credit risk on the ability of PCFC to redeem its debt in two years' time. In reality, of course, PCFC would use the *sukuk* proceeds as part of its war chest in the acquisition of P&O, along with a much bigger tranche of conventional acquisition loan financing provided by the syndicate of banks. However, no doubt the conventional nature of this $6.5 billion tranche of bank debt muddied the waters somewhat for *sukuk* investors, who consequently needed to find an untainted asset to pin their return to. The cranes happened to fulfil that brief adequately enough and the purchase of P&O was relegated to a mere description of the wider corporate activities of PCFC, which of course were loosely incorporated into the business plan. The other advantage of not linking the business plan explicitly to the acquisition was that the issuance and ongoing status of the *sukuk* would not be conditional on the acquisition.

So with the structure and documents of the transaction thoroughly vetted and signed off by the various stakeholders in the deal, it fell to the salesmen and -women of the three lead banks to go to work and sell to their investors. Driven by the bid deadline, they called hundreds of their clients, from the world's largest pension fund managers in markets such as the United States, to specialized convertible bond hedge funds in Hong Kong, to regional financial institutions in the Middle East and South-East Asia, both Islamic and conventional. In the frenzy of transcontinental telecom traffic, one common theme began to emerge. Investors had never seen an instrument like this before. Oh sure, the pension funds and hedge funds were familiar with pre-IPO convertibles and zero coupon bonds, but Sharia? Suddenly a stream of questions needed answers: 'How do we get our money back if the bond goes belly up? What's the security? What's the jurisdiction here? A court of English law? A Sharia court? Let us look into what the risk factors are. We'll get back to you.'

Whilst DIB's clients were comfortable with the risk factors related to financial investments complying with Sharia, Barclays' and Deutsche's clients were not so sure. They liked the issuing company and its parents. They knew the acquisition plan was commercially attractive though bold. The geographic and industry diversification was appealing. But Islamic? There must have been a catch.

Deutsche's sales team was getting nervous. In the absence of a dedicated Islamic sales team, the job of selling this *sukuk* fell to their conventional credit sales desk, and they were struggling. The launch date was approaching and their sales spreadsheets had too few tick marks against investor names in the 'committed' column.

'We believe there's a 45 per cent probability of selling this *sukuk*', stated the London-based head of the MENA sales team on yet another conference call to his structuring colleagues in Dubai. This time it didn't just seem as if there was a continent separating the two teams, but that the colour of the sky, too, was different in the Islamic and conventional universes. 'It's too complex, it's unprecedented. Investors won't buy.' And with that, Deutsche Bank pulled out of the arranging group, leaving a US$1 billion hole in the deal. Deutsche's Islamic structurers were furious.

A visit by Barclays Capital's chief Bob Diamond to the region seemed to step up efforts on the Barclays sales desk and before long they plugged the gap. When the deal was finally launched, DIB and Barclays sold the *sukuk* four times over to their investor base. With a total subscription of $11.4 billion, the issue size was raised from the initial requirement of $2.8 billion to a final issuance of $3.5 billion, and the bankers walked away with a cool $100 million in fees, a premium for cutting-edge work never to be repeated. The Islamic structurers from Deutsche Bank watched from the sidelines, the colour draining from their faces, as Barclays' bankers were showered with newspaper column inches and industry awards.

It is said that history is written by the victors, and investment banking is no exception. Some years later when I worked at Barclays Capital, the bond specialists maintained their unswerving belief that they had structured the PCFC *sukuk*; and no better proof of this was their logo attached to the 'tombstone' announcing their deal in the press. And yet for some reason I found it remarkably challenging to explain to them the difference between a *musharaka* and a *mudaraba*.

PCFC was a watershed for the industry. Subsequent *sukuk* issuances were measured in the billions instead of the hundreds of millions of dollars. Convertible and exchangeable *sukuk* became the fashionable method of choice for large corporations and governments to raise capital. Deutsche learnt its lesson and gave in to its structurers' pleas for dedicated Islamic sales specialists, at least for as long as markets boomed. When the credit crisis hit and *sukuk* – and indeed Islamic finance in general – came to be regarded as 'a luxury the bank can't afford',[8] the bank abandoned the market as abruptly as it had embraced it.

5

The Skunk Works Specialists

'Knowledge has no borders, wisdom has no race or nationality. To block out ideas is to block out the kingdom of God.'

Aristotle appearing to Caliph Al-Mamun in a dream

Deutsche Bank was ablaze with excitement. Safa Tower had
cemented the bank's name in the Middle East, but PCFC had
put Deutsche's Islamic team on the world map. The *Financial
Times* featured Bossuyt's bald-headed and beaming face on the
front cover of its Islamic finance supplement in June 2006,[1] and
the team expanded to accommodate its burgeoning pipeline of
deals.

Bossuyt and two Oxford-educated bankers were joined by
a team of younger structurers: a British-born Pakistani with a
physics degree from University College London, the team's only
woman, immaculately presented in business suit and *hijab* (the
Muslim headscarf); a British Nigerian, an industrial chemist from
Imperial College London, towering over his colleagues at six
foot something and an expert in derivatives; a senior Malaysian
structurer who provided reach into the world's largest Islamic

finance market; and a fast-talking Jordanian youngster. Two aggressive senior sales staff completed the recruitment process.

They wouldn't let deals like PCFC slip through their conventional colleagues' butter-fingers into the hands of competitors. They were young, dynamic and edgy in stark contrast to their socially awkward Indo-Pakistani brethren at competitor banks. Their suits were tailored, not off the peg, and they rumbled into DIFC's underground car park every morning in Italian supercars. Junior team members were encouraged to challenge their seniors and robustly defend their ideas. Morning meetings were informal and non-hierarchical, ranged around a flip chart with scattered diagrams and equations. Bossuyt eschewed his prerogative to luxuriate in a glass-enclosed corner office, choosing instead to be a man of the people and seat himself at the end of a row of desks. He even declined the seat closest to the giant window overlooking Dubai's incredible panorama, and passed it on to me instead. I wasn't about to complain.

The Belgian boss of Deutsche's Islamic finance team was socially egalitarian but intellectually elitist. Our office environment at the Dubai International Financial Centre was non-sacrosanct, verging on a social club for well-dressed geeks, on one occasion transforming into an impromptu venue for an arm-wrestling tournament. The enormous Nigerian took on his diminutive Pakistani senior across a filing cabinet, locked grimly together for what seemed like an age as the office egged them on loudly. The kerfuffle prompted Deutsche's country head to poke his head out of the glass door of his office. At first the throng swarming around the two combatants quietened and nervously parted to allow the big boss through. But he giggled at the sight and the throng resumed raucously. This is what he wanted. A team that didn't live by the dry conventions of title and conformity. It had to have an intense and sharp quality, to do things the others didn't. As if to confirm the team's unpredictability, the smaller man won, *hijabi* match referee declaring the Nigerian's loss by technical default by bending his wrists to avoid touching down. An unsuccessful attempt to exploit a legal loophole on this occasion, remarked one office comedian.

Islamic finance was hot and suddenly everyone wanted a piece of the action. But the complexity of Sharia-compliant products was ratcheting up and few had a grip on the structural and legal nuances.

Arif Naqvi wanted to be in on it badly. A well-known deal maker based in Dubai, Naqvi was the suave chief executive of an upstart regional private equity house, a financial institution that buys and sells privately held companies with their clients' money. Naqvi had an eye for a cheap company with potential for growth. He bought it, re-engineered its balance sheet, installed new management, and sold on the enterprise for a tidy profit. The Middle East had rarely before seen an operator of his type. He dared to have the same global ambitions as the big bad American 'buy-out' houses, and modelled his firm on his brash American cousins.

Nowhere were those ambitions more apparent than in Naqvi's bold courting of Deutsche Bank as a partner in the regional buy-out market. With Deutsche's help, Abraaj Capital raised US$2 billion internationally to invest in infrastructure in the region. Islamically.

The Infrastructure and Growth Capital Fund would be Abraaj's flagship fund and the relationship with Deutsche would grant the private equity firm access to an Islamic structuring capability that Naqvi's own otherwise impressively capable investment executives lacked. The $2 billion that Abraaj and Deutsche had raised was eye-catching enough, but Naqvi set his sights higher. If his team could pull off just one massive leveraged buy out, the type of heavily debt-financed acquisition of a rich trophy asset that would make headlines in the *Financial Times* or *Wall Street Journal*, then he would cement his local reputation on an international scale. And Sharia compliance would be his unique selling point.

On 30 May 2007, together with some co-investors, Abraaj
Capital's Sharia-compliant fund purchased all the shares in
a company called Egyptian Fertilizers Company – or EFC –
Egypt's largest private-sector producer of integrated nitrogen
fertilizer (known by its chemical name, urea). It cost the fund
$1.4 billion plus the $465 million already owed by the company's balance sheet in existing (conventional) debt. Including
transaction fees, the total purchase price was a whopping
$1.9 billion and the fund would need to raise debt financing
from a syndicate of banks to make it happen.

At first, the deal team at Abraaj worried that the short bid
timetable for the acquisition would not enable them to structure Sharia-compliant financing in time. This is Egypt, they
said. The legislative framework is hard enough for a conventional financing, let alone Islamic. The deal requires a
'multi-tranche' structure – that is, one that requires the debt
to be cut up into a number of discrete packages owing to the
huge size of the acquisition. It requires a refinancing of existing
conventional debt in the company. It's a structural nightmare,
they protested.

Over at Deutsche Bank, the bankers on the emerging markets
financing desk were similarly pessimistic. Schooled in conventional acquisition finance, Islamic finance was too exotic, too
unknown, to be trusted. But their colleagues on the Islamic desk
begged to differ and asked Sheikh Hussain to solve the impasse.

We met the scholar in his office in downtown Dubai. 'Bring
your client and the bankers to me', he said, then reiterated a
now familiar mantra in his rich Egyptian accent: 'If you go to the
doctor but you do not tell him all your symptoms, your background, your lifestyle, then he cannot give you the best advice.
They must give me all the information – balance sheet and cash
flow, which party earns what, who takes what risk, and all of
the requirements of the different parties to the transaction.' He
meant not only the principals in the transaction, but also the

government, the regulators and tax authorities. 'If they provide me with all the symptoms, I will find a comprehensive cure.'

So convinced was he that a commercially viable solution was possible that he offered to complete the structuring and documentation in conjunction with the legal teams within three months of the official tender offer. Three months for an unprecedented deal in a nascent industry, where the pessimistic emerging markets bankers at Deutsche might have baulked at the thought of two years, just like the Safa Tower deal before.

The conventional bankers at Deutsche and their client at Abraaj didn't believe him. The pugnacious scholar was either crazy or a genius. They understood the concept of a sale and leaseback – a real economy transaction that relies on a real underlying asset – but couldn't find a way for the underlying assets of the target company to be bought and leased back to the company by a foreign financial institution in Egypt without a tortuous licensing process, certainly one that would take longer than the mandatory offer period. Nor were they at ease with security and enforcement issues related to such a structure in the Egyptian legislative environment – the only way to enforce their security rights over 'their' assets would be via a local agent bank. This wasn't the comfortable and familiar jurisdiction that Western bankers were used to. It was a volatile emerging market. International banks don't like locals having control over their assets when the deal goes pear-shaped. What other solution could there be?

The default option of the ubiquitous commodity *murabaha* structure had been vetoed by the conservative Sheikh Hussain for looking too much like a conventional loan. If it looks like a loan, smells like a loan and acts like a loan, it *is* a loan, he reasoned – it doesn't matter what fancy Arabic words you attach to the finance documents. So the bankers in Deutsche's offices on London Wall did what all bankers do when chasing their year-end bonus: choose the path of least resistance. They would pursue a conventional interest-bearing loan to finance the deal and worry about Sharia later.

Undeterred, the Dubai-based Islamic specialists approached the scholar with an idea. In a meeting room we huddled round a white board covered in the scrawl of contractual structure diagrams and wondered out loud: what if the banks bought the finished product from the company for future delivery? What if the 'senior' tranche of the financing – the piece that is lowest risk for lenders as it gets paid back to them before anyone else gets their money – was in fact not a loan, but a contract of exchange, a sale and purchase agreement between the banks and EFC?

The idea had precedent, except that such a precedent was from 1,400 years ago – from seventh-century Arabia, in fact. At that time, a farmer lived a tough life, his fortunes subject to the vagaries of a harsh desert climate. If he couldn't lock in a price for his produce before the harvest, he risked not feeding his family for eleven months of the year. So he sold his crop in advance to different buyers, spreading out his income over the year. This forward sale of a commodity became known as the *salam* contract, allowing the farmer to ensure his family's financial security by receiving money today for delivery of a specified quality and quantity of produce at a specified point in the future. We wanted to transform a classical concept into its modern-day equivalent.

'As the bank, we buy the urea from EFC for $850 million on day one', we suggested to Sheikh Hussain, 'and they deliver the product to us for selling on into the market over a period of eight years, the term of the equivalent debt financing.' This would be a real economy transaction, one where the bank acts as a merchant, buying and selling on a product – an Islamic transaction.

Sheikh Hussain paused, smiled and slowly nodded his head. 'Praise be to Allah', he affirmed in Arabic in a low voice, as if speaking to himself. 'You have learnt well.'

The bankers in London were furious. 'Insanity!' screeched Deutsche's senior director on the emerging markets structuring desk during a conference call with her colleagues in Dubai. 'That is a ridiculous idea, and will never work. Let's move on and look for something else.' But the Dubai team wouldn't let it drop and continued to explore the idea with the sheikh and the bank's legal counsel at the elite English law firm Clifford Chance.

In the automotive and high-technology industries, this kind of behind-the-scenes unsanctioned project, typically undertaken in secret by a small group of technical experts, bypassing the normal bureaucracy of an organization, would be termed 'skunk works'. Skunk works can often result in a radically new product that may later gain official sanction. With a Samadiite sitting in each of the three firms – Deutsche, Abraaj and Clifford Chance – somehow a critical mass of ideas could be crystallized into an executable plan, building on the personal relationships between these skunk works specialists. It would be an opportunity for us to roll out a six-hundred horsepower fire-breathing monster from the secret shed to show off to our colleagues, who in contrast might perhaps spend their days building humble family sedans on the factory floor.

Would the idea work? And would such a radical financing be possible without this proximity of lifestyle and community that the Samadiites were blessed with? This would become the largest ever buy out in the Middle East, and indeed the largest Sharia-compliant buy out the world had ever seen. Failure would be highly visible and Naqvi's bold ambitions would not tolerate it, nor indeed, in turn, the careers of those involved.

The skunk works specialists needed to do more than just theorize. They had to convince their colleagues that the concepts of a millennium-old legal system could be applied to a modern cross-border acquisition financing in an emerging market. This was the type of transaction that would normally require an investment bank to simultaneously juggle jurisdictional, regulatory and tax challenges, challenges that are typically more nebulous in emerging markets than in developed markets. By adding Sharia into the mix, acquiring high-value companies through a multi-tranche financing might ordinarily lead a deal team to believe that the financing was impossible, and perhaps even abandon the cause.

To appease the conventional bankers, the initial injection of debt funding was arranged on a conventional basis in order to meet the acquisition timetable, albeit with a clear expectation of refinancing via a Sharia-compliant take-out within a pre-agreed time frame. This time frame was set at six months, but subject to a number of transaction-specific provisos.

At first, the suggestion circulated among the London bankers that their colleagues in Dubai simply didn't understand the commercial and risk parameters that a global investment bank operated under, and that perhaps the Dubai bankers simply weren't up to the task. To the sophisticated London bankers, their Dubai colleagues were the underachieving cousins sent off to far lands to tend to peripheral matters in the family business. A seventh-century contract to sell farm produce in an ultra-sophisticated twenty-first-century multi-tranche cross-border acquisition financing? These guys were nuts. But as the Samadiites put together the legal terms for their proposed forward purchase of the underlying manufactured product – fertilizer – the credit traders at Deutsche Bank began to give serious consideration to this fantastical trade. Banks, after all, are in the business of making money. If they see an opportunity for profit, then providing their risk management committees are satisfied with various levels of security and collateral in a deal, then why not? An *istisna* contract – that is, the forward purchase of a manufactured commodity over time – may have had its origins in the *salam* contract of seventh-century Arabia, but it was just a contractual tool. And contracts, after all, are what modern banks are geared to analyse and quantify.

Despite the internal conflicts, the *istisna* structure started to come together. Deutsche Bank entered into an agreement to purchase the urea on day one for $850 million, the amount of 'senior' debt required – that is, the piece that gets paid back to lenders before anyone else gets their investment back. The urea would be manufactured and delivered in pre-agreed quantities and quality, and to a pre-agreed delivery schedule. Thus, Deutsche Bank became a buyer of urea via a forward sale agreement according to a delivery schedule that gave it the same economics as a conventional loan. The forward sale agreement provided the standard protections found in a conventional senior debt financing, including various financial covenants, standard representations and warranties, events of default; all the features that one might find in any large-scale complex conventional financing – so the screechy conventional bankers back in London need not worry that an apparently archaic system of contract law might disadvantage them in some way.

Naturally, investment banks are not in the business of warehousing vast quantities of stock unrelated to their core business. In order not to inundate a bemused mail room on London Wall with millions of sacks of fertilizer over eight years (the term of the 'loan'), and to minimize the commodity risk and maximize the credit quality of the transaction, the bankers arranged a long-term buyer – an 'offtaker' – for the urea. This assurance of 'offtake performance' – in other words an assurance the goods would find buyers – was provided by a performance guarantee from the company itself, and from the company's owners.

This was a little awkward from a Sharia perspective: after all, an Islamic financing was not supposed to guarantee its repayment, otherwise it would be a conventional debt. But Sheikh Hussain deemed there to be sufficient risk in the transaction to allow the company to provide an obligation of performance. Instead of an outright guarantee of repayment, the company would be required to replace the offtaker within a specified time frame in the event of an inability to offtake.

Despite the rigour of the structure from a Sharia perspective, some compromises had to be reached. Ownership of the underlying assets of a company is not always commercially palatable to international banks. They deal in debt and cash, not bags of fertilizer. Local ownership laws in many emerging markets, especially in Egypt, may be incompatible with the transfer of title to foreign entities. Tax regulations might also have made this transaction legally and economically prohibitive. However, in such extenuating cases, scholars may be comfortable with 'constructive' ownership and possession of an asset by passing beneficial interest in an asset to the bank or its SPV without changing legal title.

In addition, the choice of jurisdiction of the various legal entities incorporated for the purposes of executing the different legs of such a transaction may require specific tax considerations in respect of dividends or profit rates, and the treatment of withholding taxes. How such payments were construed by the Egyptian tax authority was of paramount importance in determining such details, and a significant due diligence exercise was undertaken in this regard. Additionally, the purchase and resale of an asset (in this case due to the banks' requirement for an offtaker) may incur multiple stamp duties, and once again the final structure and choice of jurisdiction go hand in hand with such considerations. Ironically, sophisticated non-Islamic jurisdictions like the United Kingdom dealt with the subject of punitive taxes for Islamic transactions better than majority-Muslim nations in the emerging markets.

So it wasn't a perfect structure from a Sharia perspective. Full legal ownership and physical possession had to concede to beneficial interest and constructive possession. But without the appropriate tax and ownership concessions from the relevant authorities, this mild fudging of the Sharia issues was deemed by Sheikh Hussain to be an acceptable compromise.

Finally, the transaction would not have been complete without refinancing the piece of debt that sat in between the senior debt tranche and shareholders' equity in priority of repayment, the so-called 'mezzanine' tranche since it is repaid before the shareholders who take on the most risk (in the form of shares) and get paid in dividends from the bottom line profits, but after senior debt providers who take on the least risk and get paid out first from the business expenses. The mezzanine financing proved to be a much more straightforward structure, since its very nature was ideally suited to a refinancing via a type of investment partnership contract known as a *musharaka* – the same type of contract used in the PCFC *sukuk*. Thus, the two partners of this *musharaka* were the issuer (in other words the note holders or investors) who contributed cash of $400 million, and the company itself, which contributed capital worth $675 million in the form of equity. Job done.

As is typical in such investment partnership transactions, the company, EFC, acted as the managing partner entrusted to manage the joint venture capital in order to generate a profit according to an agreed business plan. Just like the PCFC *sukuk*, under the terms of a purchase undertaking, the assets in the partnership would be repurchased on maturity of the financing by the obligor – the company itself. Thus, just like the PCFC *sukuk*, investors in this tranche of financing were promising to buy back their investment at a pre-determined price. In time, Mufti Taqi Usmani would have something to say about this apparent breach of Sharia guidelines on true risk sharing, but for now it seemed to work, and Sheikh Hussain had no objections.

Given the enormous size of this acquisition, and the consequential need for multi-tranche financing, it was clear that conventional banks in the syndicate – particularly those participating only in the least risky senior tranche – would require the same protection of their position that they typically enjoyed in conventional transactions. They wouldn't want to have the same loose protections as the more risky mezzanine financiers. In a conventional transaction, this would be solved relatively simply by the addition of an 'intercreditor agreement', that is, an agreement between financiers to give preference to those institutions who have invested in the senior tranche. Thus, in the event of a default by the company in repaying its obligations, all the various banks involved in the transaction would look to the intercreditor agreement and be repaid in order of their risk preference: senior creditors first, mezzanine next, and equity shareholders last.

Unfortunately this was not so straightforward. In Sharia, capital providers in a venture may not enjoy economically preferential terms over any other investor, since to do so might encourage the rich and powerful to exploit the poor and weak. In this case, the need to balance the requirements of conventional banks with the Sharia was overcome by the use of a Sharia-compliant intercreditor agreement, the first of its kind in acquisition financing.

The solution was mutuality. Mutual insurance companies have operated in the West for over 300 years, though their ancient ancestors may have been the public institutions established by men like Umar ibn al-Khattab, the second caliph after the Prophet's death. Today, *takaful* insurance companies – the Sharia-compliant equivalent of conventional insurance companies – may operate by pooling the funds of policyholders on a mutual basis, with each policyholder 'guaranteeing' the financial wellbeing of fellow policyholders in the event of a calamity.

The intercreditor agreement in this case worked on a similar premise, the resulting document balancing the needs of senior versus mezzanine finance providers, and conventional bridge finance providers versus refinanced Islamic tranches. Junior capital providers mutually guaranteed the payment of senior providers in certain circumstances by promising to give up payment in those circumstances, a radically new and proprietary technique for an Islamic financing.

The EFC deal had been an immense effort, and a vindication of the Samadiites' skunk works approach. It remains the largest Islamic buy out ever conducted, and bigger even than the biggest conventional buy out in the Middle East. And yet, despite the success of the transaction, as the deal approached its closing stages, a deal-weary senior executive at Abraaj Capital called me to express his concern over the Sharia requirements of the fund that he had set up alongside the bankers from Deutsche.

'We've been having a think internally', he told me. 'We're wondering if we can make this a "best efforts" Sharia fund. It's just unnecessarily complex to do these acquisitions under the fund, and we don't think the additional Islamic liquidity justifies the effort.'

It seems he was telling me he wanted to be half pregnant. Either he was or he wasn't, I advised. The investors in the fund have already put their money in. If he returned to them now and said we tried to do deals on a Sharia-compliant basis but it was just too hard and we had gone conventional instead, how would they respond? Quite apart from the reputational impact of a 'best efforts' fund, there might have been the very real possibility of legal action by investors who thought they were buying a permissible (*halal*) product.

Islamic finance had proven more alien than he and his colleagues had at first imagined. This need to find a real asset and share in its risk was not an easy way to make money. Trading of debt, of cash flows, was so much easier: lend a buck, make a few cents – a paper trade. A financial transaction, not a real economy one. It doesn't matter what comes in between.

In the end, Abraaj relented and realized that as such financings would become commonplace as the region's economy continued to grow, understanding of Sharia structures and processes would become an essential ingredient to success. After the pain of this transaction they would be well on their way to that understanding and would find each successive deal easier to close. Without the will to overcome the constraints set by law, by regulators and by tax authorities within a Sharia framework, and without the technical skill set to execute, such deals will falter.

Investors were becoming increasingly aware that they could now invest in all sorts of assets on a Sharia-compliant basis, and many would no longer be willing to accept excuses that a deal could not be closed because of Sharia constraints. As Sheikh Hussain often said, 'For every one door in Sharia that closes, a hundred others will open.' Financing an asset conventionally now meant that issuers and borrowers could potentially close the door on a massive demographic constituency, and thus possibly deny themselves the opportunity to realize the maximum value of their assets. No deal was now too sophisticated for Islamic finance. You just needed to work a little harder at it.

***

The Malaysian *sukuk*: raising ethical standards

Commercial tensions surface regularly in the Islamic finance industry, more so than in conventional transactions. After all, participants are consciously attempting to balance commercial needs with an ethical outlook. And since the ethical basis of Islamic finance does not exist in a readily codified form, it can be frustrating for those unused to this new form of financing. Often conventional bankers perceive Islamic finance as nebulous and shape shifting, impossible to tie down to a simple set of rules, as well as likely to result in diminished returns.

The issue of balancing ethics with the pursuit of profit is not confined to Islamic finance alone. In December 2013, an investigative journalist from the BBC uncovered an unpleasant consequence of giving to charity in the UK: some of the country's leading charitable organizations, including Comic Relief and Save the Children, invest their surplus funds in companies whose activities might not accord with the sentiments of donors.[2] Comic Relief, for example, holds tens of millions of pounds at any one time, and invests those funds in companies across the asset spectrum including arms manufacturers, tobacco and alcohol companies. The charity claims that those funds 'deliver the greatest benefits to the most vulnerable people' – including those fighting tuberculosis caused by tobacco – and has a mission statement to '[work] to reduce alcohol misuse and minimise alcohol related harm'.[3] Is that what donors would want, the pursuit of profit at all costs?

And was it right that at a time when the public is especially mindful of the impact of high energy prices on the weak and vulnerable, that such a prominent charity as Save the Children had censored criticism of energy firms who acted as corporate partners to the charity? Save the Children's fuel poverty campaign had run for only one winter, one former senior executive claiming that his efforts to highlight the issue of rising energy prices having been quashed internally. One multinational energy firm had been singled out for praise in that campaign – on account of its corporate relationship with Save the Children – and subsequent internal emails revealed that the charity was pitching to become a charity partner to yet another multinational energy supplier.[4] Not only would impoverished families be denied a champion for their cause, but justice and ethics had also become victims.

In much the same way, the Church of England had come in for recent criticism following the Archbishop of Canterbury's public condemnation of high street 'payday' lenders – charging vulnerable borrowers usurious rates – only to discover that his own Church endowment funds were an investor in the controversial UK payday lender, Wonga.[5] There was a delicious irony in the thought that if the Church had appointed a Sharia-compliant asset manager, it might not have been so embarrassingly exposed. That's not to say the Islamic community is immune from such a faux pas: my local mosque's endowment fund has unwittingly become the landlord to a convenience store selling liquor. It's not easy to keep such a dirty little secret for long, and clamours by the local Muslim community to divest may eventually force the mosque to offload the property in a depressed real estate market.

The argument put forward by proponents of such investment policies is that an organization acting in the interests of others – whether they are shareholders or charity recipients – must invest with a view to generating the highest possible returns. In many cases, there is an unquestioned assumption that introducing ethical parameters will automatically diminish those returns. However, events of the last several years have revealed that ethical funds – including Islamic ones – have tended to avoid those types of investment that were excessively risky, highly indebted, or participated in activities whose ethics were dubious. The financial services sector is an excellent example: the sector's exposure to intangible and exotic derivative instruments that brought down the world's economy has meant that conventional funds severely underperformed ethical funds that avoided financial stocks or companies with large debt burdens or heavy exposures to derivative contracts. Islamic funds have therefore done remarkably well by comparison to their conventional peers in recent years.

The bare facts themselves may not be enough to convince the decision makers. It took a confluence of factors – not least of which was the geographic proximity and close friendships of the Samadiites – to ensure a successful acquisition of Egyptian Fertilizers Company. As the largest and most complex Islamic financing of its time, it may not have happened had the Islamic skunk works specialists at Deutsche not carved their own path. The financing of the Dubai government's purchase of P&O had been a similar trial in many ways. But now, slowly, the conventional banking industry was becoming familiar with the role that Islamic finance could play in executing the biggest and most complex deals, adding extra liquidity to the market, bringing a new breed of investor to the table. And as more deals would come to market, the standards applied to those deals would tighten, and conventional bankers and clients would grow even more frustrated that the framework of Islamic finance wouldn't stand still long enough for them to understand it fully.

This was particularly apparent in the raising of a *sukuk* by the Malaysian government in 2010. The *sukuk* industry had been left reeling after Mufti Taqi Usmani's now infamous comments to the Reuters reporter in 2008 that most *sukuk* at the time were not compliant with Sharia. Since those comments, *sukuk* issuances had been sporadic and cautious, a slowdown further exacerbated by the downturn in the global economy.

But in 2010 the Malaysian government invited banks to raise US$1 billion of financing on its behalf in the Islamic capital markets, the kind of deal size that warrants the description of 'benchmark'. In the post-2008 era of increased scrutiny from Sharia scholars, the lucky banks and law firms selected to raise funding for the state were acutely aware of the need to set a higher standard for this transaction than had been observed in earlier *sukuk* transactions. Whereas treasury officials insisted on replicating contractual documentation from previous Malaysian sovereign *sukuk* and the more recent Republic of Indonesia *sukuk*, the assembled bankers and lawyers – many of them Samadiites – suggested that in such a case their scholars would struggle to sign off on the deal.

The asset structure had already been decided – that is, the underlying real economy transaction that would underpin the financial one. Government officials and their bankers selected a portfolio of twelve government-owned hospitals as the assets that would form the basis of the sale and leaseback. The assets were, of course, engaged in a Sharia-compliant activity and had no conventional debt or other encumbrances associated with them. They would be placed in trust on behalf of *sukuk* holders and leased back to the government for the duration of the *sukuk*, following which ownership would revert to the government.

The big-picture structure had been approved, relevant governmental approvals granted to transfer the assets and issue the bond, contracts were drawn up, and the banks' syndicate desks, manned by armies of salesmen and -women champing at the bit, waited on standby to sell the securities to investors. So far, so good.

As the deal approached its closing stages, the bankers from HSBC, Barclays and CIMB arrived in the tropically leafy town of Putrajaya at the government offices just south of Kuala Lumpur. They were here to deliver bad news to their counterparts across the table from the Malaysian Ministry of Finance. The scholars were not willing to provide their *fatwa*, or legal certification, on this transaction: the adherence of this deal to Sharia was not of a sufficiently high standard.

In transactions of earlier years, scholars had tended to look at the overall structure of a deal, checking off the big-picture Sharia requirements rather than wading through 1,000 pages of dense contractual language and commenting on each and every applicable clause. But times were changing. Mufti Taqi Usmani had inspired a new approach. A worldwide insistence from both investors and scholars on increased Sharia scrutiny meant that no scholar could afford to be seen to be the one who let *riba*, *gharar* and other prohibitions slip through his net, no matter how tiny the infringement. In previous *sukuk* transactions, the scholars, lawyers and bankers had simply not devoted as much attention to ensuring that the tiniest of details in the contractual documentation had been thought through.

Seated at the boardroom table in the Ministry of Finance, the government treasury solicitor and her team of finance and legal specialists blinked disbelievingly and looked at each other. They didn't quite understand what they were hearing from the gentlemen from HSBC and Barclays. The weekend was approaching and volatility of debt capital markets meant the client was in no mood to delay this any further. This deal had to be launched to investors right now, before market conditions turned against them.

Then the tone of the meeting turned nasty. To the head of the treasury team, it sounded like the banks were saying 'thanks for playing, game over'. Any reticence of the banks to go through with this would probably irreparably damage their chances of being offered a government mandate again. Any delay would seriously hamper their chances of winning any mandates in the near future. It was a sobering thought: HSBC, the pioneer of global Islamic banking for the masses, denied entry to one of Islamic banking's biggest markets. Not for the first time, ever-tightening standards of Sharia were causing some to question whether raising Islamic capital was really worth the effort.

To make matters worse, the government's own legal and Sharia advisors were not themselves seasoned Islamic capital markets veterans, and could not advise their client on the reasonableness of the banks' request to rewrite the deal docs. To the civil servants seated on one side of the table, this seemed like an attempt to delay the transaction for reasons that weren't clear. They turned to their advisors, a partner from the English law firm Allen and Overy, and their in-house Sharia advisors, who merely shrugged their shoulders pathetically: the law partner was not familiar with matters of Sharia, and the Sharia advisors knew little of international capital markets nor – evidently – current Sharia standards.

'What are the scholars objecting to?' asked the head of the treasury team, bristling at the suggestion that a Malaysian *sukuk* could not be Sharia compliant. They were, after all, a predominantly Muslim country, their government a pioneer of the industry. How dare these peddlers of usury tell them they weren't Islamic enough.

'Are you telling us the last *sukuk* we did was not Sharia

compliant?' She turned her head towards her own Sharia advisors who stared vacantly across the table, desperately trying to
avoid eye contact with the bankers who seemed to know more
about their subject than they did.

For perhaps the first time on a South-East Asian *sukuk*, the
banks and the scholars were taking a belts-and-braces approach to
certifying the transaction. They would leave no stone unturned
and no clause in the documentation unexplored. Their objections were to individual clauses, the impact of which would only
be felt in exceptional circumstances, and therefore had tended
to be glossed over in past deals.

What happens, for example, if for whatever reason it became
illegal for a non-governmental entity (like the *sukuk* investors'
special purpose vehicle) to own government-run hospitals? Let's
imagine the government were to pass legislation independently
of this transaction that public sector assets, or assets of a specific
nature that included hospitals, could not be owned or leased by
a private sector entity. The solution in previous *sukuk* contracts
– enshrined in the so-called 'illegality clause' – was for the government to continue to pay the rental amount to *sukuk* holders.
Surely investors would not have a problem with this? After all,
they would be paid even though they no longer own the asset.

At that point, the whole deal becomes null and void, argued
the bankers on advice from their scholars. Even if the government
is prepared to continue to pay the bond coupons, this would be
classified in Sharia as an 'unjust enrichment': the trading of cash
flow, not a real asset. Money for nothing, in other words. The
Sharia insisted that there had to be an underlying reason for
the payment – an asset legally owned by the lessor with true
usufruct for the lessee (from the Latin *usus et fructus* – usage and
enjoyment). If the assets are no longer owned and used by the
SPV, then the SPV has no basis to charge a rent against them,
and the transaction must be wound up instead.

'But why should we not pay rent if we agree to pay and

investors agree to receive payment?' argued the exasperated treasury officials.

'This goes to the heart of Islamic finance', answered the Samadi banker from HSBC. 'Without an underlying asset, there is no *sukuk al-ijara* [rental-based *sukuk*]. If we agree to the language which has been in place on countless previous trans- actions, our scholars will not sign off, and you will not have the Islamic distribution you were looking for.'

The banker from Barclays, also a Samadiite, concurred. 'Sure, we can sell this to our conventional investor base, but without the changes requested, we don't get the *fatwa* and we don't have a *sukuk*. We have a bond. And the investors will not be the people you are looking to attract.'

The Malaysian treasury team refused to back down and the bankers furiously texted and emailed their scholars – amongst them Sheikh Nizam Yaquby – thousands of miles away in the Gulf to seek a compromise. The scholars would not budge. This is a new era, they said firmly. If companies and governments do not want to conform to the rules of Sharia, they are free to issue conventional bonds. Our job is not to acquiesce to commercial pressures. Our job is to see that Sharia is upheld.

And though the industry had been criticized for the acquies- cence of scholars in the past, and the inherent conflict generated when scholars are paid by the institutions who seek their approval, finally Taqi Usmani's message was getting through. Maybe his services might also have benefited the rating agencies, the organizations paid by banks to approve nonsense ratings on the banks' complex investment products, which ultimately pre- cipitated the global financial crisis.

With no choice left and the weekend almost upon them, the unhappy treasury boss shook her head and approved the changes. Perhaps inwardly she felt that her own advisors had not fought her corner hard enough, though perhaps she also felt that they just weren't in the game. The all important *fatwa* was issued, and banks' syndicate teams sprang into action, placing the *sukuk* with investors across the world.

So strong was the oversubscription that the Ministry of Finance opted to increase the original size of the placement to $1.25 billion, the biggest ever dollar-denominated sovereign *sukuk*, and so strong was it a template for future deals that the *sukuk* was named deal of the year by two industry journals.[6] Perhaps, just perhaps, investors really did care about the standards of Sharia applied to Islamic finance.

***

Hedge funds meet Islamic finance

The murky world of 'alternative investments' and hedge funds seems apparently far removed from Islamic notions of transparency and fair profit. Notorious for their aggressive trading strategies, and perhaps unkindly maligned by those who believe them to profit out of volatility and others' misery, hedge funds have been described by one prominent German politician as 'swarms of locusts',[7] voraciously devouring all in their path in the quest to make profit for their elite investors. If greed is good, then hedge funds are presumably the best.

Their purpose is a simple one: to make returns that are hedged against market volatility. In other words, to give investors a stable return, or an 'absolute return' – one that remains relatively constant (and positive) even in turbulent times. But over the years, hedge fund managers have discovered increasingly exotic ways to invest, employing complex and arcane methods to boost their investors' returns. Not content with merely going long (buying shares) and shorting (selling shares they borrow but do not own) to balance their portfolios, they now engage in the trading of convertible bonds, derivatives and other exotic instruments. Some hedge funds specialize in so-called 'event driven' opportunities, effectively taking a punt on a certain event occuring, such as a merger of two companies or the default of a nation's debt obligations.

As rich investors with the means to invest in their funds have gravitated away from the traditional asset manager – the 'long only' manager whose job is typically to manage a portfolio of shares over decades of steady growth – the size of hedge funds has grown and so has their influence. Now, the stock price of large corporations can be heavily influenced by one trade by a large hedge fund, leading many to question whether more should be done to rein in their power.

Trading of such an aggressive nature – profit being apparently the sole motivator – would seem incongruous in the context of Islamic finance. Do Islamic investors want absolute returns generated by this kind of fund manager? According to one hedge fund advisor, the answer was yes.

In 2007, just before that previously staid British investment bank Barclays Capital was starting to make waves in international waters by closing the net on failed US bulge bracket firm Lehman Brothers, Barclays was approached by a little known US hedge fund advisory firm based in Connecticut to provide a brokerage service – known in the hedge fund industry as prime brokerage – on a Sharia-compliant basis.

'What would we need to do that for?' asked the prime brokers. 'What's the value add for our business?' The answer from the hedge fund advisor Shariah Capital was a brand new customer, one who had previously had zero access to absolute return strategies through 'long/short' hedge funds – funds that simultaneously buy some equities in the form of publicly traded shares and hedge their position by selling others that they borrow from the market. A new product, a new class of investor, never previously accessed in this manner: 100 per cent market share of the Islamic hedge fund market.

Shariah Capital had gigantic ambitions: to become the first universally accepted Sharia-compliant hedge fund manager; to raise US$1.5 billion from Barclays' investor base in the Middle East and elsewhere; and to source the very best hedge fund managers through Barclays' prime brokerage relationships in order to make use of the proprietary methods they had pioneered.

Although Shariah Capital's ambitious plans were driven by a brash US management keen to bring their uniquely American style to the Islamic finance industry, the intellectual driving force behind this proprietary Sharia-compliant shorting method – selling stock that one does not own – was Shariah Capital's rather more phlegmatic chief Sharia officer, Sheikh Yusuf Talal DeLorenzo.

Though conservative and unassuming by nature, Sheikh Yusuf had nevertheless previously been unreservedly vociferous in his condemnation of the conventional banking industry's cynical manipulation of Islamic finance. His greatest ire was reserved for recent techniques adopted by bulge bracket firms to replicate conventional derivatives under the wrapper of Sharia compliance. It would be ironic that the product he would bring to the market a couple of years later was itself the subject of criticism from some quarters: the thought of maverick 'hedgies' punting their unique brand of aggressive trading strategies was anathema to many conservative Islamic banking specialists.

But that tired stereotypical description would not have been fair to Sheikh Yusuf, not by a long stretch of the imagination. A softly spoken and thoughtful man with a trim white beard, his gentle personality brought a much-needed balance to the fast-talking hedgie culture of Shariah Capital. A specialist in the jurisprudence of Islamic transactions, he had previously served as a Sharia advisor to dozens of firms before he came to the attention of Shariah Capital.

Unusually, they asked him to join their management team, a departure from the usual role that scholars fulfil within financial institutions. Typically scholars tend to sit on a number of independent Sharia boards, and act in concert with other scholars to vet and approve products for compliance with Sharia. But perhaps in this case, Shariah Capital had felt it necessary to capture the services of one of the US's only internationally recognized advisors in the field, rather than fight other firms for a chunk of his time.

Born Anthony DeLorenzo, he was the grandson of half-Catholic, half-Methodist Sicilian immigrants to the US, but was raised in neither religion. Whilst a student at Cornell he elected to spend some time studying abroad and found himself in Casablanca reading the Quran, before moving on to Cairo and Karachi. His conversion to Islam was cemented by a change of name and marriage to a Pakistani.

During his thirty-year career, Sheikh Yusuf served as an advisor on Islamic education to the Pakistani president in the early 1980s, working at the time with the eminent scholar Sheikh Hussain Hamed Hassan, and later published *A Compendium of Legal Opinions on the Operations of Islamic Banks*,[8] the first English/Arabic reference work on the *fatwas* issued by Sharia boards. As the number of advisory roles with financial institutions grew, a hedge fund manager in Greenwich, Connecticut, came knocking on his door, looking to create a Sharia-compliant hedge fund.

Despite an underlying unease in the Islamic finance industry at the thought of Islamicizing an 'advanced form of speculation',[9] Sheikh Yusuf kept an open mind. If Islamic finance was predicated on the prohibition of interest and uncertainty, and abhorred the creation of wealth through idleness or gambling, then was there an intrinsic harm in creating a financial instrument that generated absolute returns by hedging itself in a Sharia-compliant manner?

It took years of running back and forth between London and New York for Sheikh Yusuf to crack the code with fellow scholars, and draw up a set of workable prime brokerage documents with Barclays Capital. In what would become a radical breakthrough for the industry, he settled on a type of contract in Sharia known as the *arbun* as a viable basis for replicating the economics of a short sale, the fundamental trading strategy necessary to balance a stock portfolio in the simpler hedge funds.

In 2008, Sheikh Yusuf published his white paper 'The Arboon Sale: A Shariah Compliant Alternative to Selling Short with Borrowed Securities'. In it, he reasoned that there was unanimity of agreement amongst scholars on the impermissibility of the sale of borrowed shares and, as a result, in Sharia the seller must first establish ownership of the subject of the sale. One cannot sell what one does not own.

He suggested that it was a mistake to assume that hedge funds could never become Sharia compliant, but criticized the use of 'artificial solutions' aimed at circumventing Sharia by 'swapping' returns from hedge funds, a clear dig at a recent technique developed by Deutsche Bank to replicate synthetically any economic effect, no matter how impermissible the underlying asset. The architect of Deutsche Bank's derivative products was none other than Sheikh Hussain Hamed Hassan, a one-time colleague of Sheikh Yusuf, and so the seeds of a scholarly spat were sown: *my method is more Sharia compliant than yours.*

Sheikh Yusuf was not alone in this opinion. A long-time critic of what he called 'Sharia arbitrage' techniques – that is, the provision of products whose exorbitant cost is justified by an apparent adherence to religious guidelines – fellow US scholar Mahmoud El-Gamal had previously likened Islamic finance to an elaborate con, preying on people's religious insecurities. 'Don't take my duck, sprinkle holy water on it, and say it's a chicken', he told *The Wall Street Journal*.[10] Perhaps Professor El-Gamal would have been equally critical of Shariah Capital's efforts in the field, in spite of Sheikh Yusuf's involvement.

So what is an *arbun*? In a conventional sense, it's like an 'option', a type of financial instrument that gives the buyer the right – but not the obligation – to buy an asset. So a share option is the right to buy a share for a particular value in the future. An investor might buy an option for shares in Microsoft instead of the shares themselves (called the 'underlying'). The price of the option would be much less than the price of the share itself. This price is called the premium, and its value is dependent on the likelihood of the underlying asset – in this case Microsoft shares – passing a predetermined 'strike price'. If the share price of Microsoft fails to pass the strike price, the option is worthless and the investor has wasted his premium, a bit like losing his deposit on goods he has decided not to purchase outright. If Microsoft rises in value, the investor cashes in his option and reaps the difference between the actual market price of the shares and the strike price (minus, of course, the premium he has already paid). So it is a way for investors to 'gear up' their returns for a small outlay.

In classical Islamic jurisprudence, the *arbun* contract was a downpayment by a buyer towards the purchase of an item from a seller. So, a bit like a modern financial option: if the buyer opted to complete the sale, the *arbun* would count towards the total purchase price; if the buyer didn't complete, he would forfeit his deposit.

Sheikh Yusuf's white paper went on to refer to the 1993 ruling by the Fiqh Academy on the *arbun* contract, as well as classical narrations, as evidence of the *arbun*'s suitability for the purchase of shares.[11] Shariah Capital, like Deutsche Bank before them, opted to reveal its proprietary methodology to the market, though of course for any competitor to implement a similar Sharia-compliant prime brokerage platform would not be trivial, requiring a significant allocation of time and resources. Let's use Sheikh Yusuf's own worked example to understand how the *arbun* is used to enable a prime broker to short sell a stock.[12] It's a little involved but it's also an insight into how Sharia scholars and structurers find ingenious solutions to conventional problems.

   Imagine a long/short hedge fund analyses the performance of a company, ABC, and concludes that its stock price is likely to fall within the next sixty days. The parties to this trade are the hedge fund trader and his prime broker; a first seller looking to divest its shares in ABC; a buyer or investor willing to buy shares of ABC at the market price; and a second seller willing to sell shares of ABC at market price in sixty days. Now imagine the share price of ABC on day one is $10. Let's assume the hedge fund trader decides to buy ten shares of ABC under certain conditions of sale: he makes a downpayment to the first seller of $10 through the prime broker and the first seller delivers all ten shares. If the hedge fund trader happens to sell the stock within sixty days, the first seller gets to keep the original $10 downpayment and the hedge fund will pay him in kind for the remaining nine shares that are owed to him. If the hedge fund trader does not sell the stock in sixty days, then the first seller will keep the downpayment and the hedge fund will return all ten shares. This sale can be documented as an *arbun*.

   Immediately after the purchase by the hedge fund, the hedge fund trader negotiates a sale with a buyer through the prime broker. The conditions of the sale are cash for immediate delivery of ten shares at $10 per share. The trader receives $100 and delivers ten shares to the buyer. The trader's current position shows he has $90 in cash ($100 from the sale minus $10 in downpayment to the first seller), and owes the first seller nine replacement shares.

   Now let's go to day sixty. The hedge fund trader buys nine replacement shares from a second seller in the market (via the prime broker). The stock price has fallen to $9 per share as the trader had predicted, and he pays $81 to the second seller. He delivers nine shares of ABC to the first seller as per the terms of the original sale agreement. The first seller has now received the original $10 downpayment and has nine shares of ABC. The hedge fund trader now has $9 net in cash (the previous balance of $90 minus the $81 he just paid for replacement shares to the first seller) and no shares. Thus, as a result of the fall in share price, he made a small profit *without selling stock that he did not himself own.* Conversely, if the share price had risen against his original prediction, he would be out of pocket by a similar magnitude.

We have just replicated a short trade but we didn't sell something we didn't own. Is it unethical, or contrary to the spirit of the Sharia, to employ Sharia-compliant contracts to replicate the effect of shorting? Are critics of Islamic finance right in thinking there can be no such thing as an Islamic hedge fund? Even in developed Western markets, in recent years there has been a clamour from politicians to outlaw so-called 'naked shorting' of the market – that is selling a security one does not own, without first borrowing the security or ensuring that it can be borrowed before it is due to be delivered to the buyer. Indeed, the Securities and Exchange Commission (SEC), the federal agency responsible for regulating the US securities industry and US exchanges, enacted a new ruling in September 2008 immediately after the collapse of Lehman Brothers and Bear Stearns, as well as the government bailout of insurance company AIG. The ruling banned the practice of naked short selling, thus mitigating the possibility of market participants driving down the price of a company's stock. The US was not alone in this action.

Free market advocates contend that short selling brings much needed liquidity to the securities markets. Just as liquidity is important when share prices are rising so that a true and fair share price is reached as quickly as possible in the market, there is a powerful argument that share prices should also reach equilibrium as quickly as possible on the way down, and short selling is the oil that lubricates those downward price movements – an aid to price discovery and a natural brake on overvaluation of share prices. Even the more extreme practice of naked short selling – short selling without borrowing the security – has its advocates (though few) since the practice can be beneficial in enhancing liquidity in shares that are difficult to borrow. However, critics often point to the usage of naked shorting in market manipulation, damaging companies and threatening markets that are broader than merely the company whose stock is being manipulated. After all, one can sell an unlimited amount of shares if one doesn't need to borrow them.

I don't know about you, but I'm starting to feel a little uneasy. Hedge funds that short stock are notorious for driving down the price of those securities until companies are bled to death. As much as free market advocates may defend the practice of shorting as contributing to efficient markets, there must have been an underlying moral principle against Islam's ban on selling something that one doesn't own.

Sheikh Yusuf recognized these concerns in his white paper and addressed them. 'In a garden', he wrote, 'a hedge is used to protect flowers from the feet of people walking by.' Hedge funds are designed to protect investors' capital against volatility, not to make wild speculative gambles, he suggested. The funds that his colleagues would be sourcing for this Sharia-compliant platform would be 'risk averse and profitable',[13] and indeed some of the most respected hedge fund managers had opted to join the platform. He went on to refute the suggestion that hedge funds intrinsically engage in speculative behaviour. 'All business is based on a degree of speculation because no one, other than the Almighty, knows the future.' Risk and reward are linked and need balance, and the prohibition against uncertainty is not intended to dissuade the merchant from seeking reward. The scholar differentiated between 'undisciplined and uncontrolled speculation' and the kind of detailed analysis employing sophisticated tools that hedge funds engaged in to balance risk and reward.

And what of short selling? Given that Muslims believe there to be an inherent wisdom in the prohibition against selling that which one does not own, how can one justify a technique that mirrors the same effect? Sheikh Yusuf argued that selling a stock in the expectation that its price will fall was morally little different to buying it in the expectation its price will rise, providing one does not breach the Sharia requirement on ownership. Indeed, he suggested, short selling has, historically, often been a trading strategy employed on heavily overvalued securities, thus providing a much needed balance and integrity to markets.

Shariah Capital was now in business.

But the timing was horrendous. It took a year of complex structuring and negotiation between the Sharia advisors and the prime brokers to establish the platform. Shortly after the green light had been given to raise funds for the platform, Wall Street stalwart Bear Stearns collapsed under the weight of its exposure to mortgage-backed securities, and vultures circled Lehman Brothers, the US's fourth largest investment bank, as it desperately negotiated a rescue deal. A few months later, a wealth manager named Bernard Madoff was arrested on charges of defrauding investors of $65 billion in the largest fraudulent pyramid scheme ever uncovered. *The Wall Street Journal* described his Ponzi scheme as contributing to 'a national crisis of confidence and distrust of the financial system'.[14] In the melee of meltdowns across asset classes, hedge funds around the world made enormous losses and hedge fund investors gripped their wallets tightly. Shariah Capital was able to raise only $200 million from the Dubai government instead of the $1.5 billion it had hoped for, and the Islamic finance industry was forced to admit that the time to introduce such an ultra-sophisticated investment product had long since faded.

6

The Doomsday *Fatwa*

For they have sown the wind, and they shall reap the whirlwind.

Hosea, 8:7

On an oppressively muggy June 2010 evening in Dubai, smartly dressed young executives took refuge in the opulently chilled luxury of the Emirates Towers to hear Tarek El Diwany discuss his latest book project. The book was a wide-ranging attempt to bring together views both for and against the current direction of the Islamic finance industry, and a proposal for basic reforms at institutional and contractual levels.[1] Perhaps unwittingly, El Diwany had attracted something of a cult following among the professional Muslim community around the world, particularly those in the financial services industry. Shunned by mainstream bankers and conference organizers, he found his invitations to speak to the industry had become increasingly infrequent, and indeed (excepting his appearance at this glamorous location in Dubai) glittering ballrooms in five-star hotels had long since given way to dingy community halls in the East End of London.

Not that this bothered him. He had long since freed himself from the trappings of a former life as a credit derivatives dealer at Prebon Yamane in the yuppie heyday of the late 1980s. Now in his forties, gaunt but energetic, he exuded a youthful intensity and passion for his subject: the eradication of interest from the modern financial system and the return of the Islamic banking industry to its core values.

'Actually, do you mind if I step off the stage, and come down to talk?' he enquired of the assembled young men and women, many of whom had heard about the lecture at Friday prayer in Masjid Al-Samad. He stepped off the stage, microphone in hand, and proceeded to wander among the audience.

'I've been told I look like a lunatic when I do this', he laughed self-deprecatingly. He liked to get up close to his crowd, to engage them on a human level – a refreshing change from the London Business School stiff in an immaculately tailored suit pitching his latest magic beans from the safety of a conference lectern.

To the MBA alumni he was indeed a lunatic. The mainstream had stopped trying to debate with him long ago, perhaps because the one-dimensional world that some of them inhabited had not equipped them to imagine new possibilities or perhaps simply because they struggled to match his razor-sharp intellect. With a sound knowledge of economics and modern banking practice, as well as a keen sense of the principles of Islamic jurisprudence and the spirit of Sharia, El Diwany delivered his arguments precisely, convincingly and intensely in his plummy English accent. But despite the beard and bookish demeanour, he was no journeyman accountant or academic. He was an evangelist.

In the Emirates Towers' Godolphin Ballroom he set the scene, as he often did, with a description of the relationship between the goldsmith moneylender and today's fractional reserve banking system. That money could be created out of money was contrary to sense and morality, he argued.

He sought to draw parallels between the clever ruse employed by medieval financiers to circumvent the Church's ban on usury, the *contractum trinius*, and the *hilah*, or legal tricks, employed by modern bankers to produce apparently Sharia-compliant financial products.

Several centuries ago, since Christianity formed the backbone of judicial systems in Christian nations, in such countries it had been made illegal to charge interest on a loan. Financiers entered into three contracts with borrowers: an investment, a sale of profit and an insurance contract. Each individual contract was permissible under Church law, but in combination the three contracts produced an interest-bearing loan, a transaction explicitly outlawed by the Church.

'Imagine I made an investment of money into your business and we agree to share profits', he suggested. 'Then I agree to sell to you future profits on the investment for a price we agree today. Finally you agree to insure me for a loss on my investment. In the end, you have ended up paying a fee to me for money which I "invested" in you.' Thus three contracts – the *contractum trinius* – are combined, leaving a loan with interest. Many in the audience shifted nervously as they recognized the parallels with the modern Islamic finance industry.

Over the course of centuries, various justifications were made by laymen and financiers for the charging of interest. They argued that money was a useful commodity: it had usufruct and thus could be rented. Christian scholars rejected this position on the basis that a rental of money was equivalent to a sale of money, and it would be unjust to sell one quantum of money for a different quantum. Lost opportunity cost was another argument put forward: the lender of money must abstain from its consumption and is therefore deprived of pleasures that he might otherwise have enjoyed, or is restricted from entering into other business activities or necessities as a result of his loan. El Diwany's answer to this was thought provoking. 'Do we prefer to consume now or in the future?' he asked his audience. 'Most people say now. But don't you prefer to consume one breakfast every day or would you prefer all seven of your week's breakfasts today? Of course, you want to have one a day.'

But let's hold that thought for now. We will come back to this line of thinking when we look at how modern financial analysis techniques can defeat common sense in Chapter 8. A voracious appetite for economic growth fuelled by debt not only contributed to the post-2007 global credit crisis, but may arguably also have other side effects, such as environmental degradation or the sudden dismantling of communities. A gradual acceptance by society of usury may be a contributory factor.

In time, Church theologians would come to the position that the usury that had previously been outlawed could in fact be reclassified as an 'excessive' interest charge, though quite what 'excessive' means is a function of the borrower's standing. And so interest became legalized and – leaving aside the clergy's grandstanding on the greed of bankers in the light of the contemporary banking crisis – the modern Church rarely raises any objections to the practice of modern banking.

Murabaha and *tawarruq* as modes of financing

In the previous two chapters I mentioned the *murabaha* contract, a type of Islamic contract of exchange primarily intended as a method of financing goods on a 'cost-plus' basis. By means of this contract, a financier or merchant buys a product in the market at cost and sells it on to a buyer at a cost plus mark up – a real trade, in accordance with the Quranic injunction: 'Allah has permitted trading and forbidden interest.'[2]

Although beneficial in this guise, use of the *murabaha* has become so distorted from its original intent that it has become the single most common method of funding inter-bank liquidity and corporate loans in the Islamic finance industry. How does it do this?

Sometimes known as a '*murabaha*-to-order', the modern incarnation requires two sales to take place in order to effect the purchase of a single item with payment on a deferred basis. Imagine the customer of a bank wishes to purchase a car worth $10,000. The Islamic bank may agree to purchase the car at its known cost price of $10,000, and resell it to the customer at, say, a specified 10 per cent mark-up, the resulting $11,000 to be repaid by the customer to the bank in instalments over the specified repayment period, let's say two years. So far, there's absolutely nothing wrong with this: the bank is acting as a trader of goods in accordance with the Quranic injunction.

However, if the bank purchases the car, naturally it will wish to be reassured that the customer will in fact then purchase the car from the bank. The bank is, after all, not a car dealer wishing to hold inventory in stock to be resold at a later date. Thus, the bank will require the customer to sign a promise that the customer will purchase the car from the bank.

Is this combination of contracts – two sales and a promise – Sharia compliant? Although moving away from its traditional form as a simple cost-plus-profit sale agreement, it may be argued that this form of the *murabaha* does allow for the bank to take on asset risk to the extent that the overall effect meets the basic conditions for a valid sale and does not breach the general prohibitions stipulated in the Sharia. Nevertheless, conservative scholars such as Mufti Taqi Usmani argue that *murabaha*-to-order should be viewed as a transitory step towards a true profit-and-loss-sharing mode of financing, and where such modes are not practicable.[3]

Now let's take this concept a stage further. What if we use the *murabaha* to purchase assets, let's say liquid, readily available assets such as commodities, in order to finance other assets? In other words, use the *murabaha* to form the basis of a debt-financing structure. The so-called commodity *murabaha*, sometimes known as *tawarruq* financing, has become one of the most common tools in money-market transactions and asset financing among Islamic institutions today, and is perhaps the most controversial. According to those like El Diwany, it is the kind of legal trick employed by Christian financiers several centuries ago.

A legal trick – *hilah* in Arabic – is a contractual ruse to defeat a specific Sharia ruling by employing permissible contracts. The combination of contracts to form the medieval *contractum trinius*, is an example of a *hilah*. One ruse used by some Islamic banks until fairly recently was the *bay al-ina*, intended to produce the effect of an interest-bearing loan by employing two separate contracts, each individually compliant with the Sharia: the lender buys from the borrower goods for cash and then sells those goods back to him for a higher price on credit, the difference in price being the interest charged. Despite the condemnation of *ina* by classical and contemporary jurists,[4] a number of modern financial institutions employed this method as a purported Sharia-compliant method of financing, though condemnation is so widespread that its usage is very much limited nowadays. In general, the concept of combining two sales within one is universally prohibited and supported by various recorded sayings of the Prophet in the Hadith.

Now imagine an individual wishes to purchase a car. What if the bank – recognizing that it may not combine two sale contracts into one – introduces a third party in the transaction to move the form of the contract away from the banned *ina*? Let's say the bank uses a commodity as the subject of the sale, say copper. Here comes the clever bit. Assume the bank buys a quantity of copper from a supplier in the market and pays the spot price for that copper, say $10,000, which happens to be the same value as the car that the bank's customer wishes to purchase. On the same day, the bank sells the copper to the customer on a cost plus profit basis, let's say for $11,000, payable by the customer on deferred terms back to the bank. Also on the same day, the customer sells the copper (having already appointed the bank as its agent to sell the commodity on its behalf) into the market to another supplier on a spot basis at cost price, in other words for $10,000. The two suppliers are unrelated. Since the resale of the copper by the customer to the second supplier is organized in advance of the customer's purchase of the copper from the bank, this type of transaction is known as 'organized' tawarruq. The customer now has $10,000 cash in hand today, which will enable him to purchase his car, and will repay $11,000 to the bank over an agreed duration. Just like a conventional loan.

Some scholars have permitted *tawarruq* where it is not organized in advance. Thus if a person buys an asset on a deferred payment basis but then decides to sell it for a spot cash price, provided the purpose of the purchase was not to sell immediately, this would not be classified as organized *tawarruq*. The two legs of the transaction just 'happened' to follow each other. However, since the majority of banks who practise *tawarruq* actively market their financial product as one that allows the customer to obtain cash immediately, and therefore overtly acknowledge the purpose of the product, they do not have the liberty of hiding behind the argument that the intention to resell did not exist.

Even the introduction of a third party has not persuaded the majority of scholars that this series of transactions is valid in the Sharia. By not financing against the asset, the bank has taken the same risk as in an interest-bearing loan, and the customer has received one amount of cash for another. The erudite Mufti Taqi Usmani's view, for example, is very clear in his argument against this kind of transaction, as he espoused in the Pakistan Supreme Court's judgement on interest.[5]

As Islamic finance has grown in recent years, so conventional banks have dipped their toes in the water by trying out a commodity *murabaha*. At first, their intentions are often to gauge demand with the simplest type of ostensibly Islamic transaction, then decide whether and how to expand the scope of their Islamic business, and some prominent scholars have tended to tolerate this practice 'for the growth of the industry', as they like to put it. In practice, commodity *murabaha* ends up becoming not only the conventional banks' primary source of 'Islamic' business, but also acts as the default structure for any type of Islamic financing need.

In 2007, a consortium that included two Sharia-compliant Kuwaiti investment companies, Investment Dar and Adeem Investment, made international headlines by acquiring just over 50 per cent of James Bond's vehicle of choice – the British luxury car maker Aston Martin – for a share purchase price of US$464 million. Journalists had a field day with the idea that something so quintessentially British could be funded with Islamic money: 'The name is Bond. Islamic bond.'[6] I must admit, even I allowed myself a little snigger at that one.

The acquisition financing package included a $393 million commodity *murabaha* arranged by the German bank West LB. At one of the many Islamic finance conferences in London that year, West LB executives proudly presented their award-winning transaction to an admiring audience. Though the deal was labelled as Islamic, the bankers nevertheless stumbled when asked by an audience member what was so Islamic about this form of financing. Perhaps a true *murabaha*, where the bank takes the asset on its balance sheet, might be a step too far for a conventional bank, but was not a simple sale and leaseback of the underlying asset possible instead? One flustered junior banker countered by suggesting that his bank's credit committee struggled to get comfortable with a lease, and that the risks inherent in a commodity *murabaha* structure were close if not equal to those in a conventional loan structure, which is not surprising given that some scholars say it *is* a conventional loan structure.

The disconnect between the view of conventional bankers on the subject of Sharia compliance and the view of scholars (and often the Islamic banks) is neatly illustrated in an article written by a real estate banker at a bulge bracket firm for an 'expert' publication on Islamic investments. I write 'expert' in quotation marks as invariably this type of industry publication tends to cobble together a tired collection of essays, rehashed from internal memos of bankers who happened to stumble across an Islamic deal once, or academics who have been trying for years to get a job in a bank. Embarrassingly, I myself am forever tainted for having contributed a chapter to it.

After three or four pages of trite nonsense, the banker in question proffers a pearl to the reader when describing how Islamic investors may invest in a conventionally financed real estate deal:

> The Islamic investors effectively sell a quantity of non-precious metal to the SPV, the value of which is equal to the amount which the Islamic investors desire to invest in the SPV. The SPV immediately sells the metal to receive cash with which it finances its real estate investment. The SPV does not immediately pay a price for the metal to the Islamic investors, so it now owes the price for the metal to the Islamic investors. The whole transaction involving the metal is usually effected through commodity derivative transactions with no exposure to market movements in the metal. When the SPV eventually sells the real estate, it uses the proceeds to repay the conventional financing and to settle its payment obligation with the Islamic investors by exchanging this obligation against equity of the SPV.[7]

So the Islamic investors never really took any real asset risk in the real estate, they merely lent money at a fixed mark-up. I have no doubt that this particular banker tells his colleagues that Islamic finance is a complete crock.

So we have uncovered our modern-day version of the *contractum trinius*, though in this case the transaction, and particularly the *bay al-ina* before it, more closely resemble the cruder and simpler *retrovenditio* ('selling back') used by Christian financiers of yore. And over at the Emirates Towers, El Diwany is not having any of it.

Islamic derivatives: the Manhattan Project and the Doomsday *Fatwa*

Geert Bossuyt had a problem. The Safa Tower deal, two years in the making, had still not closed, and the life expectancy of Deutsche Bank's Islamic structuring team was rapidly diminishing. The flamboyant Yassine Bouhara had been patient up until now, but there was only so long that the Godfather of the Middle East could hold back the barbarian hordes, the conventional bankers for whom only the pursuit of profit mattered. What did the hordes care about a strategic initiative if after two years it was still not generating meaningful revenues? Why should they subsidize the salaries and bonuses of their Islamic colleagues? Dump this initiative and move on. No one needs Islamic. No one needs socially responsible investing. This is an investment bank, not a hippy commune.

But Bossuyt had a brain the size of a planet – and a plan to blow the market wide open. It was time to act on Bouhara's call to arms, to 'commo-dee-tize ze industry', to 'mek ze Eeslameec finance Beeg-uh-Mac-uh'. Bossuyt's equity derivatives background was unique in the industry – his competition consisted of third-rate relationship managers and *murabaha* desk jockeys at parochial firms with limited ambition. A Belgian Catholic with a conventional derivatives background, he afforded himself the luxury of thinking about Islamic finance in unconventional, non-traditional ways, and the people he assembled around him reflected this ethos. His team would be edgy, intellectual and ambitious, just like him. And it would invent an entirely new market – Islamic derivatives.

Bossuyt had access to a small group of first-class structurers – the individuals who would design and build the structure and contracts of financial instruments from a blank sheet – and the world's leading scholars, a structuring dream team assembling the finest minds in the industry, robustly defending their ideas over scrawlings on a flip chart in closed-session meeting rooms. Intellectual elitism may have bred some aloofness, perhaps even arrogance, in their ranks – they were the best and they knew it, but Bossuyt encouraged them to challenge each other, and challenge the scholars in the quest to invent a new industry.

But while the bank's sales force were used to selling product to the leading institutions throughout the Middle East and Malaysia, educating them in the nuances of these new products would be a challenge in itself.

Islamic investors were poorly served. They had limited access to the kinds of asset classes that their conventional counterparts could buy off the shelf. Walk into any high-street retail bank in London or New York, and within minutes you can open an account, make term deposits, take out a mortgage, and buy shares and mutual funds online. For those with the means to open a premier or private account, a more sophisticated world of investments awaits: derivatives, structured products, hedge funds, exchange traded funds, real estate and private equity funds.

Walk into an Islamic bank and you can deposit your money, perhaps earning a return on a commodity *murabaha* basis (though some in the UK merely offered no return at all, just a safe place to keep your money at a zero interest rate). The more sophisticated Islamic institutions offered home-financing products, but without the flexibility of their conventional counterparts, and at substantially greater cost. They were doing the Muslim community a favour by catering for their needs.

Muslims in the UK felt a sense of alienation from the banking industry, a bitterness at the so-called Islamic banks that seemed to make a business out of ripping them off. Want to finance a home without compromising your faith? Here's an Islamic mortgage. It looks the same, the technical terms are in Arabic, and we charge you more.

What do Islamic investors lack? Bossuyt mulled over the question and decided that where the industry was failing was in its inability to hedge the exposures of Islamic investors to various risks: macroeconomic risks such as currencies, commodity prices and rates, volatilities in equity markets, geopolitical risks around the world. Islamic financial institutions had failed to hedge themselves adequately against their various exposures, and private investors had no way to protect themselves against falling market prices, or were unable to participate in alternative investment methodologies such as the pursuit of 'absolute returns' through hedge funds.

Yassine Bouhara had already made a commitment to fund a 55 per cent owned subsidiary of Deutsche Bank, a company called Dar Al Istithmar (DI). A self-proclaimed think tank, DI was a joint venture with an affiliate of the University of Oxford – the Oxford Centre for Islamic Studies – and a vehicle of the Saudi Binladin Group, Saudi's largest construction company. The Safa Tower deal had been a pilot project for the new venture and its real value add had been demonstrated in the access it provided to some of the world's leading scholars. The Deutsche structuring team approached the chairman of DI's Sharia board, the same Sheikh Hussain Hamed Hassan, to help them devise an all-purpose methodology for investment products, a framework on which to build a whole new range of financial instruments.

Bossuyt promised Sheikh Hussain that any structure he devised in conjunction with the Deutsche team would be attributed to the sheikh's newly appointed management team at DI, a forceps-enabled delivery dragging the think tank into the cold harsh air of the commercial marketplace. And so the Deutsche team began to create what would become one of the most controversial pieces of work the industry had seen: the 'wa'd structure', also known as the 'double wa'd structure' or the 'Islamic total return swap', which would come to underpin the development of modern Islamic derivatives.

Let's for a moment clarify our understanding of a 'derivative'. A derivative is a financial contract whose value is derived from the asset or pool of assets that underpin it, also known as the underlyings. An underlying can also be in the form of an index or anything that the counterparties in the contract can choose to derive a value from. The weather, for instance. Imagine, for example, that Party A says to Party B, 'If you give me $10 today, I will pay you $100 if it rains for more than fifteen days of this month.' The two parties have created a derivative contract using the weather as an underlying. The value of the contract varies as the weather varies.

Derivatives need not be quite so speculative in nature, however. The value of a contract may be linked, for example, to macro-economic movements, and the consequent payout may be part of a counterparty's essential hedging strategy. Say, for example, that Company A manufactures cars in Germany, but sells them in the US. Its cost base is denominated in euros, but its revenues are in dollars (at least the revenues from American customers). Naturally, as currency exchange rates move, its profits will either gain or diminish. If the rate moves massively against Company A, it stands to make a loss, and there may be consequences for its shareholders, its employees and their families. The sensible thing to do would be to buy a type of insurance policy, a contract that hedges its exposure to such movements.

Company A might decide to enter into a currency forward with a counterparty, that is, it agrees to buy an amount of euros at a given point in the future for a dollar amount, the rate for which it locks in today. Let's assume that Company B has an inverse requirement. It manufactures a product in the US but sells in Germany and wishes to purchase dollars in the future in order to pay its cost base out of the revenues it generates in euros. So Company B wants to lock in a euro price today. Assuming the two parties have equal and opposite requirements, they may agree to 'swap' their cash flows at pre-agreed rates on both sides for a specified duration of time. A currency swap is born. But finding two counterparties with synchronous requirements is unlikely, hence the need for investment banks to act as intermediaries in the process. These intermediaries warehouse the underlying asset class (in this case, euros and dollars), and act as the counterparty to those who wish to hedge their currency positions.

A similar type of derivative contract is used to hedge against movements in interest rates. These are known as interest rate swaps. When an individual arranges home financing, he will usually be presented with a range of pricing options including, for example, a mortgage whose rate of interest remains fixed for a duration of time, and thereafter reverts to floating in line with central bank base rates. A fixed-rate mortgage enables the buyer to manage his future cash flows on a more predictable basis but requires the bank to enter into a rate swap or similar derivative contract with other counterparties. This is because the bank generally borrows its funds in the inter-bank market on a floating rate basis, but is lending to the customer on a fixed rate basis, and therefore needs to manage this 'gap' risk.

The sophistication of derivative contracts can go well beyond the simple examples used above, and might include, for example, a mechanism to reassure counterparties that as the economics of a transaction moves against one party, it has the ability to repay its obligations. This might be in the form of depositing additional collateral (sometimes known as 'posting margin') based on what are known as 'marked to market' calculations, that is, the ongoing determination of the value of a derivative contract based on current market conditions. The contracts will also generally include the kind of sophisticated terms and conditions to be expected in any complex commercial transaction, such as the various representation and warranties of the counterparties involved, events of default, arbitration provisions and so on. The end result is often a lengthy and complex legal document.

There are myriads of other kinds of derivative contracts, though the only other generic derivative we will refer to for the time being is what have come to be known as 'structured investment products'. This wide-ranging group of financial instruments is difficult to encapsulate in one single definition, but in general they are products that investors can buy in order to participate in the gains and losses of any underlying asset class (such as shares on a stock market or interest-bearing bonds). The manner in which these instruments participate in such gains or losses is rarely correlated on a perfect one-to-one basis.

For example, an investor may wish to 'gear up' the returns from an investment. If he wants to participate in the returns from real estate, for example, he can either buy a property outright with cash, or he can borrow money in the hope that the value of the property rises fast enough for him to pay off his loan. Generally speaking, in a rising property market investors look to leverage themselves to the greatest extent possible in order to maximize their profits from real estate investments. Conversely, of course, in a falling market, they may get badly burnt and that is the risk of gearing one's investments in such a manner. Structured products can replicate this gearing effect without forcing the investor to buy the underlying, or engage in other trading strategies (such as taking out loans), though the economic risk they take may be the same. In some cases, they can also buy and sell these instruments in the secondary market like shares on a stock market, though of course the available universe of buyers for a typical structured investment product may be much smaller and specialized than that of share traders.

As we discovered earlier when we looked at Sheikh Yusuf

DeLorenzo's *arbun*-based long/short hedge fund, a 'call option' gives investors the right, but not the obligation, to buy a commodity or security, typically an equity share in a company. By doing so, their downside is limited to the cost of the option (typically a fraction of the cost of the underlying share), and their upside is the difference between the market price of the share and a pre-agreed 'strike price' set at the beginning of the contract, in other words virtually unlimited. This is a derivative (since it derives its value from the value of the underlying share) and is often used as a basic component of a structured investment product. As options and other simple derivative contracts are linked together, the net effect can become as sophisticated as the investor desires.

Let's take an example. Imagine an ultra high net worth individual walks into the oak-panelled client room of his wealth manager in Zurich. For a while he chews the breeze about his vintage car collection and can't help but be impressed at his relationship manager's extensive knowledge of the difference between a 1961 Ferrari 250GT SWB SEFAC and its successor, the 250GTO.

'You're right, I must arbitrage this opportunity. Can you help me source one of those through your contacts?' 'Of course', says the relationship manager (he read about it in *Octane* magazine last month), and now that he's got his client's undivided attention, he turns to the important matter at hand.

'I see that you have $30 million parked in your account, which is earning you not much over the bank base rate. Have you considered redeploying these funds?' The client is curious, but has no idea how different asset classes will perform in the near future and doesn't want to take any undue risks. If only he could hedge his bets.

'We have an investment product that gives you exposure to three different asset classes: commodities, global equities and bonds over the next three years. The product lets you participate in returns from the best performer among these three asset classes but without actively investing in all three. You won't lose money in the event all three asset classes lose value, but the trade off is you'll have to sacrifice some upside.'

The investment bank has created a structured investment product that pays out, say, 75 per cent of the increase in an index, whose value is equal to the highest performer out of the three different asset classes (let's say the benchmarks are published global indices for commodities, equities and bonds) over a three-year period. That same product might include 'capital protection' such that in the event all three asset classes fall below the initial investment level, the investor still gets his initial investment back in full. So the investor now has a chance to participate in the returns from one of the three types of investment, with protection against losses. He doesn't get to participate in the full extent of the gains (he only gets 75 per cent), but the trade off is he gets to protect his downside if his bet goes wrong. He also gets three chances to make money: if commodities don't do well, then maybe equities will. If they don't, then maybe bonds will rise.

The ultra high net worth client likes this product. It allows him to play the markets with minimal risk. Of course, he won't know that the investment bank may be making as much as 10 per cent in fees off the back of this product, but then few clients really know how these products are priced and sold, and as long as he makes money he's unlikely to demand a forensic audit trail. And because these products can be so complex and so expensive, we can't buy them over the counter of our local high-street bank. Regulators generally don't like retail customers being sold stuff that can be extraordinarily complex.

So now that we have a basic understanding of a derivative and the more complex structured investment products, we turn our attention to Islamic derivatives, an apparently oxymoronic concept if the traditional scholarly view is to be followed. After all, why would an Islamic investor wish to speculate on future prices of an asset by purchasing intangible constructs such as 'rights' or engaging in the swapping of mere cash flows? Where is the real asset? Who has legal title? Who may buy and sell this asset, or lease its usufruct? Where is the certainty, the transparency?

As far as Geert Bossuyt was concerned, the derivative was a benign and magnificent tool, something to be made freely available to people of all creeds. Why should Muslims be restricted from harnessing the power of financial markets? Surely they needed to hedge their economic exposures as well? Did they not also deserve a wider menu of investment flavours?

I mentioned earlier the *murabaha*-to-order, a method by which banks could help customers finance goods. This combination of two sales and a promise enabled the bank to be reassured that the customer would in fact purchase the goods from the bank through the use of the third contract: the undertaking, or promise. And it is this unilateral undertaking, known in Arabic as a '*wa'd*', that underpinned Bossuyt's precocious brainchild, given corporeal essence in the form of a 2007 paper published by Deutsche Bank, 'Pioneering Innovative Sharia Compliant Solutions', otherwise known in the industry simply as the White Paper.

The White Paper was the theoretical basis for the 'total return swap' methodology pioneered by Deutsche Bank to replicate the returns from any and all conventional financial instruments, though at first the intention had been merely to create hedging products for the treasury departments of Islamic financial institutions. In other words, although this technique was aimed at helping Islamic banks to find ways to protect themselves from rate movements or currency fluctuations, it could in theory allow an Islamic investor to do anything that a conventional investor could do, such as earn profits from market movements in pork belly futures. Now that doesn't sound very Sharia compliant, does it?

The paper described the investment structure developed by the Deutsche Bank team, which would form the basis of their structured products platform, and provided Sharia justification for the methodology, such as the nature of promises and contracts in the Sharia. This Sharia justification took the form of a narrative to present and critique the argument that the promisor in a promise has a 'norm-creating power'.[8] It may have been the first time that an investment bank had ever written such a paper, and it surely must have been the first time that an interlocutor named Ali was the central character, the fictional creation of a former University of Oxford law lecturer turned banker, Hussein Hassan (no relation to the eminent scholar), who was the primary author of the paper and the dream team's resident expert on the jurisprudence of transactions in the Sharia.

The throngs pouring through London's Landmark Hotel at the Euromoney Annual Islamic Finance Summit that year gawped at the glossy booklet lining the Deutsche Bank exhibition stand. Simultaneously bizarre and impressive, the White Paper was a brain dump of immense effort and achievement. One wag flicked through twenty-four pages of Sharia analysis, moral philosophy, structure diagrams and mathematical formulae to declare the glossy as nothing more than 'intellectual masturbation', though there was no disguising his obvious covetousness. Despite the theoretical detail, the paper did not dissect the individual contracts underpinning the overall structure, nor provide operational details of how the investment products were engineered and sold, and competitors were left wondering precisely how they would go about replicating the factory to create their own products. And although it admirably suggested that one of its intentions was to allow other financial institutions to use the fundamental elements of the structure for the benefit of their clients (thus growing the size of the market), and to encourage the use of the structure 'in its correct context', it also concluded by tantalizingly stating that 'the Structure may not be applied to the provision of capital protection for Sharia-compliant structured products'.[9] By keeping this critical weapon in its armoury hidden, even in its apparent magnanimity Deutsche was determined to stay one step ahead of the competition.

I've thought long and hard about whether to discuss in these pages the theory of the 'double *wa'd*' structure – 'double' since the technique employs two simultaneous unilateral undertakings. I had to balance whether I might help the reader understand the most sophisticated contractual structure in Islamic finance today against the fact that the intricate details are, well, intricate and detailed. So in the end, I've compromised and consigned the technical explanation to another time, which is a shame as it means that we will have to assume that (a) the structure works from a purely technical perspective and (b) there is a disconnect between letter and spirit of the law when it comes to the Sharia compliance of the technique, if the buyer or seller of the product so desires it.

But, irrespective of the technical details, perhaps it is not hard to understand whether there are occasions when the spirit of the Sharia is breached when using this technique to replicate conventional derivatives. Let's take an overview of the double *wa'd*. The structure allows the investor to place a sum of money with an institution via an investment vehicle, a black box if you like. A shell company, which takes in cash, chews it up and spits out a derivative contract at the other end.

The investor places the cash with the special purpose vehicle, or SPV, established by Deutsche Bank for the purpose of issuing Sharia-compliant notes or certificates. The SPV issues these certificates to investors and deposits the cash proceeds into a segregated account. Segregation means a legal and physical separation of the money from any other funds, so that under no circumstances can there be a 'co-mingling' of investor's cash with non-Sharia-compliant funds from other sources.

Using these segregated funds, the SPV buys Sharia-compliant

assets from the market. These assets can be anything provided they meet the requirements of the Sharia, but ideally they should be liquid and tradeable so that the SPV can buy and sell them at a moment's notice, with maximum efficiency and minimum transaction costs. Typically, the SPV chooses the public equity shares of a large multinational company, say Microsoft (assuming the company fulfils the necessary criteria – such as low levels of interest-bearing debt – to be considered Sharia compliant). Remember, these Microsoft shares are just a liquid commodity, something easily exchanged for cash whenever we need to. That's their only real purpose, not their actual investment potential.

Here comes the clever bit. Now with full legal title to these shares, the SPV enters into a 'total return swap'. Deutsche Bank (as the originator of the Islamic certificate) sits on one side of the trade, with the SPV (as the issuer of the certificate) sitting on the other side. The investor holds a piece of paper in his hand telling him he will one day in the future receive a return on his money linked to a given benchmark. Let's say the investor is sophisticated and wants to make a play on the markets. He thinks there are three asset classes with a chance of rising in the future, but he's not sure which one: they are US equities, US corporate bonds and the price of gold. So Deutsche Bank agrees that the benchmark stated in the piece of paper he holds is a formula that calculates the highest riser among those three published indices. This is now a structured investment product, much like the one bought by the vintage car connoisseur in Zurich we met earlier.

Deutsche Bank undertakes (via a promise, or *wa'd*) to purchase from the SPV the Microsoft shares held by the account – and, don't forget, those Microsoft shares have arbitrarily been chosen as something liquid and tradeable – for a price equal to the benchmark (and remember, that benchmark has nothing to do with the share price of Microsoft). On the other side of trade, the SPV undertakes (via a second *wa'd*) to sell the Microsoft shares to Deutsche Bank for a price equal to the benchmark. Because the benchmark price has nothing to do with the actual market value of the Microsoft shares, it's as if I promised to sell my house to you in a year's time proportionate to the rise in gas prices, even though gas prices have little to do with house prices.

The conditions under which these two undertakings are exercised by the promisee are mutually exclusive, and therefore only one undertaking can be exercised. However, the nature of the promises means that the shares will always be traded for a price equal to the benchmark. Since the conditions related to the two undertakings are mutually exclusive, and both cannot be exercised at the same time, scholars who have approved this structure argue that they do not constitute a bilateral contract, thus avoiding Sharia prohibitions of 'two sale contracts in one'. They also argue that investors' monies remain pure since they are held in a segregated account and used to purchase only Sharia-compliant assets (in this case, shares in Microsoft).

So, without actually buying directly the underlying assets (the US equities, US corporate bonds, and gold), the Islamic investor has gained exposure to their returns according to a pre-determined formula. Deutsche Bank has managed to 'swap away' the return of the Microsoft shares held in the segregated account with the return on something completely unrelated. Investors' money has not touched anything non-compliant – it hasn't been invested in interest-bearing US corporate bonds, for example – and yet it is getting exposure to the return on those non-compliant assets. Ingenious and yet troubling at the same time.

Deutsche Bank's Hassan understood that critics of the technique would seize upon the use of the *wa'd*, as opposed to a binding sales contract, to circumvent the prohibition of a bilateral contract, and the swapping of an intangible cash flow. He therefore addressed these specific issues of jurisprudence in some detail in the White Paper.[10]

This piece of fundamental research was a turning point for the Islamic finance industry: scholars who had hitherto baulked at the mere mention of the word derivative were now prepared to engage in a reasoned discussion on the need for investors and institutions to hedge their risks. What had once been a discussion about speculation was now turning into a discussion about introducing stability to an industry subject to a previously unacceptable level of volatility. But it was not without significant controversy.

One of the first products Deutsche Bank created under this platform was a capital-protected investment certificate linked to the return on a Goldman Sachs hedge fund, naturally a non-Sharia-compliant underlying. The buyer was the private banking department of Dubai Islamic Bank, a client that would turn out to be the single biggest buyer of Deutsche's Islamic structured products, its private high net worth customers being some of the hungriest investors in the retail Islamic space. It helped, of course, that Sheikh Hussain was also the chairman of DIB's Sharia board, thus ensuring that the Sharia certification effort would not need to be duplicated for the buying institution.

In June 2007, at the press launch of the new product,[11] Deutsche's Geert Bossuyt sat alongside Sheikh Hussain and out-lined the far-reaching consequences of the total return swap for the future of the industry.

'It allows investors to meet their specific investment objectives without resorting to conventional methods, in a Sharia-compliant manner', said Bossuyt, and went on to outline the specific investment certificate that was being sold to DIB's high net worth Islamic investors. But in private he also made what would become his trademark remark at many subsequent conferences at which he pitched his bank's services: 'We create conservative products for conservative investors and aggressive products for aggressive investors.' Away from the microphone that day, the press missed those words, yet it was undoubtedly a momentous statement of intent by the behemoth financial services flow monster, and one that would be repeated in public in the months to come.

Slowly but surely, some scholars and investors started to feel deep unease about the way in which a global investment bank was able to churn out vast quantities of sophisticated investment products, typically instruments that linked their returns to non-Sharia indices or benchmarks, and apply a 'wrapper' to the package, apparently miraculously rendering it *halal*, or permissible. The technique may well have been originally intended as a force for good, but Deutsche's pushy Middle East sales executives were beginning to recognize the technique as an incredible cash cow, to be milked for all it was worth. No benchmark or underlying asset was too sacred to replicate, and anything was possible. Suddenly the market was wide open and 99 per cent of it belonged to Deutsche. It was a mouth-watering feast of fees and year-end bonuses too good to pass up, though at some point perhaps it had mutated from a cash cow into a golden goose, and that goose was about to die.

Shortly after the White Paper was published, Sheikh Hussain called me and my Deutsche colleagues into his office and excitedly waved a letter in front of us. 'Look what he is saying', he exclaimed furiously. The pugilistic scholar had a manner that could scarcely be described as delicate or reticent even on a quiet day, but on that day his magnificent vocal chords and table-thumping fist would be particularly well exercised. 'LOOK at it! He is saying to the newspapers. To the NEWSpapers!' BANG. Clenched fist meets table. In adjoining offices, members of Dubai Islamic Bank's Sharia Coordination Department looked up for a brief moment as their thin walls shook, then went back to their paperwork. 'He is calling it a DOOMSDAY *fatwa*!' BANG.

A one-time colleague of Sheikh Hussain, Sheikh Yusuf DeLorenzo (now the chief Sharia officer at Shariah Capital) had not been able to hold his silence any longer and had made his views on the total return swap very public. In a paper entitled 'The Total Returns Swap and the "Shariah Conversion Technology" Stratagem', he proposed it to be a sham methodology, allowing investors to reap the benefit of *haram* (impermissible) returns, dressed up in Islamic clothes. He had written a lengthy letter to Sheikh Hussain, setting out his deep distaste for the methodology that was transforming the landscape of Islamic finance. But it was too late – a very public spat was forming where instead a scholarly forum behind closed doors might have cooled passions on both sides.

The older scholar was dismissive of the criticism and bristled at the suggestion that he had sold out. He suggested at first that Sheikh Yusuf had simply not taken the time or effort to understand the Sharia issues, and was trying to protect his job. Sheikh Yusuf, on the other hand, was explicit in his condemnation of the many scholars who were, by now, approving this structure for a number of global investment banks: 'They have made a serious mistake. So serious, in fact, that in my paper on the subject I have called their decision the Doomsday *Fatwa*. . .it is likely that those scholars fell into the trap of literalism.'[12] He went on to suggest that scholars should consider the details of a whole transactional series, not only one part of it, perhaps mindful of the Church's own changing attitude to usury which came about through acceptance of the *contractum trinius*. 'While a promise to exchange returns may be lawful, if the returns promised have been earned by illegitimate means (by funds that invest in Treasury futures, for example), then the promise may be declared unlawful as it has become a means, an ostensibly legitimate means, for illegitimate ends.'[13]

Here, Sheikh Yusuf was making a critical point in his analysis. In a head-to-head debate at a conference in Dubai in early 2008, the primary author of the White Paper, Deutsche's Hussein Hassan (confusingly with the same name as the scholar), defended the methodology through the application of *sadd al-dharai*, the legal device from classical jurisprudence that blocks ostensibly legitimate means when these are employed for illegitimate ends. Hassan suggested the *wa'd* methodology does not inevitably lead to conventional exposures, and that the end that is in question is not a certainty to the means. If there is no necessity to use the *wa'd* in order to arrive at the required end, then why should this means be prohibited and not the others?

But Hassan was fighting a losing battle for the hearts and minds of the audience. Sheikh Yusuf had no issue with the *wa'd* itself. He suggested instead that the application of *sadd al-dharai* was unwarranted in this case, on the basis that whatever leads to involvement in the unlawful will either lead to the unlawful as a certainty or lead to the unlawful as a possibility. 'This product', wrote Sheikh Yusuf in his paper, 'includes investments, even though they are entered into indirectly, that are clearly unlawful. Moreover, there is no doubt whatsoever that the transactional series leads incvitably, and repeatedly, to what is unlawful. . .as a certainty and not as a mere possibility.' He concluded, 'There is no need to resort to *sadd al-dharai* because the transaction is clearly unlawful.'[14] On the basis of the aggressive pushiness of Deutsche's gung-ho sales team, eager to sell all manner of credit derivatives and hedge funds wrapped in this technology, he had a point.

At the conference, Sheikh Yusuf responded to Hassan's patient explanation of the methodology by pointing to the money flow. 'When you accept this investment product, you accept the whole series, whether you know it or not. As the money moves, its character changes.'[15] Thus, he suggested that a Muslim investor taking part in a total return swap is implicated in every investment decision, trade and cash flow that the bank subsequently takes with his funds. If the bank hedges itself on the other side of the transaction (say, by buying units of the Goldman Sachs hedge fund for its own account), the Islamic investment certificate holder is implicated in this *haram* trade, though he may not himself be investing directly in the non-compliant instrument.

In Sheikh Yusuf's paper he suggested that it may be argued that conventional banks use the money of Islamic institutions with whom they trade in non-compliant ways. However, he set out a fundamental difference: that when the conventional bank receives money from an Islamic institution that money becomes its own to do with as it pleases. Money used to buy investment products under the *wa'd* methodology, on the other hand, has 'direct, predictable and immediate consequences. . .the Islamic client's investment in this product triggers a series of transactions, none of which is Sharia compliant'.[16]

And what of the use of a benchmark, just as LIBOR is used as a benchmark for the pricing of *sukuk?* His paper clarified: 'A benchmark is no more than a standard and therefore non-objectionable from a Sharia perspective. If it is used to determine the rate of repayment on a loan, then it is the interest-bearing loan that will be *haram* [impermissible]. LIBOR, as a mere benchmark, has no direct effect on the actual transaction or, more specifically, with the creation of revenues.'[17] He went on to say, 'Most importantly, the use of LIBOR as a benchmark for pricing in no way means that interest has entered the transaction itself. . .The attempt to draw a legal analogy, *qiyas*, between the use of LIBOR for pricing and the use of the performance of non-Sharia compliant assets for pricing is both inaccurate and misleading. The only similarity is that both are used for pricing.'

He offered a further reason why the methodology was dangerous: it risked damaging the industry. 'Why should a bank bother to spend the extra time and money required to make a securitisation into a *sukuk?*' he wrote.[18] In other words, he was arguing that there was no longer any need for a company to raise capital based on a real underlying asset, like a property that is sold and leased back from investors: 'For less money and in less time, it can simply offer conventional bonds and then use the "mechanism" to match performance, appear to sanitise the money, and satisfy the investor that the investment is *halal* and lawful.' He went on to question the need to ensure the Sharia compliance of Islamic stock indices, mutual funds, real estate, infrastructure projects, private equity and home finance. If the industry did not address this potentially pernicious new product, he feared that fund managers of all descriptions would never be motivated to comply with requirements of Islamic jurisprudence to trade and do business in Islamic – in ethical, in real economy – ways, and investor confidence would eventually erode, destroying an industry that has demonstrated so much promise in recent years. 'The question [the industry] faces now is whether it can prove that it is moral and responsible.'

Cleverly, and perhaps with the intention of repairing relations with the older scholar of whom he admitted he was a great admirer, Sheikh Yusuf left the door open for the methodology to be acceptable, under one strict condition. At the conference he concluded, 'If you're going to swap returns of one basket of performing assets for another, then you must insist that the assets in both baskets are *halal*.'[19] Thus, for example, linking the return to the performance of a basket of Sharia-compliant stocks would be acceptable to him.

Some time later I caught up with Sheikh Yusuf. 'Sheikh Hussain is one of the most thorough and thoughtful men I know', conceded Sheikh Yusuf in private, noting a relationship that spanned almost three decades. Perhaps he regretted the manner in which the media had portrayed a schism in the industry, since not for a moment did he wish to question the ethics of a man described as the father of the modern Islamic finance industry, and one from whom he acknowledged to me that he had learnt so much. And perhaps as the debate unfolded, I noticed a softening in Sheikh Hussain's response.

Indeed, in time, Sheikh Hussain would implicitly take on board the comments of Sheikh Yusuf by adapting the certification process that produced the *fatwa* for each new investment product. He undoubtedly recognized the magnitude of the concerns raised, and took pains to ensure that he be involved in both the development and distribution phases of each new product. He would even go so far as to approve the language for newspaper advertisements. What had started with the potential for acrimonious mudslinging had instead turned into an opportunity to refine the standards employed by the industry.

But it was impossible to beat the bankers. Across the industry, other firms picked up on the methodology and began issuing their own products using their own scholars, many of whom were not as intimately familiar with the structure. Corners were cut and products of dubious provenance continued to pour out from the sales desks of less scrupulous institutions.

Even Deutsche continued to consider the *wa'd* at every opportunity. Deutsche Bank's Islamic conveyor belt was now in full flow. Transactions became increasingly bizarre and far removed from the original intent of men like Sheikh Hussain. One that came to the team's attention involved the financing of a portfolio of hotels in Europe: the Qatari buyer demanded a *fatwa* so that he could continue to earn from the revenues of the hotels' restaurants, not generally considered to be Sharia compliant since a significant proportion of hotel revenue is derived from alcohol. Just as Sheikh Yusuf had foreseen, Deutsche suggested the total return swap: finance the purchase of the hotels through an investment vehicle that buys a Sharia-compliant asset (copper, Microsoft shares, whatever takes your fancy), swap away the return of the asset for the return of the hotels, and wine would miraculously turn into water. The suggestion led to some furious arguments amongst Deutsche's rocket scientists, and the first cracks began to appear in what had been a closely knit team.

Those cracks widened as the team considered some of the more detailed issues of Sharia compliance in their investment products platform, a brand known as Al Miyar. Incredibly, the investor had no legally enforceable security interest in the Islamic assets (the liquid and tradeable investments whose returns get swapped away), but somehow there was an acceptance by all parties that these assets belonged to him.[20] This couldn't be right, but the effort involved to restructure the security package and seek reapprovals for the platform was too much. So the issue was quietly brushed under the carpet and ignored. Imagine if Deutsche Bank were to meet the same fate as the hapless Lehman Brothers. Would Islamic investors get their money back directly from their 'segregated' accounts? Probably not.

Equally significantly, the Al Miyar platform allowed for the Islamic assets – apparently 'owned' by the investor – to be reused for Deutsche Bank's own trading purposes.[21] In other words, the Islamic assets (such as Microsoft shares) could be pulled in and out of the apparently segregated Islamic investment account, as and when Deutsche Bank desired, and without the investor being informed.

In the tens of thousands of words of documentation he had reviewed in his capacity as the chairman of Dar Al Istithmar's Sharia board, this (very fine) print had not been been brought to the attention of Sheikh Hussain. To what extent this oversight had been a deliberate obfuscation on the part of bankers and lawyers is not clear, though they were certainly aware of it in private.

As a member of that edgy Deutsche structuring team, I personally felt I had participated in the Islamic finance equivalent of the 'Manhattan Project', a Second World War initiative that assembled the Allies' leading physicists in the seclusion of the Los Alamos desert to build the atom bomb before Hitler. We knew the *wa'd* technology we would create could be used in good ways or bad, and had a global application, and yet in our hearts we also knew its primary use would be as a financial weapon of mass destruction by aggressive sales teams. Perhaps Sheikh Yusuf's doomsday description of the total return swap was apt, after all.

7

Standardizing the Industry:
Accelerating Chaos
or Bringing Order?

'I think that some of it is socially useless activity.'[1]

Adair Turner, referring to the derivatives industry
and its role in the post-2007 global financial crisis

Deutsche's *wa'd* technology had opened up new horizons.
Whilst its salesmen and -women criss-crossed the Middle and
Far East selling exotic structured investment products to the
private banking departments of Islamic financial institutions,
Sheikh Hussain and the Deutsche skunk works structurers
were more concerned with addressing the gap risk that Islamic
institutions suffered as a result of their inability to hedge their
macroeconomic exposures. Here was a real issue facing the
industry: a ticking time bomb of unhedged currencies and rates
on a massive scale, not some esoteric trophy investment bau-
bles for the ultra high net worth Gulf prince. Billions of dollars'

worth of institutional exposure, not the crumbs of a few tens of millions in speculative nibbles in the hope of financing one's next megayacht.

Treasury departments of the Islamic institutions knew they had a problem. The Islamic Development Bank, a multilateral development-financing institution owned by fifty-six member states, was haemorrhaging cash as if it were funding a war. It simply couldn't swap dollars for euros or vice versa on an ongoing basis without resorting to the conventional markets. It couldn't enter into rate swaps or currency forwards. Islamic institutions everywhere were funding long-term assets with short-term deposits. Without a Sharia-compliant solution to managing these risks, their volatile existence was owed to booming equity and real estate markets in the Middle East. For now, at least.

Some institutions pretended the problem didn't exist. Turkish institutions, in particular, wouldn't even use the word 'Islamic' in their name for fear of upsetting the country's secular sensibilities. Instead they were 'participation' banks, though the commodity *murabaha* trades that were their lifeblood lacked the participation that classical Islamic concepts of risk-sharing demanded. Their notions of what constituted Sharia compliance were at odds with almost everywhere else in the Islamic finance industry: they discussed Islamic 'repos' – or repurchase agreements that enabled them to borrow money against liquid assets held by them such as bonds – using interest-bearing Turkish inflation-linked bonds that somewhat stretched the definition of *sukuk*. They were content to transact swaps on a conventional basis despite their outward adherence to Sharia principles, on the basis that there was apparently no alternative.

Even in conservative Islamic environments, treasury departments of banks often entered into currency or rate swaps and forwards on a conventional basis, simply because the effort involved in preparing the necessary documentation was so daunting, and the process of Sharia certification so alien to departments whose staff were generally sourced from conventional banks. Do the trade, hide it in the books, and almost no one will know. What's the harm – it's only a hedging transaction, right? It's not as if we're trying to profit from these trades, or selling investments to the bank's customers. We're just protecting our institution from external risks.

The Sharia structuring process and legal documentation was indeed daunting. Regional Islamic banks in the Middle East and Malaysia had almost no specialized personnel trained to understand and negotiate Sharia-compliant treasury swaps, nor were they generally willing to pay the kind of fees demanded by the few appropriately qualified external legal counsel and third party structuring specialists.

A stalemate was playing out. Fast-talking rocket scientists in pinstripes from the global investment banks could structure the product, but getting their counterparts at the regional Islamic banks to focus their attention on it and procure internal legal and Sharia approvals was proving tricky. When the international bankers suggested a direct approach to the Islamic banks' Sharia boards, their counterparts often found excuses. Perhaps it was the fear of losing face in front of their colleagues in a one-on-one with their counterparts – always a cultural hot potato in much of the Islamic world (remember the Malaysian treasury official and her Sharia advisors?) – or perhaps such a direct approach threatened their own role as gatekeeper to the scholars.

The industry was crying out for a standardized set of documents. It would provide immediate access to liquidity and prudent management of balance sheets for the Islamic banks, lowering their exposure to macroeconomic volatility.

The ISDA Master Agreement

Standardized documents could be used under almost any circumstances, with changes to the key commercial parameters in the form of a schedule to a pre-formed master agreement. This type of templated transaction was already prevalent in the conventional world. An international trade organization of participants in the derivatives market, known as the International Swaps and Derivatives Association, or ISDA, had created a standardized contract known as the ISDA Master Agreement. This agreement allowed market participants to enter into 'over-the-counter' derivatives transactions – so-called because they take place directly between counterparties in the form of a bilateral contract rather than on an exchange – via a contract that both parties understood and were comfortable with. The specific commercial terms of the transaction are negotiated and set out in a Schedule to the Master Agreement.

The ISDA Master Agreement first came into being in 1992 as a result of work performed by ISDA on specific derivative transaction documents in the mid to late 1980s. It provided derivatives counterparties with standard terms that applied to all derivatives trades entered into between those counterparties. For every new trade, the terms of the master agreement applied automatically without the need for renegotiation.

Following the global economic turmoil of the late 1990s, the ISDA Master Agreement underwent a strategic review leading to wide-ranging revisions incorporated in the resulting 2002 Master Agreement and, at the time of writing, that is the central document around which the rest of the transaction structure is built for most over-the-counter derivative trades. This standardized document is never altered other than to insert the names of the counterparties. Global investment banks and the treasury departments of their large corporate clients tend to be intimately familiar with the agreement, as well as the credit and risk management issues associated with it. The trade is customized through the use of a schedule containing elections, additions and amendments to the master agreement. Once the master and schedule are executed by the counterparties, any future trade merely needs to make mention of the commercial terms, typically over the telephone and subsequently confirmed in writing.

The result is an industry that has mechanized the production of trillions of dollars' worth of derivative contracts every year, and unwittingly accelerated the rate at which an institution such as the infamous AIG could stuff its balance sheets with half a trillion dollars' worth of unhedged credit default swap contracts – a type of insurance policy in which AIG would act as the insurer against the default of loan repayments by companies and nations.[2] When the economy went belly-up, AIG was forced to make good on its guarantees to creditors by writing cheques for US$562 billion. Not having this kind of money down the back of the sofa, the risk junkies of AIG were forced to beg for a bailout from the American taxpayer, who duly obliged. It was a damning indictment of the modern financial system – that the larger and more entwined a financial institution was in the fabric of a nation's economy, the more likely it was to take larger and larger risks in the expectation that the hapless public would pay when it went wrong.

Would Islamic finance institutions benefit from a standardized template for swaps and derivative contracts, thus more efficiently managing their balance sheets and stabilizing their long-term earnings? Or would such a template lead to the creation of another uncontrollable monster of naked speculation, a harbinger of moral hazard?

Let's first take a look at the Islamic equivalent of a conventional swap transaction before we address this question. One of the most useful types of treasury product used by Islamic financial institutions is the profit rate swap, which seeks to swap away one type of rate exposure for another, in the same way that conventional institutions may swap away a floating interest rate payment for a fixed one. Imagine you have a mortgage with a conventional high-street bank. It's a fixed-rate mortgage with an interest rate that doesn't change for, say, five years. However,

the bank itself probably borrows money on a floating rate basis
– as the 'base rate' changes up or down over the next five years,
so will the bank's liabilities to depositors, the capital markets and
other banks in the inter-bank lending market. Clearly the bank
doesn't want to be exposed to these fluctuations in the base rate,
so it hedges itself by entering into a 'floating to fixed' swap with
a counterparty. Now its assets match its liabilities and its balance
sheet is being prudently managed.

At this point, the reader may be permitted to do a double-take.
Doesn't it sound strange that Islamic financial institutions pay
and receive interest-like amounts and describe them as 'profit'?
Well, whether they like it or not, these institutions exist within
the fractional reserve banking system and are subject to similar
capital adequacy and risk management requirements as their
conventional counterparts. So they take depositors' money and
pay a return to those depositors that is benchmarked against
their conventional counterparts. They invest in or lend to
companies at a rate that is benchmarked to their conventional
counterparts. How they pay that return and charge that rate is,
of course, the critical consideration for them to be considered
Sharia-compliant institutions. (Are these trades backed by some
real asset? Is there perhaps some form of risk sharing involved?
Have they avoided the prohibitions typical of Islamic commercial transactions?) But there is no question that benchmarks such
as LIBOR continue to be a necessary metric for Islamic banks,
and the overwhelming majority of scholars have come to accept
this, however imperfect a solution this may seem.

The profit-rate swap utilizes the same technique discussed in
the previous chapter, the *wa'd* structure, though this time not
to build an investment product. Previously we benchmarked the
price of underlying liquid tradeable assets (such as the Microsoft
shares) in the 'black box' SPV to the price of a set of published
indices, so that the investor could participate in the returns from
different asset classes. By contrast, this time we are considering

a hedging product rather than an investment product. On one side of the trade, the client has a floating rate liability and wishes to swap into fixed rate, and on the other side, the bank provides the hedge. The aim of a hedging transaction is to minimize risk, not maximize profits from a speculative trade.

The two parties on either side of the trade have reciprocal undertakings. They each enter into promises to enter into *murabaha* arrangements, with one side generating a series of fixed payments (with the the underlying Islamic assets – such as the Microsoft shares – priced at a cost price plus a fixed profit element), and the other side generating a series of floating payments (priced at a cost price plus a floating profit element).

So far, we have merely described the structure and essential transaction documents of the profit-rate swap. If you have understood all of this, you have done extremely well: few banks, whether Islamic or conventional, have personnel who truly understand how Islamic treasury products are designed and manufactured. Even were they to get past the basic structure, the detailed terms and conditions become an intellectual effort best left to the brightest lawyers in the industry. No wonder, then, that Islamic treasury products have been so slow to take off, even though the product exists and is evidently replicable. The balance sheets of Islamic institutions remain ticking time bombs until such time as they staff up or pay up for external advisors to project manage the implementation of such products.

What's the solution? There is no shortcut to the product: it is complicated, and no credible alternatives have been proposed at this point in time. The Islamic finance industry needs its equivalent of the ISDA 2002 Master Agreement, and each relevant institution needs to devote its resources to making standardization a reality. The first steps towards a Sharia-compliant derivatives template have been taken by ISDA in a joint venture with a standard setting body for the Islamic finance industry, the International Islamic Finance Market (IIFM). ISDA and IIFM have drawn on the pioneering work done to date by leading banks and law firms. With the help of a consultation process with both conventional and Islamic banks, and the advice of their eleven-man Sharia board, they have produced a template master agreement known as the ISDA/IIFM *Tahawwut* Master Agreement.

The *Tahawwut*

The *Tahawwut*, as it is generally referred to, attempts to unify the various swap documentation that has been transacted on a bespoke basis from bank to bank, the net result being a single master and schedule that has strong parallels with the 2002 ISDA Master and Schedule, and is therefore well understood already by the conventional industry. Why should it matter that its format should reflect its conventional equivalent? Simply because the conventional banks – such as Deutsche – have been driving the creation of Islamic derivatives, and continue to act as counterparties in the majority of trades. If their credit risk management departments can get comfortable with the credit risks, then it is likely that so will their regional counterparts.

Using the 2002 ISDA Master as a basis for the *Tahawwut*, ISDA and IIFM initially set about amending some of the big-picture principles. For example, transactions under the *Tahawwut* may only take place for the purpose of hedging, not speculation, though quite how this may be policed is a moot point. Interest may not be charged on transactions, and no compensation may be paid for defaulted or deferred payments. All fairly straight-forward, so far.

Then it gets a little more complicated: how do we allow for the valuation and settlement of outstanding contracts in the event of an early termination? Resolving this particular thorny issue may have been a primary reason as to why it took twenty-four drafts and a consultation period spanning three and a half years to complete the *Tahawwut*.[3]

In conventional swap transactions governed by the ISDA Master Agreement, the master and the confirmations entered under it form a single agreement. Therefore the counterparties may aggregate the amounts owing to each other in separate trades and replace them with a single net payable amount by one party to the other. This is known as netting. Of particular importance is the concept of 'close-out netting', where the transactions under a master agreement are terminated, perhaps due to a 'credit event' such as one party failing to pay the other on time. In order to calculate the net amount payable by one party to another in the event of termination, an independent third party may be instructed to calculate the cost of entering into trades with identical commercial terms to the terminated transactions. This is known as the settlement amount, and its enforceability in the event of termination is of critical importance to financial institutions entering into derivative trades, since netting allows them to allocate capital only against the net figure they would have to pay on close-out of an ISDA Master Agreement.

Not only are credit lines more efficient, but close-out netting also facilitates the taking of collateral to offset exposures and lowers reserve requirements to satisfy regulatory capital requirements. With lower reserves and collateral posted for net and not gross exposures, financial institutions experience lower costs, increased liquidity and reduced credit and systemic risk. Indeed, in the aftermath of the collapse of Lehman Brothers, its counterparties were able to close out their over-the-counter trades relatively smoothly under the ISDA Master Agreement, largely because close-out netting is legally enforceable in the United States. The financial system would have experienced a much tougher test had the counterparties of Lehman Brothers needed to determine their exposures on a gross basis instead of net.

There are two areas of concern here for Sharia-compliant swap transactions: the first is the Sharia permissibility of the principle of netting, and the second is the enforceability of netting in jurisdictions where Islamic financial institutions operate.

Given that a Sharia-compliant swap requires the counterparties to enter into a sequence of *murabahas*,[4] then naturally, in the event of early termination, a future stream of *murabahas* has not yet been transacted. At this point, bankers want to be reassured that only a net liability is due, and not the gross notional value of each trade individually, something that they refer to as 'gross settlement risk'. Imagine a $1 billion notional swap value: this might potentially require the Islamic investment account to trade $1 billion worth of copper (or other Sharia-compliant asset) in order to fulfil outstanding *wa'd* obligations. The credit risk management department and commodities trading desk at even the largest global investment bank will have trouble signing off on the possibility of having to find such a massive amount of copper (or Microsoft shares) to be traded at a moment's notice, and they certainly don't want to be left exposed on one side of the trade if their counterpart fails to honour its obligation on the other side. Clearly, bankers are looking for a close-out netting similar to that allowed under the 2002 ISDA Master Agreement. However, as we discovered earlier, in the Sharia one may not net off one sale against another within one contract in order not to fall foul of the prohibition on combining sale contracts. Nor indeed are the calculation methods available to conventional bankers – such as determining the 'present value' of future obligations by discounting future cash flows – necessarily considered a Sharia-compliant method of calculation (given the inherent recognition in such a calculation of interest rates and the uncertainty of future circumstances).

Outside of the ISDA/IIFM initiative, those banks that have already transacted Islamic swaps have solved the close-out netting issue in various ways. One way is to force the amount of the Islamic assets that are the subject of the *wa'd* to be much smaller in value than the notional value of the swap itself, thus substantially reducing the quantum of the gross settlement risk. For example, the counterparties may agree to trade Islamic assets worth, say, one-tenth of the notional value of the swap. So a $1 billion swap may only require $100 million worth of copper as the underlying, this being the cost price of each *murabaha* in the sequence. Not all scholars are comfortable with this, however, since the paper value of the trade doesn't match the real value and, after all, Islamic financial transactions are supposed to be based on something real and tangible rather than being mere paper contracts.

The *Tahawwut* Master Agreement deals with close-out netting by splitting the calculation of the settlement amount into two, with one calculation for concluded transactions within a swap (where delivery of an asset has been made under a *murabaha*), and the other for non-concluded transactions (where assets have not been fully delivered). In the former case, the originally agreed payment price is accelerated and becomes payable immediately. All payments due from one counterparty to the other under concluded transactions are accelerated and set off against each other to determine a single close-out amount.

Non-concluded transactions within the swap are a little trickier. An index is calculated based on the market quotation and loss framework as used in the 1992 ISDA Master Agreement, which determines a replacement cost for the terminated swap trade. IIFM's scholars were able to agree to an index instead of a replacement cost valuation. The final termination settlement amount is then paid through a *musawama* sale contract, which is a bit like a *murabaha*.

The second area of concern for swaps traders is the enforceability of netting in jurisdictions where these products are traded. Typically, Islamic banks in the Middle East and South-East Asia operate in 'non-netting' jurisdictions, that is, jurisdictions where the legislative framework does not allow for such trades to aggregate and net each other out in the event of early termination. As a lobbying body for its member institutions, ISDA is tasked with working to achieve recognition for netting under the insolvency laws of countries around the world. Since ISDA has currently procured opinions on the legality of netting in only fifty-five countries,[5] there is still much work to be done to ensure that banks and their counterparties are comfortable with the risks of entering into Sharia-compliant swap transactions.

Has the *Tahawwut* been a success? To date, sadly, no. Critics point to the close-out netting arrangement as being incomplete, requiring as it does the entry into a new transaction when a default has taken place. Can one bind an insolvent party into entering into another commercial transaction? In addition, the issue of non-netting jurisdictions in the majority of the Islamic world remains, and thus counterparties remain unsure of the legality of the document in the markets for which it is generally intended. Others say the *Tahawwut* has not gone far enough in addressing critical supplementary issues such as the Credit Support Annex that attaches to the ISDA Master Agreement, and governs the posting of collateral in derivative trades, a major tool in mitigating counterparty credit risk.

But these issues can be resolved, though they may take some time. There is something more immediate for the industry to work on: a cultural issue. Some local and regional Islamic finance institutions complain that they have not felt involved in the consultation process. In contrast, ISDA and IIFM officials have privately expressed their frustrations that early drafts were circulated to some one hundred institutions across the world but only twenty-five took an active interest, the majority of these being conventional financial institutions. Some international bankers echo this frustration. After hearing a treasury sales manager at a Middle East bank complain that the *Tahawwut* documents were simply too complex for ready digestion, I was tempted to advise him that sadly there is no big print version with colour pictures, there is no 'guide for students', and there is no shortcut to understanding it. It's a complicated product, so man up and get studying.

International bankers found the process to be so drawn out and frustrating that in those three and a half years they corralled their own resources – legal, Sharia, credit risk management, compliance, structurers, traders, sales staff – and went ahead, producing their own internally approved Sharia-compliant liquidity management and hedging tools. The market is now awash with contracts documenting the profit-rate swap, all using roughly the same structure, but in different colours, shapes and sizes. As a result, each swap transaction continues to be negotiated on a unique, bespoke basis, and the regional Islamic institutions are overrun with the 'suitcase' bankers from global firms, each trying to pitch their own version of the same product.

And some bankers are still missing the point of Islamic finance's necessary relationship with the real economy. At the World Islamic Banking Conference in November 2010, a technical workshop on the *Tahawwut* Master Agreement yielded a revealing question from one treasury banker in the audience – 'Can we use this for credit derivatives?' he asked. 'I mean credit default swaps. How can I use this document to buy protection against sovereign defaults?' The Islamic institution represented by this gentleman had no known exposures to Greece, or Portugal, or Ireland, or indeed many of the nations on the critical list at the time, and yet he wanted to buy an insurance policy against their default. He wasn't trying to hedge a position, he was looking to make a sizeable profit on a speculative punt. Perhaps his institution might also try to drive that particular sovereign into default through other means.

Would the Sharia board of this institution check for existing exposures to the risk in question, or would they assume in all cases this kind of protection was a necessary hedge and allow it to take place? One of the fundamental premises of the *Tahawwut* is its use as a tool for hedging, not for speculation, but how does one draw a line between the two? It has been reasonably argued, for example, that without the existence of speculators in the market, there might not be sufficient liquidity for those looking to hedge their positions.

Once, MBA courses taught that firms like AIG were shining examples of the modern finance industry. And yet basic truths enshrined in Islamic law would immediately suggest otherwise: without dissecting such an institution's balance sheet, the very fact that they encouraged counterparties to bet on the default of entities in which they held no interest should be cause for concern. Would you like your neighbour to take out a fire insurance policy on your house? Let's hope he's not an arsonist. That's how the modern financial services industry works, and now Islamic bankers want what their conventional cousins already have.

Critics of the Islamic finance industry often point to the industry's mimicry of the conventional industry, both in its products and, more importantly, in its philosophy. If the Islamic finance industry is to gain the respect of the wider (particularly Muslim) public, then it may wish to consider a step change in the way its practitioners operate within it, or give greater powers to its Sharia boards to examine ongoing trades for adherence to the spirit, as well as the letter, of Sharia.

Without such changes, there is every possibility that trades like the speculative credit default swap above could become prevalent in the Islamic finance industry, just as they have in the conventional industry. Perhaps Islamic finance might end up creating the same types of asset-backed securities linked to subprime mortgages that brought down conventional financial institutions such as Lehman Brothers. Without cultural change, the introduction of a standardized Islamic derivatives agreement may simply become the catalyst for the creation of a new monster.

8

The Credit Crisis and Islamic Finance

I believe that banking institutions are more dangerous to our liberties than standing armies.

Attributed to Thomas Jefferson[1]

When I sat down to write this book, it had always been my intention to make the connection between the global credit crisis and the dominance of the 'financial' economy over the 'real' economy. In other words, creating financial instruments – the derivatives we read about earlier – that provided exposure to different types of investments without actually *investing* in those assets created an economy powered by pieces of paper. Like a game of musical chairs, when the music stopped and underlying assets were no longer performing to expectations, suddenly investors found themselves without a chair. It's not surprising that many outside the industry see the financial economy as a giant Ponzi scheme.

I haven't set out to describe in detail the events and causes of the financial crisis of late 2007 onwards, nor do I suggest that Islamic finance in its contemporary form would have prevented the crisis in the first place, or indeed be the definitive solution to recovery. There are many excellent narratives of the events that led to the collapse of major banking institutions and subsequent government interventions, and the reader may wish to develop his or her understanding of these events.[2] These events provide a context for the challenges that faced the Islamic finance industry during this crisis, and the role that it may play in preventing future crises.

What are the origins of the credit crunch? To help us answer this question, I turn to an irreverent and anonymous cartoon that circulated the internet in 2008, entitled 'The Subprime Primer', and I paraphrase it below, though I regret being unable to unearth the author in order to credit him or her:

At Ace Mortgage Brokers ('We Make Your Dreams Come True'), a customer walks in and declares his wish to buy a house.

'But I haven't saved any money for a downpayment and I don't think I can afford the monthly payments', he says. 'Can you help me?'

The mortgage broker is bullish. 'Sure, since the value of your house will always go up, we don't need downpayments any more! And we can give you a really low interest rate for a few years and raise it later.'

'Sounds good', says the customer. 'But there's one thing: my employer might not verify my employment. Is that a problem?'

'Not at all. Here, take a look at the "Liar's Loan" and you can verify your own employment and income.' The broker hands over a brochure with a smile and a wink.

The customer is delighted. 'Wow, you're willing to finance me?'

'Well, we don't actually lend you the money', explains the broker. 'That's the bank's problem. As long as they lend you money, we get commission.'

A few weeks later, at the First Bank of Bankland, Inc, ('We Don't Waste Your Time with Due Diligence'), the head of loans has a problem. The new mortgages file doesn't look too hot and he's worried about the credit risk on his books. 'These crappy mortgage loans are really stinking up my office. I'll sell them to the smart guys in New York and they can do their magic on them.'

Over in New York, at the Stearns Brothers Investment Bank of Wall Street ('So Sharp, We Cut Ourselves'), the stinking mortgages are attracting flies.

'Who's gonna buy this crap, boss?' asks one of the smart guys.

The boss is very smart. 'We create a new security using these mortgages as collateral. Let's call it a CDO, short for collateralized debt obligation. We sell the CDO to investors and promise to pay them back as mortgages are paid off.'

'But crap is crap, isn't it? I don't get it', says the junior investment banker.

'Sure, individually, these loans stink', explains the boss. 'But if we pool them together, only some of them will go bad, thus spreading out the risk. Since housing prices always go up, we have very little to worry about. To categorize the risk, let's cut up the loans into three pieces or tranches: the Good, the Not-So-Good, and the Ugly. If some mortgages fail, we'll pay investors holding the Good tranche first. Then we'll pay the Not-So-Good holders, then the Ugly.'

'Oh, so you mean we'll pay the highest interest rate to investors in the riskiest Ugly tranche, and the lowest rate to the least risky Good tranche.'

'Yes, and I have an even cleverer idea', continues the boss. 'We buy bond insurance for the Good tranche. The rating agencies will give it a great rating, somewhere between A and AAA. The Not-So-Good will get rated B to BBB. We won't bother rating the Ugly tranche.'

'Boss, you're a genius. You've created AAA and BBB securities out of a stinking pile of crap. So, who do we sell to?'

'Well, the SEC [the US Securities and Exchange Commission] won't let us sell this to orphans and widows', says the boss, clearly frustrated, 'so we'll have to go to our sophisticated institutional clients. Insurance companies, banks, pension funds for small villages in the English countryside, school boards in Kansas. Anyone looking for a high-quality safe investment.'

'Who's gonna buy the Ugly piece, boss?'

'We keep it for ourselves', says the boss. 'We'll pay ourselves a handsome interest rate.'

'This is great, boss. But even though the mortgages are collateral for an entirely new security, it's still on our balance sheet, right?'

'Don't be stupid. The accountants will let us set up a shell company in the Cayman Islands to take ownership of the mortgages. We move the crap off our balance sheet onto theirs. It's called a Special Purpose Vehicle or SPV.'

Over at the Office of the Czar of Accounting ('The Finest Box Tickers in the Land'), an investor and concerned citizen is demanding that the Czar forces financial institutions to show greater transparency and openness in their financial reporting. But the Czar is in the middle of a fiendishly difficult sudoku puzzle and waves the concerned citizen away.

At the Crinkley-on-the-Wold Village Pension Fund in rural England ('Safer than Geoffrey Boycott's Forward Defence'), the fund manager has a problem. 'I say, old boy', he says to his contact at Stearns Brothers. 'What is going on here? We're not receiving our monthly payments!'

'Sorry, bud, it's really crazy round here. The mortgagees are not paying up so the CDO is struggling', replies the investment banker.

'You mean the AAA piece, the "Good" one? We're supposed to be paid out first!' exclaims the incredulous fund manager.

'It seems the loans are worse than we originally thought and there's very little cash coming in. Frankly we're as disappointed as you are.'

'You told me the housing prices would always go up and borrowers could always refinance!'

'Yeah, bad assumption. My bad. Sorry.'

'And the AAA rating from the rating agencies?'

'Their bad.'

'What about the insurers?'

'They don't have enough money to cover this mess. Their bad.'

'What do I tell my villagers?'

'Your bad.'

The cartoon may have been overly simplistic, but it contained some considerable truth. At the point at which French investment bank BNP Paribas identified in August 2007 that three of its funds could not value assets within them owing to a 'complete evaporation of liquidity',[3] in a clear sign that banks were refusing to do business with one another following a slowdown in the US housing market and increasing default rates on US subprime loans, the authorities began to mobilize their resources to prop up the financial system. At first, the European Central Bank pumped €95 billion into the banking market to improve liquidity, then followed up with a further €109 billion a few days later. The US Federal Reserve, the Bank of Canada and the Bank of Japan also began their own interventions.

Whilst the Fed cut its bank lending rate, warning that the credit crunch could be a risk to economic growth, the rate at which banks lend to each other rose to its highest level in nine years: banks started to worry about being repaid by other banks, or urgently needed funds themselves. By September 2007, Northern Rock, the fifth largest British lender, had approached the Bank of England for emergency support in its capacity as the 'lender of last resort'. Northern Rock's mortgage lending relied heavily on the capital markets, rather than savers' deposits, for funding and this funding was now drying up. The day after this information became public, depositors withdrew £1 billion, the largest run on a bank in more than a century, forcing the British government to step in to guarantee depositors' savings.

By October, Swiss bank UBS announced US$3.4 billion of losses from subprime investments, and its chairman and chief executive stepped down. Merrill Lynch's chief executive also resigned after revealing a $7.9 billion exposure to bad debt. These numbers seemed like small fry over the next six months as Citigroup was to reveal losses of $40 billion.

By December, central banks around the world engaged in a concerted effort to stabilize the global economy by offering billions of dollars in loans to banks, including a $500 billion package from the European Central Bank to assist commercial banks over the Christmas period. Though the Fed and the Bank of England repeatedly cut rates, global stock markets continued to fall, and the first monoline insurance company, MBIA, announced a major loss, blaming exposure to the US subprime sector. Companies like MBIA specialize in insuring bonds, guaranteeing to repay loans in the event the borrower collapses, and now ratings agencies would look to downgrade these previously AAA-rated bastions.

In February 2008, the British government announced that Northern Rock would be nationalized; a month later, distressed US investment bank Bear Stearns was acquired by JP Morgan for a paltry $240 million, where only a year earlier it had been worth $18 billion. Shortly afterwards the International Monetary Fund warned that the contagion of the credit crunch was spreading from subprime mortgages to commercial property, consumer credit and corporate debt.

Rights issues – that is, asking shareholders to subscribe for new shares – and other capital-raising exercises were announced by Royal Bank of Scotland, UBS and Barclays, and by September the US government had stepped in to aid the country's two largest lenders, Fannie Mae and Freddie Mac, both owners and guarantors of $5.3 trillion worth of home loans – simply too big to be allowed to fail. US Treasury Secretary Hank Paulson stated that the two institutions' levels of debt posed a 'systemic risk' to financial stability and that without action the financial position of the two firms would rapidly deteriorate.

Almost immediately afterwards, on 15 September 2008, Lehman Brothers became the first major bank to collapse since the crisis began. Days earlier, it had posted a loss of $3.9 billion for the three months to August and had been frantically searching for a buyer, but to no avail. Simultaneously, Merrill Lynch was agreeing to a takeover from Bank of America. The next day, the

US Fed announced an $85 billion rescue package for the country's largest insurance company, AIG, in return for an 80 per cent stake.

But the largest bank failure was yet to happen: on 25 September, the mortgage lender Washington Mutual, with $307 billion of assets, was closed down by regulators and sold to JP Morgan Chase. Around the world, governments were bailing out their financial champions and guaranteeing depositors' savings at the expense of the taxpayer. The US House of Representatives passed a $700 billion government plan to rescue the US financial sector, even using some of the money to support the three big car manufacturers, General Motors, Ford and Chrysler. In Michael Moore's documentary film, *Capitalism: A Love Story* (2009), he described the bailout as a 'financial coup d'état', with particular venom directed at the investment bankers turned politicians and senior civil servants, now apparently bailing out their buddies with little thought to moral hazard.

British taxpayers also felt the pain, with £37 billion injected into Royal Bank of Scotland, Lloyds TSB and HBOS as part of a £50 billion rescue package. Around the world, the US jobless rate rose to a sixteen-year high, the Bank of England's base rate dropped to its lowest level in its 315-year history, Chinese exports registered their biggest decline in a decade, and world economic growth fell to its lowest rate since the Second World War. The effects of the crisis will be felt for generations to come.

Did Islamic investments and institutions survive? Did they thrive in the vacuum left by conventional financial services? Let's first take a look at what industry analysts tell us about the conventional financial services industry.

In a fictional narrative produced in 2011 by the consulting firm Oliver Wyman, 'The Financial Crisis of 2015' reconstructs the events of 2011 to 2015 through the eyes of a senior investment banker who witnesses a cyclical repeat of the credit crisis that gripped the world only a few years earlier. The narrative contends that there are three potential reasons for a financial crisis to re-emerge: the resurgence of shadow banking, the formation of emerging markets asset bubbles, and sovereign debt restructurings in developed markets. In other words, the growth of hedge funds, irrational exuberance in emerging markets and a change in developed nations' debt obligations could result in a perfect storm. 'Shadow banking', that enormous sector of finance that exists outside the purview of mainstream banking regulators and out of mind of the general public (like hedge funds), was projected to be subject to greater scrutiny by policymakers and regulators. Despite this, the report surmised that the world of structured investment vehicles, credit hedge funds, asset-backed commercial paper conduits and securities lenders would remain on top in the game of regulatory cat and mouse. The amount of risk warehoused in the global financial services industry would continue to get squeezed across from the carefully monitored banking industry into the murkier world of the shadow banking sector. New, stricter, regulatory regimes would fail to persuade, threaten or penalize the financial sector into behaving more prudently and responsibly.

As for the emerging markets, to where many institutions might end up migrating in order to escape constricting regulatory environments, an asset bubble would form. Western banks would lend to emerging markets' banks and governments in order to generate a positive margin over the rising costs of funds in their home markets, moving down the credit spectrum to increase their yield – in other words, riskier loans with higher interest rates. Favourable demographics and increased liberalization of such markets, catalysed by cheap money, would lead to rising commodities prices and consequent strong incentives to launch expensive development and infrastructure projects. An overemphasis on commodities-related activities such as mining would create a massive oversupply relative to demand from the real economy, and governments would spend beyond their means in the comfort of their unrealistic asset valuations.

Western banks would build concentrated credit exposures in these markets, and previously risk-averse banks would feel pressured into acquiring previously downsized banks.

Rampant inflation in China as a result of dramatic rises in commodity prices and loose Western monetary policy would lead to a raising of Chinese interest rates and an appreciation of its currency. The Chinese economy would slow and global demand for commodities be profoundly affected. The commodities crisis of 2013 (remember this is a fictional scenario postulated in 2011) would render expensive commodity exploration projects half finished, just as the tumbleweeds had blown through real estate developments around the world only five years earlier. (In this respect at least, the consulting firm's fictional scenario turned out to be partially right, with a Chinese slowdown leading to reduced demand for raw materials and a consequent correction in commodity prices.)

Finally, the developed world's sovereign debt mountain would reach a crisis point. Heavily indebted US, UK and European nations would experience rising long-term sovereign bond yields as their solvency rapidly deteriorated. Their debt burdens would become unserviceable, forcing restructuring and bailout money from healthier nations, leading to the biggest post-war rebalancing of economic and political power.[4]

A far-fetched scenario? Not according to some of the more introspective observers in the Islamic finance industry. To them, the modern obsession with growth, and leverage to achieve that growth, is fundamentally philosophically at odds with the notion of creating a harmoniously balanced society, leading as it does to repeated cycles of debt-fuelled lunacy. Like a long-suffering father bailing out his alcoholic son's gambling debts, governments have become accustomed to entertaining moral hazard by subsidizing risk taking by their financial institutions.

This observation is not exclusive to observers from the Islamic world. In Oliver Wyman's report, the projected scenario contends that speculative investors will head for the exits at the first sign of trouble when the Chinese economic juggernaut applies the brakes, leading to the next global financial crisis. One of their suggestions to avoid this 'avoidable history', as they call it, is to stop the subsidization of risk taking by governments. They contend that market failure is commonly caused by governmental distortion of prices, often by way of taxes or subsidies.

Governmental policies causing market failure is an interesting observation for our purposes, because tax legislation has been one of the primary reasons why both lenders and borrowers turn to debt financing instead of equity financing. Though the report goes on to discuss implicit government support for bank creditors – in the form of reducing risk premia on banks' debt funding – a primary reason why an entity would wish to finance itself with one form of capital over another is largely distorted by the unequal tax treatment of debt versus equity. Interest repayments on debt are typically tax deductible, dividends on equity shares are not. Governments incentivize us to use leverage to grow, instead of to seek equity investors, who typically focus on long-term strategic issues with a view to growth, not merely payback. In addition, the acceptance of an economic system that allows banks to maintain low reserve ratios is anathema to the real economy perspective of Islamic finance, where the offer of finance by one party to another does not create wealth in and of itself.

Other types of governmental price distortion include the effects of quantitative easing, the printing of money, which can help to cause the formation of bubbles. In our discussion on the nature of money in Chapter 2, we heard from Justice Mufti Muhammad Taqi Usmani at Davos. His vision of an Islamic economy leads to the suggestion that a just economy could not be based on an interest-bearing fiat currency. Fiat money – that is, money that has value established by decree – is based on faith in the government issuing the money rather than on a physical commodity such as gold.

According to the Mufti, the credit crisis can be distilled into four basic causes: money is no longer a medium of exchange; the sale of intangible contracts (the modern derivatives industry) has ballooned out of control; the sale of debt is not considered objectionable; and the sale of assets one does not own caused a spiral of collapsing prices.[5]

He no longer appears to be alone in his views. Western commentators have started to question the way in which the world's financial institutions do business. Riots and protests from Athens to London to Wall Street suggest that the general public – the holders of low- and middle-income jobs, mortgage payers – agree and demand change. Some are also starting to question our established conceptions of leadership. Are the mistakes that have been made in recent years that led to the global financial crisis a result of the manner in which we collectively view risk, and appoint our leaders to chase that risk?

Jeremy Grantham, the chief investment strategist at US fund management company Grantham Mayo Van Otterloo, certainly believes so. In his letter to the firm's investors in autumn 2008, he identified what he believed was the underlying cause of the global financial crisis. He contended that his firm knew dozens of people who saw the crisis coming, who had good historical data, were thoughtful and intuitive. He described them as right-brained: given to developing odd theories, taking their time to sift through and ruminate on mountains of data. They considered outlier events, the ones the financial services industry believed couldn't possibly happen. They were introspective, reflective and patient, but their personality traits are not generally considered those of natural leaders. In contrast, said Grantham, not one of the bosses of the bulge bracket investment banks, nor US Treasury Secretary Hank Paulson, nor the chairman of the US Federal Reserve Ben Bernanke, saw the crisis coming. Grantham writes:

I have a theory that people who find themselves running major-league companies are real organisation management types who focus on what they are doing this quarter or this annual budget. They are somewhat impatient and focused on the present. Seeing these things requires more people with a historical perspective who are more thoughtful and more right-brained – but we end up with an army of left-brained immediate doers.

So it's more or less guaranteed that every time we get an outlying, obscure event that has never happened before in history, they are always going to miss it. And the three or four dozen-odd characters screaming about it are always going to be ignored.[6]

Today's CEOs and political leaders have been picked for their left-brainedness: focus, persuasiveness, political acumen, energy, decisiveness. Patience does not figure. If they do not act decisively and immediately, they would not hang around in their jobs for too long. Their job performance is measured on a quarterly basis and their career risk is high. If the herd is piling into financing real estate development projects, or collateralized debt obligations of mortgage-backed securities, then so must they, or they risk being thrown out onto the street. Investment banking does not reward thinkers. It rewards doers.

So what has all this got to do with Islamic finance? Let's return to the scene at the Godolphin Ballroom in the Emirates Towers Hotel on that muggy summer night, where our derivatives trader turned Islamic finance evangelist, Tarek El Diwany, was in full flow.

'The seventeenth-century goldsmith banker had realized the incredible opportunity presented to him in the behaviour of his customers', explained El Diwany. The gold deposit receipt presented to the depositor by a trusted goldsmith would increasingly be accepted in the marketplace by merchants selling goods and

services to those holding the paper receipts. As a result, depositors sought redemption of their gold receipts in ever decreasing
numbers, gradually dispensing with the need to frequently
withdraw gold. The goldsmith was no longer the manager of a
gold vault, instead he now offered to lend paper receipts, instan-
taneously created in the back office. Paper money was born.

'Naturally, many businessmen wanted to join in this new game
of banking', said El Diwany, describing the fractional reserve
banking system, an evolution of the argument of goldsmith
bankers that they need not keep the same amount of gold in
their reserves as the amount of paper money they lent out. Since
the majority of depositors did not come back to the bank to
claim their gold in any given period, one could safely issue paper
receipts in excess of the amount of gold in the vaults. Bankers
thus created multiple legal claims of ownership for every gold
coin in their safe keeping. Now the reserve ratio was born.

So notes had become legal tender instead of gold and were lent
in the inter-bank market for banks to fulfil day-to-day activities.
Every time a bank made a loan, the supply of money circulating
in the economy increased. El Diwany put forward the argument
that reducing debt would merely cause a reduction in the money
supply and lead to recession. 'Pay your debt, or lose your job,
that's the choice.'

He illustrated the point by way of an example.[7] Imagine there
is one bank in the economy, holding $10 of cash in its vault as
its start-up capital. Customers A and B are issued with cheque
books. A buys goods from B for $100 and pays by cheque.
B deposits the cheque at the bank, leaving A with an overdraft
and B with a credit for $100.

If B were to withdraw his money, the bank would not be able
to redeem the deposit since it only has $10 in its vault. If B buys
goods from A for $100, the $100 of money would disappear
in B's account. Money created by the bank is destroyed in the
act of repaying a bank loan. Thus bank money is fundamentally

different in nature to commodity money: gold coins, for example, would continue to exist after the act of repayment.

Let's go back to A's overdraft of $100. At an interest rate of 20 per cent, A would need to pay $120 back to the bank in a year. Since there is only $110 of money in existence – that is, $100 of bank-created money and $10 cash in the vault – A cannot repay the money unless he borrows it from the bank (creating new bank money and merely deferring the problem), or the state creates new 'state money' (cash issued by the state, such as, say, welfare payments), or A sells goods or services to the bank in return for bank money.

'Much of the effort of society to produce is in fact an effort to obtain sufficient money to repay debts owed to banks', concluded El Diwany. He described the monetary system as being responsible for 'forcing unnecessary and sometimes aggressive forms of economic growth on the world', fuelled by long-term increases in debt.

When in late 2007, the problems of Northern Rock became public knowledge, memorable images were broadcast around the world, the very definition of a run on the bank, as customers flocked to their local provincial high street, queues snaking for blocks out of the branch doors in locations around the UK. If the photos had been in black and white and the customers had worn flat caps, you would be hard pressed to know it wasn't the Great Depression of the 1930s.

If the bank's customers all asked for their money back at the same time, and the inter-bank market slammed the door on an institution, what then? In Northern Rock's case, the Bank of England stepped in with £20 billion of what was described as taxpayers' money, though El Diwany contended that this was in fact 'new money, created in a few keystrokes by the Bank of England' and backed by the taxpayer if Northern Rock could not repay the bank.[8] The consequences of a wider bank run would clearly be an economic catastrophe.

Should the legal privilege to create money be removed from private hands? What about government hands? Do we trust our political leaders not to issue money for their political advantage? Islamic economics experts suggest a gold-based currency: its quantity is finite and it has intrinsic value. This argument has not been restricted to Islamic commentators, though. Even America's founding fathers saw the benefit of throwing off the yoke of enslavement to private banks, with Thomas Jefferson variously attributed as having written:

> If the American people ever allow [private] banks to control the issue of their currency, first by inflation, then by deflation, the banks and corporations that will grow up around them will deprive the people of all property until their children wake up homeless on the continent their Fathers conquered[9]. . .I believe that banking institutions are more dangerous to our liberties than standing armies. . .The issuing power should be taken from the banks and restored to the people, to whom it properly belongs.[10]

Whilst it is difficult to establish the outright veracity of the above quotations (since they were printed many years later), Jefferson was one of a number of early American presidents distressed by the greed of money manufacturers, arguing that the Republic and the Constitution were in constant danger from the so-called 'money power', an elite who manipulated the political power of the state to gain a monopoly over money issue.[11] Andrew Jackson, having struggled to demand the withdrawal of government deposits from the privately owned Bank of the United States, arguing that debt from private monopoly was being wielded as a political weapon, passionately addressed the American public some years after Jefferson, in 1837:

The distress and alarm which pervaded and agitated the

whole country when the Bank of the United States waged war upon the people in order to compel them to submit to its demands cannot yet be forgotten. The ruthless and unsparing temper with which whole cities and communities were oppressed, individuals impoverished and ruined, and a scene of cheerful prosperity suddenly changed into one of gloom and despondency ought to be indelibly impressed on the memory of the people of the United States. If such was its power in time of peace, what would it have been in a season of war, with an enemy at your doors?. . .if you had not conquered, the government would have passed from the hands of the many to the few, and this organised money power, from its secret conclave, would have dictated the choice of your highest officials and compelled you to make peace or war, as best suited their wishes.[12]

Jackson had earlier argued that 'the only currency known to the Constitution of the United States is gold and silver. This is consequently the only currency which that instrument delegates to Congress the power to regulate.'[13] No doubt Jackson would have considered today's US Federal Reserve, a private bank-owned monopoly, to be unconstitutional.

The last of many populist presidents to fight against the money monopoly, Abraham Lincoln faced a heavy burden financing the Civil War from a banking system under private control. A shortage of coins meant the private banks were unwilling to finance the Union Army, and so Lincoln presented to Congress a bill in 1862 to make United States notes full legal tender, thus enabling the Federal Government to print sufficient paper to finance the war. Not surprisingly, the issue of paper money by the government was opposed by banking interests, and they argued that they be allowed to act as agents of the government in issuing money, thus rendering the state a perpetual borrower in thrall to the private money monopoly.

In the end, it didn't matter. By 1913, the Federal Reserve Act was signed into law and the private banks had triumphed. Now the laws of nations across the world permit and encourage money creation by the banking system, and its lending at interest, increasing indebtedness. The banking system will continue to benefit from a society that cannot repay its debt, and debt will continue its inexorable march upwards as a proportion of GDP. El Diwany argued that in previous centuries Western nations had often avoided interest-based debt in order to build their infrastructure, with the hospitals and universities of England financed by donations and endowments. In contrast, today's massive infrastructure projects such as the Channel Tunnel toil under the debilitating effects of debt service. El Diwany clicked on the next slide of his presentation to illustrate the stark contrast in quality of modern infrastructure, its cost base burdened by debt: a picture of St Pancras Station in London, its fine craftsmanship evident in the brickwork and masonry, juxtaposed against an extension to the station made of prefab panels.

Another click on his laptop and another photograph, this time the rural charm of the English village of Kelvedon, before a house-building firm changed the face of the village by borrowing such a huge amount of debt that rather than make incremental changes to the village, it turned it into a characterless housing estate. Knowing that it could employ leverage at a lower rate of interest than the rate of return on its investment had spurred on its greed to the detriment of what once had made that village unique. One more click and a photograph of a giant out-of-town shopping centre in north London, where at least five of its clothing retailers are owned by the same family-owned investment vehicle of one private individual. El Diwany comments:

House-building firms, out-of-town supermarkets, enormous shopping malls whose clothing stores are owned by the same man, these are all fuelled by leverage. Employment becomes more common than self-employment. Small businesses disappear. Product choice and variety decline as fewer producers dominate the market. Local communities lose control over their affairs as distant centres of influence grow in power.

He painted a grim picture, although some of the harder bitten bankers and lawyers in the audience rolled their eyes. Was there any intellectual credibility to this doctrine of anti-globalization? Was El Diwany identifying with the mass of disorganized and misinformed protest on Wall Street, aimlessly railing at big corporations and government control? Or was he perhaps identifying with America's founding fathers, who foresaw a future of enslavement to debt?

In Austrian economist Eugen von Böhm-Bawerk's theory of time preference he proposed that money available today is worth more than money available tomorrow, simply because individuals prefer to consume now and not later. Thus one may consider having $100 today as the equivalent of having $110 in a year's time, and therefore be willing to borrow $100 today from a bank in return for a repayment of $105 in a year. Although a theory that had much credibility in the nineteenth and early twentieth centuries, few economists questioned the central assumption that consumption today is better than consumption tomorrow. To illustrate the point, El Diwany asked his audience whether it was better to consume one breakfast every day or all seven of the week's breakfasts on one day.

A further argument was put forward. Consumption today can deny consumption in the future. If one decides to take a holiday now, in one year's time one may feel it would have been better to wait a year to take the holiday. Thus consumption in one year may have been preferable to consumption today. El Diwany illustrated the point with an environmental example using a tool employed by corporate financiers to calculate the mathematical value of a business opportunity: the discounted cash flow methodology. Let's imagine a farmer is faced with a choice: either he can produce a sustainable level of output at 100 units of profit per year, or through an intensive pattern of farming, produce 150 units of profit per year but only for fifteen years, after which the land becomes desertified.

Discounted cash flow is a simple piece of maths that determines which projects to invest in by attributing greater importance to profits closer to day zero than those in the future, and the contrast between near-term and long-term profit is determined by a 'discount rate'. This discount rate is usually the opportunity cost of capital, in other words the rate foregone by investing in the project rather than investing in, say, tradeable securities on a stock exchange.[14] Thus, in our example above, if the farmer uses a discount rate of 10 per cent – representing the rate he would normally earn by investing elsewhere – he would quickly discover under the discounted cash flow methodology that he should adopt the highly intensive process that will ultimately desertify his land.[15]

In this case, modern financial analysis has defeated common sense. It is impossible to maintain perpetual growth for ever because the planet will not sustain it. A modern obsession with GDP growth as the only objective measure of the health of humanity forces us to consider ourselves failures when our nation achieves less than a 5 per cent per annum growth rate. And when we fail to achieve these numbers we mobilize sheer physical force. Early stock markets in Britain and Holland traded the shares of East and West India companies, who were themselves engaged in both military and trading ventures; ventures that were ostensibly private and profit seeking, but which governed exploited far-off populations as an arm of an overseas conqueror. For post-industrial Europe, capitalism has invariably meant a perpetual state of war.

El Diwany poses the question: 'Do we not have a duty to future generations in the decisions we make today?' He responds:

'By and large, Western financial economics answers "no" to this question, and interest is the reason.' Suddenly, El Diwany no longer sounded like the lunatic that his left-brained critics painted him to be. Though much of the audience were already sympathetic to his views, none of the small core of conventional bankers and lawyers present felt that he had spoken anything but common sense. Perhaps there was a point to Islamic banking, after all, and provided the industry found the courage to plough its own path, perhaps there was a chance it might have a workable solution to the adverse effects of modern globalization.

Did Islamic financial institutions thrive during the global financial crisis? Not really. Subject to the same regulatory and legislative constraints, and plugged into a global economy from which they cannot decouple, they suffered their own slowdown in tandem with the rest of the world's banking institutions. However, they at least managed to avoid the excesses of gorging on increasingly intangible derivative instruments, though much of this may be attributed to their general lack of sophistication rather than their lack of want. Hedge funds, collateralized debt obligations, structured investment products – these products were largely absent from their shelves. However, many such institutions were overexposed to shares on local stock markets in the Middle East and bricks and mortar, particularly in the Dubai bubble. Those who had put all their eggs in one basket suffered the most. To their credit, any lending activities they had undertaken in the boom years at least correlated with the real economy. For those who had not employed commodity *murabaha* transactions as a proxy for loan financings, they at least owned real estate through sale and leaseback (*ijara*) contracts.

***

By way of conclusion, let us return to the Landmark Hotel in London in February 2010. The Euromoney Annual Islamic

Finance Summit is in full swing and the first panel session of the two-day conference has begun. At the Annual Heads of Islamic Finance Panel Discussion, six senior bankers are quizzed by the moderator, a transparent PR exercise to satisfy egos and justify the budgets each banker has expended on sponsoring this annual jamboree.

'Has the global financial crisis been an opportunity missed for Islamic finance?' asks the moderator. At first the responses are, predictably, platitudinous nonsense. Of course not, say the bankers. The industry has grown by x per cent, y number of new institutions have been formed, z number of new funds. Our products are even more innovative than ever, we invest more in talent creation, our value add to our clients puts us at the top of our industry.

But two of the bankers disagree. 'Why do we use numbers of institutions and awards won as a measure of success in our industry?' says one.

'What about the man in the street?' says the other. 'Why do Islamic finance products have to be about financing luxury residential developments in central London for ultra high net worth individuals? What about pension funds, retail home financing products, mutual funds, venture capital for small and medium enterprises? We missed a trick. We missed the chance to tell the world that Islamic finance can achieve something that conventional finance could not: real economy transactions leading to real wealth distribution. Ethical finance.'

The head of an Islamic institution sitting in the next chair bristles. 'I fundamentally disagree with this gentleman', he fumes. 'In the last twelve months, we have demonstrated significant progress in this industry. My firm has invested billions in prime luxury real estate in London and the Middle East, including a Sharia-compliant commodity *murabaha* financing which has helped us to win the industry's leading awards.'

The left-brained rule the world.

9

When *Sukuk* Go Bad

Oh my son, I leave you three pieces of advice: don't rely on what you have not yet attained, be pleased with what the Lord gives to you, and be patient with your loss when the Lord takes from you.

Prophet Dawood (David) to his son Prophet Sulayman (Solomon), *Lore of Light, Lives of the Prophets According to Traditional Islamic Sources*

It looked like the party would never end. To the incessant thumping beat of rubber stamps at Dubai International Airport's immigration desks, wide eyed British, American and European expats swarmed into the country: construction project managers, investment bankers, airline pilots, and those who had come to reinvent themselves as real estate brokers in Dubai's steroidal property boom. The newcomers were conspicuous on arrival. Ambitious executives with young families staring upwards, agog at the vastness of this international gateway, the largest building in the world by floor space; its floors laid with perma-polished white marble, immense fluted colonnades stretching up to vast ceilings, palm trees dotting its avenues; a duty free shopping centre stocked almost exclusively with designer labels to rival the plushest of malls, its armies of cleaners and maintenance men in a state of maximum alert to attend to the slightest blemish on its vast surface.

Outside, the visitors were greeted by lines of immaculate cream coloured taxi cabs, plying their trade on arrow straight multi-lane highways lined with a riot of architectural diversity, a testament to the egos of construction magnates vying with each other for the title of biggest, best, most visionary. And, everywhere the eye could see, construction cranes building the city of the future. Some said that 25 per cent of the world's cranes were right here in one city, and who would disagree?

Life would turn out to be extraordinarily good for these white-collar workers. Pakistani gardeners would tend their lawns and fill their swimming pools, Indian electricians and plumbers would maintain their houses, their wives would leave behind the drizzle and the drudgery of school runs and domestic chores, leaving their Filipina housemaids to clean the house and rear their kids, and freeing them to sashay from gym to nail spa to coffee morning.

The international media, especially the British red tops, raged apoplectically at the injustice of this modern-day slave trade, though the reality was somewhat more prosaic. Most menial workers were content to live in this two tier society, earning multiples of their earnings back home. Employment law was gradually catching up with more developed parts of the world. Because of the inherently imbalanced demographics – Emiratis represented perhaps only a quarter of the country's population – it would never be an ideally balanced and free labour market, but it was moving in the right direction.

Despite the turmoil taking place in Western financial markets, many in the emerging markets continued to put their faith in the notion of 'decoupled' markets. Dubai couldn't fail, could it?

It had a naturally ideal geographic location to act as a gateway between East and West, first world infrastructure, management talent drawn from all parts of the globe, a world-class airline, and a globally recognized brand name built on the back of iconic landmarks to draw in a constant stream of tourists. In October 2008, the chief executive officer of a real estate developer in Dubai was asked about one regional investment bank's forecast on Dubai property prices. The bank analyst's report suggested prices would peak in 2009 and fall by up to 20 per cent by 2011.[1] With the rest of the world in the throes of a financial calamity, this particular CEO dismissed such suggestions with the following statement:

> In my opinion prices will never go down. . .First and fore-most. . .we have visionary leadership that has conducted the essential and proper studies. . .They looked at the fundamental issues such as the economic factors, the political issues, the social issues and so forth. They took all the issues and points concerning the real estate market and took the necessary steps. . .I believe there will not be a price correction in the market.[2]

Shortly afterwards Dubai real estate values plummeted in some areas by over 50 per cent. The hubris championed by apparent experts in Dubai's giddy property ride leading up to the crash was plain to see for the more reflective in Dubai's financial community. But who would listen to them whilst gung-ho doers were developing increasingly fantastical projects such as palm-shaped islands in the sea or underwater hotels. Even more concerning was the practice of 'flipping': buying off-plan properties – sometimes entire floors of apartments – with a downpayment to the developer, say 10 per cent of the property's value, then selling the property on ('flipping') in the secondary market a short while later for a small premium, say another

10 per cent of the property's value. As long as the speculators were doubling or tripling the value of their investments every one or two months, who would be foolish or brave enough to question their business model?

Secondary market buyers, typically those who hadn't stood in line at the developer's sales office since 3 a.m. on the day of the launch, or who didn't have family connections to the developer's chairman to propel them to the front of the queue, were similarly hopeful that they would find other willing buyers. Since these speculators had put down a mere 10 or 20 per cent deposit, within a matter of days or weeks they, too, were able to double or triple their money.

The practice of flipping properties before they had been built and delivered to end users was a classic example of gearing, a small upfront payment multiplying to create exponential returns. It was like using a crowbar: apply a little bit of pressure, and the further away you move from the fulcrum, the more force you apply. Debt financing of these upfront deposits increased the length of that crowbar. Like the derivatives created by companies like the American insurance giant AIG to turbocharge their profits, gearing in the Dubai property market – by flipping an asset that had not yet been created, and borrowing to finance those deposits – had created a monster. And while the monster slumbered, those like our dismissive property mogul basked in their good fortune, attributing it to their own brilliance, hard work and vision. The get-rich-quick schemes of the Dubai property market made dollar millionaires quickly but also destroyed a similar number of investors when the music stopped in 2009. Developers absconded in droves and many buyers were left holding the papers to a worthless sand pit. The unluckiest found themselves defaulting on other payments, and Dubai's non-existent bankruptcy laws meant that many endured a spell in jail.

To those who had raked the lucre of Dubai's boom years, it

had not generally been a time to introspect. If the many Muslims working in the real estate sector had done so, they might have reflected on Quranic verses and Hadith on the subject of *rizq*, a word that is loosely translated as 'sustenance' or providence from the Lord, and includes within it the simpler concept of personal material wealth. 1,400 years earlier, the Prophet Muhammad advised his followers:

'The holy spirit spoke into my soul that no soul shall die until it has completed its term (*ajal*) and has received its providence (*rizq*); so hasten to seek (from Allah)[3] and let not the apparent slowness of providence drive any of you to acquire it through an act of disobedience for indeed what is with Allah cannot be obtained except with obedience to Him.'[4] Thus, one's material wealth is pre-ordained, and how one comes to acquire that *rizq*, or sustenance, will be one's test.

Throughout this volatile period, Masjid Al-Samad, the mosque at the heart of New Dubai, remained a remarkable constant. Though its congregation of worshippers had naturally been affected by Dubai's economic troubles, largely the same young professionals continued to occupy its rows at Friday prayers. Despite the considerable drop in Islamic finance activity, the Samadiite lawyers had refocused their efforts towards litigation work, and the bankers on restructuring.

Even the neatly turbaned young Australian-Egyptian lay preacher at the Masjid Al-Samad cautioned his flock by reminding them of something his grandmother used to tell him:

'*Fuqra sutra,*' she would remind him back in the old country as she observed the world around her changing. Poverty is a protection.

'Wealth can be a *museebah*,' explained the preacher to the assembled Samadiites one Friday. A burden, something for which Allah will bring us to account on Judgment Day. Literally. Every penny or cent we earn or spend in our lives will be audited. How did we earn it? Where did it come from? Did we spend it on the permissible or the impermissible? Did we use it wisely? Did it have a benefit for those around us?

I was fortunate to be living on the Palm Jumeirah at the time, the iconic palm-shaped island that had helped to put Dubai on the international map. An early buyer of a property on the island when it had been merely a scale model in the marble-clad atrium of the master developer's sales office, I had put my faith in the vision and liquidity of the emirate's ruling family who were apparently backing the developer Nakheel. Nakheel had spared no cost in appointing the world's leading construction and dredging companies, and their marketing of this immensely significant undertaking had propelled the city of Dubai up the list of the world's most glamorous tourist destinations.

At first, the omens were wholly positive. Dredging ships began spraying sand in a rainbow arc across the waters of the Arabian Gulf in June 2001, completing the outline of an island visible from space, some 25 km^2 in area and adding 78 km to the coastline of Dubai by 2005. By the following year, compacting machines had compressed the foundations of the island allowing 1,400 villas to be built on 16 palm-shaped fronds extending out from the trunk of the island, plus a further 2,500 apartments overlooking the turquoise waters of the Gulf and the impressive skyline of Dubai's Sheikh Zayed Road. Dozens of hotels would ring the island on a crescent acting as a breakwater against the open sea. By May 2009, a futuristic monorail transit system extending down the trunk of the island was inaugurated, linking the Atlantis hotel and water theme park at one end with the mainland at the other.

But cracks started to show. A few months earlier, in November 2008, the luxury Atlantis resort launched itself to a US$20 million fanfare of fireworks, billed as the most expensive launch party in history. While Robert De Niro and Sir Richard Branson nibbled on lobster and mezze among 2,000 other glitterati at the hotel, my family and I observed the mother of all firework displays from the beach at the bottom of our garden. And yet, despite the ostentation of the occasion, and a feel-good factor that thumbed its nose at the global economic trend, I was confused and not a little disturbed. Only a few days earlier, I had chatted with an Indian handyman sent by Nakheel to perform a routine maintenance check on my villa. The labourer had arrived by bicycle at the villa but without the usual contingent of his colleagues in a minivan: 'They have gone back to India', he replied when I enquired. 'Maybe I am next', he added ruefully. 'If you have a job, please help me.'

Over the next few weeks, I would continue to receive requests from taxi drivers, maintenance workers and shop assistants. *I have not been paid for three months. The boss has run away. My visa has been cancelled. I need work. Please help me.*

Reports circulated in the international press that the island was sinking, and Dubai dinner-party chatter surmised that vibro-compacting work during the early build period had not been completed to a satisfactory standard. As a denizen of the island, I found these rumours to be unfounded, though I was discovering that the fixtures in my house had evidently been built to a cost as a result of rocketing global raw material prices. Though the villa itself and those surrounding it appeared structurally sound, it seemed that Nakheel had procured the cheapest Chinese-sourced air conditioning and plumbing systems to pare down costs as the finance noose tightened around its corporate neck. Nakheel's customer services told owners wishing to replace faulty hardware that they would need to wait months whilst a backlog of work was cleared. The maintenance staff simply weren't available. If customers required urgent assistance, Nakheel could contract out the work to third parties, but at considerable cost to the customer. Rather than live without running water or air conditioning, my neighbours and I embarked on our own systematic replacement of hardware. But this was merely a minor symptom of underlying problems in what had come to be known as 'Dubai Inc.', the wider network of government-related corporate entities.

On 25 November 2009, almost precisely one year after the fabulous firework party, Nakheel dropped a bombshell on the capital markets. At 10 a.m. that Wednesday morning, one day before the long *Eid Al Adha* public holiday began, the government of Dubai issued a statement to the press regarding its financial support fund:

> The Government of Dubai. . .today announces that it has raised a further $5 billion as part of its $20 billion long term bond programme launched at the beginning of 2009. . .The proceeds are managed by and further strengthen the financial resources of the Dubai Financial Support Fund ('DFSF'), which was established with the specific purpose of providing liquidity on a commercial basis to Government and Government-Related Entities undertaking projects deemed to be of strategic importance within Dubai that contribute towards the overall economic development of the Emirate.[5]

The money was being raised from government-owned banks in neighbouring Abu Dhabi, a clear signal that Dubai was in need of outside help. Astonishingly, two hours later at midday, the government issued a second statement regarding two of its flagship companies:

> The Government of Dubai. . .has authorised the Dubai Financial Support Fund. . .to spearhead the restructure of Dubai World with immediate effect. . .Dubai World intends to ask all providers of financing to Dubai World and Nakheel to 'standstill' and extend maturities until at least 30 May 2010. The $5 billion bond announced earlier today. . .*is not linked to the restructuring of Dubai World and is meant for the general purposes of the DFSF.*[6] (emphasis mine)

Though technically not a default, for all practical purposes the statement that Nakheel's debt servicing would be parked for a period of time whilst Dubai Inc. got its house in order was tantamount to the same thing. So if this restructuring was not linked to the new money raised from big brother Abu Dhabi, as announced earlier in the day, were residents of the Palm to believe that Abu Dhabi did not wish to see Nakheel and Dubai World survive? Or that the Dubai government itself did not deem the two companies to be 'strategically important' enough?

Bankers looked at the two statements and blinked. So, let's just get this straight, they said. First Dubai says we've raised money from our big brother up the road, hurray! Then they say, 'By the way, this has got nothing to do with Nakheel's debt obligations, which we can't honour. Maybe in May next year. Sorry about that. Oh look, it's the *Eid* holiday weekend, got to go, bye!'

It was a catastrophic mismanagement of information dissemination. Dubai discovered that weekend how not to deliver bad news to the market. The Nakheel *sukuk*, as the emirate's bellwether debt instrument, had risen from a low price of 63 cents on the dollar to 110 cents on expectation of full repayment before the announcement. When markets opened after the *Eid* holiday, the *sukuk* plummeted and touched an intraday low of 42 cents on 27 November,[7] whilst an index of shares traded on the Dubai Financial Market plunged 22 per cent over a two-week period. Dubai's sovereign credit default swap – a measure of the emirate's credit worthiness representing the cost of insuring against the debt default of an entity – jumped to a level higher than even that of Iceland, which was in a wretched economic state. Worse still, the Islamic finance industry fell into a tail spin of panic and self-doubt. A big *sukuk* was defaulting. Was it the fault of Sharia law?

Internet blogging sites buzzed with the news. Predictably, it was the comments posted by casual users on British newspaper websites that contained the most bile and venom for the emirate. One poster to the *Daily Telegraph* website couldn't contain his Schadenfreude, stating: 'It is important to remember that Dubai is an utter dump. Why anyone wants to go there is beyond me. Only the culturally bankrupt and the modern day carpetbagger will ever be enticed by this land of unending sand and unending roads and unending building sites and unending alcohol.'[8] Another had posted: 'I am sure some sheikh must have shorted their stocks before making the announcement.'[9]

While the first statement was made perhaps either in abject xenophobia and ignorance, or with the disproportionate bitterness of one who had himself been wronged in some way, the second statement was not without merit, at least according to a fixed-income salesman on my firm's trading desk. On the trading floor, some staff were picking up the rumour that an Abu Dhabi institution had sold a significant number of related bonds that morning before the second announcement. Though the bank was unable to substantiate the rumour, the whiff of foul play had always been an endemic problem in these markets.

When markets reopened the following week, I received a call from my firm's press office asking if I would speak to the *New York Times* to provide some background on the Nakheel default. From her office 11,000 km away, the reporter from the *Times* had only a sketchy understanding of the issues. 'Make it simple for me to understand. Talk to me as if I'm your mom in words of one syllable', she said. 'So what happens to the bond holders? Do they go to a *Shar-eye-ah* court? Does an *eee-maam* decide on who gets paid what?'

It became clear to me that she thought this complex *sukuk* documentation would be judged by a group of unkempt old mullahs in *shalwar kameez*, squatting in a circle on the floor of a stone mosque, like some Afghani *jirga* dispensing summary justice to the hapless investor. I asked myself in what context she would discuss Islamic transactions. Terrorist financing? The injustice of the Sharia and its incompatibility with Western standards of decency and transparency?

Nakheel is a real estate company suffering a credit problem, I replied. It is in trouble because it cannot service its financial obligations as a result of over-leveraging itself, and some questionable commercial decisions in the past. Whether it had financed itself using conventional debt or Islamic finance is not the reason for its problems. In the specific case of Nakheel's inability to repay its *sukuk* on the due date, and how *sukuk* holders might recover their investment, there are some technicalities to consider. In short, they are: what is the basis on which *sukuk* repayments are made in this case? What security do *sukuk* holders have, and how can this security be enforced?

To answer these questions, I turned to the Nakheel *sukuk* prospectus, the legal document issued to prospective investors when the *sukuk* was launched back in December 2006. The *sukuk* was predicated on an *ijara*, or lease contract, whereby the SPV, the special purpose vehicle – remember this is a shell company created to issue the bonds to investors – would take ownership of the leasehold rights for a period of fifty years over certain land, buildings and other properties within the yet to be constructed Dubai Waterfront development. These leasehold assets would be valued at 15.5 billion dirhams by an independent valuation firm,[10] or around $4.2 billion, thus amply covering the *sukuk* issuance of $3.52 billion.

Once the *sukuk* assets are safely ensconced within the SPV, they would be leased by the SPV back to Nakheel, and the ensuing six-monthly rental payments would give *sukuk* holders their periodic coupon. At the end of the *sukuk*'s three-year term, Nakheel as the lessee would buy back the *sukuk* assets from the SPV in accordance with an agreement – known as a purchase undertaking – at a pre-agreed exercise price, equal to the par value of the *sukuk* at issuance. No surprises so far: this is a fairly standard sale and leaseback *sukuk*, albeit on a 'lease and leaseback' basis (also known as a 'headlease/sublease structure') since a foreign company was not permitted by local law to have permanent freehold title. There were some bells and whistles on the instrument, not least of which was that it was a 'pre-IPO exchangeable' – in other words, the bond would be paid out in shares of a company to be floated on a stock exchange in the future – just as the PCFC *sukuk* had been before it, but this fact was not relevant to the subject at hand.

Even at the height of development mania in Dubai, Dubai Waterfront stood out as a gargantuan exercise in master planning. Nakheel would create a city within a city, able to house a population of 1.5 million in skyscrapers spread over an area twice as big as Hong Kong island, and adding 70 km of coastline to the emirate.[11] This *sukuk* would be the first capital markets instrument to finance a portion of the development, and the real assets attached to this instrument would be a clear demonstration of the tangibility of Islamic finance and its inviolable bond with the real economy. If Nakheel failed to honour its payment obligations, then investors would have ownership of something real and valuable. Right?

Is Sharia the problem?

When the repayment deadline came and went, investors worried about recovering their money. Let's first take a closer look at the salient points of the ownership and security structure of this deal, because that is pertinent to understanding whether the Sharia is a help or hindrance in modern commercial transactions. The SPV issuer of the bonds was incorporated as a UAE free zone company. Its single share was owned by a third party share trustee,[12] under the terms of a declaration of trust under which the share trustee holds the share on trust for charity. Each of the *sukuk* notes, or trust certificates, represented an undivided beneficial ownership of the trust assets (which included the *sukuk* assets mentioned above plus the security and transaction documents) pursuant to the declaration of trust, this document to be governed by English law and subject to the non-exclusive jurisdiction of the English courts. Thus the trustee was to act on behalf of *sukuk* holders. So far, so good.

In addition to the trust, the SPV also acted as an agent for *sukuk* holders in accordance with an agency declaration, this document to be governed by the laws of the UAE as applied by the Dubai courts.

A fairly convoluted ownership structure meant that three Nakheel entities acted as 'co-obligors' of the financing, each of them jointly and severally guaranteeing payment obligations under the transaction documents. Dubai World, the parent company of the three Nakheel holding companies, would issue a guarantee to the SPV issuer for the payment obligations of the co-obligors. On the surface, this looked very much like a belt-and-braces approach to security, but there was more to come. One of the co-obligors granted a pledge of shares in a subsidiary company in favour of the SPV issuer. It also granted two mortgages, free of security interest or encumbrance, on the *sukuk* assets, to be held as security for and on behalf of the SPV issuer by an agent.[13]

Now what would happen if Nakheel failed to honour its payment obligations to the SPV, and in particular the purchase undertaking granted by one of the co-obligors to repay the *sukuk* principal? At first, the SPV would have recourse to the joint and several payment obligations of the co-obligors. Then their parent company, Dubai World, would be held to its payment guarantee if its subsidiaries were unable to pay. But since Dubai World is a holding company for other huge Dubai Inc. entities, and these companies would have debt obligations of their own – and therefore requiring more immediate attention to their own creditors than a guarantee of their parent company to an entirely separate entity – it would be unlikely that the Nakheel *sukuk* holders could get very far under this guarantee if Dubai World's wider network of businesses was also cash strapped.[14] Which they were. The prospectus acknowledged as much in its section on Risk Factors: 'Dubai World is dependent on the operations of and cash flows generated by its subsidiaries. Therefore, any claim that may be made by a creditor on Dubai World will effectively be structurally subordinate to any claims made by creditors directly on Dubai World's subsidiaries.'[15]

One wonders how many prospective *sukuk* investors back in 2006 had contemplated a potential scenario in which this guarantee might actually be required, and what implications this structural subordination might have on their ability to get satisfaction. One also wonders whether these same investors had given thought to the government's explicit denials that it stood behind the corporate debt obligations of its various Dubai Inc. entities. One prominent scholar had been moved to berate such investors as 'fools' for assuming that governments were charitable organizations whose sole purpose was to bail out foreign investors who didn't read the fine print.[16]

As for the share pledge, when the *sukuk* was launched in 2006, no doubt investors felt that those shares might actually be worth something meaningful. They, too, would probably turn out to be of little real value in the event that Nakheel suffered a crisis of existence, and there would be little sense in attempting to extract a cash value from the pledge. So finally investors might turn to the mortgages over the two properties underpinning the *ijara*, the lease. Finally! They get to enforce their rights over the property itself. This is the part where Sharia makes its grand entrance and saves the day.

Well it would do, but it turns out there's a problem: despite the apparent attachment to a real set of underlying assets, investors did not in fact have access to those assets. Thankfully for the Islamic finance industry, it turns out it is a jurisdictional problem, not a problem of Sharia law as the woman from the *New York Times* suspected. The right of usufruct is a concept found in the UAE federal Civil Code and is the right to use and exploit a property belonging to another person, a 'real' property right. A lease is very similar, though according to the Civil Code, a tenant does not acquire a property right through a lease. Instead, he acquires a personal contractual right that is enforceable through a contract between himself and the landlord.[17] This distinction between real property rights and contractual rights is critical for foreign investors to understand, since, at the time of the *sukuk* launch, there was no formal registration of the lease attaching to the underlying land – which would render the lease a real property right – due to a lack of established process for registration of such a lease at the Dubai Lands Department. Welcome to the emerging markets.

Be that as it may, the security right under the mortgages could still be enforced, assuming the mortgages were fully perfected. Except that no one seemed to know if they had been – Dubai Islamic Bank acted as the *sukuk* investors' security agent for the mortgages, and not as their lender, and such a role had not been tested in the UAE courts before. Even the prospectus acknowledged this fact amongst those pesky Risk Factors: 'In the absence of clear judicial or legislative guidance or clarification on the arrangement contemplated by the Security Agency Agreement there can be no assurance of the enforceability of the Mortgages by the Security Agent in the manner contemplated by the Security Agency Agreement or any enforcement process or procedure.'[18]

If you're still reading this, you've done a lot better than the majority of the individuals and institutions who bought the Nakheel *sukuk*. Had they taken the time to analyse these risk factors, they might have come to the conclusion that the considerable legal uncertainty attached to this instrument did not perhaps justify its relatively low yield, the coupon it periodically paid out to the investors. This *sukuk* was a high-risk instrument, with a bunch of inherent risks that investors had simply not factored into the yield.

And there's more to come. Let's assume the investors attempted to enforce their rights to the property through the declaration of trust. Like the guarantees of the co-obligors and of Dubai World, this legal document was governed by English law and enforceable in the English courts. Let's take a look at those Risk Factors again:

> UAE law does not recognise the concept of trust or beneficial interests. Accordingly there is no certainty that the terms of the Declaration of Trust. . .would be enforced by the Courts of Dubai. However, the obligations of each of the Issuer under the Agency Declaration to act on behalf of Certificateholders in accordance with their instructions. . .are enforceable as a matter of contract under UAE law.[19]

Let us assume that the investors get a favourable judgement through the trust in an English court and turn up in Dubai, judgement in hand, to enforce their rights separately through the agency declaration, a UAE law document. Not that this English court judgement should have any influence on proceedings in a Dubai court, naturally, but there would be no harm. Would there be any further legal obstacles?

Sadly, yes. That Bit of the Prospectus No One Reads says: 'An establishment of the Government may be sued, but. . .no debt or obligation of such establishment may be recovered by way of an attachment on its properties or assets.'[20]

Is Nakheel considered a government entity? Or is it a private commercial enterprise, disowned by a government who – quite reasonably – states it won't stand behind the obligations of the country's private sector? Only a lengthy litigation process could determine this. And whilst Dubai World and the co-obligors had explicitly waived sovereign immunity in the transaction documents, if indeed they had been entitled to it, who knew if such a waiver would actually stand up in a Dubai court and be valid and binding?

These were all problems not unusual in an emerging markets environment, irrespective of the Islamic nature of the product. For the media to suggest that this was a default of a Sharia-compliant instrument as a result of differing interpretations of Sharia law, or the inherent structural uncertainties and lack of precedent attached to such instruments, was specious at best. I kept my phone conversation for the self-described simple mom from the *New York Times* as simple as I could, as I did for all those subsequent journalists who asked me the same questions. No it's not a problem with Sharia, I insisted, it's a problem with a nascent legislative environment.

In time, investors would also come to accept that it had been their own foolishness in jumping on an investment to which they had subscribed two and a half times over without properly assessing the risks.[21] As for the Dubai government, their options were limited. On the one hand, they could wipe their hands of the affair, allowing one of their private sector companies to default and suffer the embarrassing consequences: a long litigation process with more than 100 interested parties, a loss of confidence from the financing community leading to difficulties in future ratings and fundraising exercises, and perhaps most importantly, a loss of face. Alternatively, they could seek help, pay off their debts and live to fight another day. Marginally less embarrassing, perhaps.

The following month, big brother came to the rescue. On 14 December 2009, the government of neighbouring emirate Abu Dhabi and the UAE Central Bank announced that they would provide US$10 billion to the Dubai Financial Support Fund so that Dubai World could repay the *sukuk*.[22] The UAE

Central Bank also announced that it would inject liquidity on an as-needed basis to banks that faced exposure to the beleaguered Dubai World. Ever since the Dubai government's November announcement, it had been toiling behind the scenes with its neighbour to deliver a package to restore investor confidence. Perhaps oil-rich Abu Dhabi had determined that rather than let little brother suffer for his sins, it made more sense to contain the potential spread of contagion, though the quid pro quo was the subject of much speculation at those Dubai dinner parties on the Palm. Would it be DP World, the ports operator, that would go to the Abu Dhabians? Emirates airline, perhaps?

What was not in any doubt was the humiliation suffered by Dubai less than a month later when the world's tallest tower, up until then named as the Burj Dubai and reputed to have cost $1.5 billion to build, was renamed the Burj Khalifa, after the ruler of Abu Dhabi.[23] Hubris and greed had given way to downfall. In the heady days of the property boom, not many had stopped to reflect on their good fortune, and whether it was merely a transitory state or whether this was the fulfilment of what had been ordained for them. Whilst property speculators turbocharged their bank balances, they had perhaps forgotten the advice of the Prophet on the pursuit of wealth: 'Let not the apparent slowness of providence drive any of you to acquire it through an act of disobedience for indeed what is with Allah cannot be obtained except with obedience to Him.'[24]

Would it be fair to describe the practice of flipping contracts on off-plan properties in the secondary market as disobedience? After all, like a debt, trading was taking place in a contract, an intangible, and the underlying asset was not yet in existence. Without question, such a prevalent activity in such an unregulated market had contributed to a catastrophic failure of an economy within a short space of time. And had there been a specific injunction or restriction against the practice, or a restriction on the financing attached to such properties, we may have seen an orderly cooling of the local economy. It was ironic that a federal legal system based on Sharia had little or no provision to restrict practices that had clear prohibitions in Sharia law.

Whilst the slow hand of providence had spurred individuals to seek riches without introspection, perhaps still fewer had sought to examine the activities of companies who raised Islamic funds to catalyse the growth of their businesses. Was the activity and corporate philosophy of these firms truly Sharia based, or were they merely looking to jump on the bandwagon and 'tap Islamic liquidity' as they so unashamedly proclaimed in public? Should not the activities of a Sharia-compliant company have certain social considerations – labour practices, environmental considerations, corporate social responsibility – structurally hardwired into their basic corporate operating system? Being a good corporate citizen and a valuable member of a wider society – is this what Nakheel and others had in mind when they built islands in the sea and luxury villas for the most privileged members of society? Is this what the Islamic bank chief was considering when he raised billions for vanity development projects, picking up awards in the process?

As we have discussed previously, Muslims are not forbidden from pursuing wealth, but the manner in which they do so is held to scrutiny. *Fuqra sutra*, said the wise Egyptian grandmother. Human nature is greedy: we cannot help comparing our possessions with those of our neighbour's and we are tempted to cut corners to compete. What differentiates Islamic philosophy from conventional Western wisdom in this matter is that *rizq* – our sustenance, our wealth – is ultimately not in our control, so cutting corners in acquiring it does not affect its eventual quantum. The Quran says: 'Allah has favoured some of you over others with regard to *rizq*'.[25] In contrast, modern society expects individuals to believe that their destiny, their success or failure, is wholly in their hands. They feel empowered to achieve whatever they want to achieve and conversely that their failure is their own fault. That's not to say, of course, that Allah expects the believer to wait for *rizq* to drop into his lap. He is still expected to strive for it, and that effort stands in his favour when his deeds are measured on the Day of Judgment.

Even among Muslims, it is uncommon to find successful businessmen publicly attributing their success to a higher power. More often than not, the credit goes to hard work, or parents teaching one the value of money, or incisive decision making, all worthy Anglo-Saxon concepts adopted uniformly across the business world.

There are exceptions, of course. The co-founder and chairman of Al Rajhi Bank, Sulaiman Abdul Aziz Al Rajhi, is reported to have told a gathering of businessmen in Riyadh that he planned to distribute most of his $6 billion in assets to his children and a charitable trust,[26] saying 'I will go with only my clothing.'[27] He attributed his success to the blessing of Allah and exhorted the gathering to donate, expanding on a core Islamic philosophy by advising the audience that 'even if [a] person receives a salary of one thousand riyals only, he should consider [giving] away for Allah as much as he can since [Allah has promised] that anything spent for Allah will be returned to the giver as much more than was spent.'[28]

One other prominent businessman who seems to live his life according to similar principles is Warren Buffett, though naturally Sharia is not a driving force for him. Notable for shying away from ostentatious living, the Sage of Omaha has lived in the same house he bought in 1958, well before he became a billionaire.[29] Though ranked as one of the world's wealthiest people, he has pledged to give away 99 per cent of his fortune to philanthropic causes, most notably the Gates Foundation.[30] And perhaps the most interesting aspect of his 'value investing' philosophy is that it is 'long only'. He buys and holds companies he believes to have long-term value. Long-term equity risk. That sounds quite Islamic.

10

The Regulator Strikes Back

I don't care about the Shar-eye-ah stuff! Just get me the waiver!

New York-based acquisition finance banker
on a conference call, October 2005

Another Islamic finance conference, another unimaginative selection of corporate drones on the question and answer panel, each one of them chosen by the conference organizers for their acquiescent blandness, always on message and never controversial. From the floor, an elderly gentleman dressed in a *dishdasha* and *ghutra* – a long white robe topped by a red-and-white chequered headdress – stands up to address the panel with a question. The microphone trembles slightly in his hands and his voice is hoarse. Perhaps his thick Arabic accent and halting English knocks his confidence a little, surrounded as he is by these urbane captains of industry.

'Why do we have conventional institutions selling us Islamic products?' he asks. 'Why should we allow them in?' The hint of a titter ripples through the audience and the panellists smile indulgently. The old man baulks a little but carries on. 'Why should we trust them? They only want to make money out of us.'

Across from the main hall is a 'breakout' room in which a technical workshop is taking place on the *Tahawwut* Master Agreement. As if to reinforce the old man's point, a treasury banker is asking how he can replicate credit default swaps in a Sharia-compliant manner.

Over at the Qatar Central Bank, scholars are wising up to the dangers of allowing conventional bankers to drive the direction of the Islamic finance industry. They urge government mandarins to stem the influx of conventional institutions into the Islamic market. They are concerned that the banks are co-mingling depositors' funds with the banks' other – *haram* or impermissible – business activities, and want to see a clear separation of Islamic and conventional money. The QCB ponders the issue, its finger hovering over the red button that will ban all conventional institutions from selling Islamic products.

At the Dubai International Financial Centre, a messiah from the US is preaching his gospel of a new beginning in Islamic finance. A conventional banker himself – with no previous history of Islamic finance – he convinces the DIFC investment arm to back his venture, a shadowy Islamic finance boutique that proclaims it has invented a revolutionary financing tool that will change the face of the industry. Two years later, the venture fades into obscurity.

Rich pickings from a massive and under-penetrated customer base have brought the opportunists to the surface. Now a cut-throat industry moving faster than its conventional counterpart, Islamic finance has witnessed the rise of technocratic rocket scientists and aggressive sales staff from Western banks, relegating the idealists to supporting departments or 'back office' compliance positions.

Sulaiman has had enough.[1] An unassuming and contemplative young man with a piercing intellect, he wonders whether his work of the past few years will weigh favourably in his balance when he dies. When his fellow Samadiites brainstorm their latest deal, he remains silent, sifting through the details of the transaction in his mind. Is it true to the spirit of Sharia, or is it another 'reverse engineered' financial product?

Sulaiman's path to advising on Islamic finance transactions has been an unusual one. Intellectual academic pursuits have taken priority over career. A junior lawyer at one of the leading English law firms, he reasons that his appointed *rizq*, or providence from God, has been pre-ordained for him. Although he is an expert in classical Arabic and has a sound understanding of the jurisprudence of commercial transactions in Sharia, his English law training has come a little later than his peers and not without struggle. Despite being called to the Bar as a barrister at Lincoln's Inn, he opted to study Sharia for two years, then taught Arabic before studying for an LLM, the Master of Laws degree, in the fashionable though unhelpful area of international law and human rights – unhelpful because, as he says, 'Law firms look for a certain type of intelligence. They don't want people to look out of the window and wonder if they're doing the right thing.' Introspection and self-reflection are not prized in the commercial world. These elite English law firms, the so-called 'Magic Circle', and their bulge bracket clients want left-brained go-getters and doers.

The timing was fortuitous, though. Just as Sulaiman was concluding his intellectual pursuits, the global Islamic finance industry was taking off in increasingly exotic areas such as derivatives and hedge funds. Within the industry, a few savvy partners at Magic Circle firms began to search for appropriately qualified trainees to help them put some legal flesh on these arcane mechanisms, and Sulaiman joined up hoping to make a difference.

What he saw distressed him. This wasn't an industry devoted to offering financial services to Muslims in a manner compliant with their beliefs, he concluded. This was the reverse engineering of conventional products using template contracts that individually adhered to the tenets of Sharia, but in aggregate achieved something more dubious.

'You spend every day helping very rich people get even richer', he says in a clipped and quiet voice. 'Do I want to lie on my deathbed thinking this is what I've done with my life?' A project in Africa's poorest countries illustrates his point: a European manufacturer of high-tech prefabricated concrete panels approached his firm to help them on a development aid programme. Their proprietary concrete panels would be used to build schools and small-scale developments using a carbon neutral technology. To complete the clean-tech, green and ethical dimension to this project, they would make the investment comply with Sharia.

But why sell this product to the world's poorest? It was expensive and unnecessary – a green and ethical solution might instead have been proposed using traditional materials such as wood. It was clear what was happening. Under the terms of the aid programme, the Europeans were saying 'We aid, you buy.' Those African nations would not feel the benefit of the aid whilst they laboured under the additional burden of debt they had acquired.

'We lack perception', says Sulaiman. 'We shut off this side of our thinking.' Islamic finance was not about a holistic view of commerce, its practitioners were not interested in consequences for society and the individual. To Sulaiman it was a perpetuation of the failures of the conventional banking system: unbridled leverage, the trading of cash flows, the trading of unbundled credit and risk, a dislocation between the financial economy and the real economy, the pursuit of profit above all else.

Industry initiatives on standardization, such as the *Tahawwut* Master Agreement, seemed to be missing critical elements in their collective reasoning. Sulaiman found himself having fundamentally grave reservations about the replication of the conventional swaps and derivatives industry. 'Get rid of them completely', he suggests. 'Instead create supra-national *takaful* [mutual insurance] pools – that is what organizations like AAOIFI are for, no?' A real economy solution: a global pool of tangible assets dedicated to ensuring the participants are protected in a mutual cooperative against macroeconomic swings.

But why would the industry change the status quo?

Ignoring for a moment this philosophical question – whether an *Islamic* derivatives industry is desirable in the first place – Sulaiman was disturbed to note that there was an inconsistency in the approach of scholars. The *Tahawwut* initiative had been laborious and drawn out, and yet it had not reached a satisfactory conclusion. Close-out netting and the calculation of termination settlement amounts had been particularly vexatious discussions: scholars had insisted that a discount rate not be used in the calculation of the settlement amount, and yet they remained content to link the prices of the commodities underpinning the hedges to interest rates. In an attempt to fix the impasse, Sulaiman felt the scholars ignored the issue.

'They have a phobia of the word "interest" or "discount rate"', he says. 'They seem more fixated on the semantics and not the reality. It's a type of psychological trauma.'

The politics and intrigue of the corporate environment, though a fact of life for all those who work at large multinational firms, were a necessary trial for Sulaiman. Despite a predisposition to *hayya*[2] – a traditionally valued Islamic notion of modesty or shyness – he learnt to develop a thick skin. As he observed his colleagues and clients become trapped by their material success, reluctantly complying with every demand of their employers but unwilling to leave the industry, he wondered if he would become like them. Perhaps outwardly he would project piety – long beard and white Arabic dress, the *thawb*, at Friday prayers – but he would be forced to practise his craft slyly. The interests of the firm would come first and he would have no right to refuse a transaction. 'You become a being of that environment', he reflects sadly. Sulaiman sought spiritual guidance. But rather than approach a scholar for guidance, he sought his guidance from the source, from God Himself.

Since the concept of a formal priesthood does not exist in Islam – nor the concept of vicarious atonement, for that matter – when guidance or forgiveness is sought, it is best sought from Allah. And so Sulaiman performed the *salat ul-istikhara*, the formal prayer of guidance performed in a manner similar to the five times daily prayers. The *istikhara* is a prayer for Allah's favour in commencing on a course of action, or alternatively to have that course of action taken away from the supplicant, and to remain content with either outcome. His devotions completed, the next day Sulaiman handed in his resignation and felt a burden lifted. He would no longer work on commodity *murabaha* transactions and Sharia-compliant development aid projects.

As we part company, an early Christian comment on this subject may be illuminating. A third-century bishop of Carthage, St Cyprian, had himself despaired at the state of his fellow clergy:

> Among the priests there was no devotedness to religion. . .
> Very many bishops who ought to furnish both exhortation and example to others, despising their divine charge, became agents in secular business, forsook their throne, deserted their people, wandered about over foreign provinces, hunted the markets for gainful merchandise, while brethren were starving in the Church. . .they increased their gains by multiplying usuries.[3]

Sulaiman's experience of the past few years is nothing unusual. At the World Islamic Banking Conference, one banker described Islamic banks as trying to play water polo against teams whilst wearing the protective clothing of American football. Islamic institutions operate under the rules of central banks, the lenders of last resort in the fractional reserve banking system. Their methods and corporate philosophy have not developed in radically new directions, instead adopting and adapting those of their conventional counterparts. The simplest instruments they require to function and those that they sell to their customers are constrained by the norms of the wider banking industry. In the inter-bank money market, for example, whilst conventional banks may fund themselves in highly liquid instruments with maturities as short as one day, Islamic institutions seek to replicate these funding sources through the cumbersome commodity *murabaha*. Not only is the *murabaha* money market insufficiently well developed and illiquid, but the very Sharia compliance of it has come to be questioned, often by those very scholars Sulaiman laments. After all, how does it differ from an interest-bearing debt instrument?

The Sharia board of some banks, such as Abu Dhabi Islamic Bank, have taken a stance against the commodity *murabaha* and are increasingly looking at 'purer' forms of funding, involving the more equity-like structures of *musharaka*, *mudaraba* and *wakala* (an agency contract). But as long as such institutions remain tied to the same rules on capital adequacy and reserve ratios, as long as they are forced to operate within a financial system that rewards the use of debt over equity, and as long as they seek to provide the same services and products that conventional institutions provide, they will always be playing catch-up.

Perhaps Islamic finance missed its opportunity to carve its own path in the 1990s, when Gulf-based financial institutions entered the London market to offer retail products to Muslim customers. As a student at the turn of the decade, I attended a presentation by the sponsors of my university's Islamic society, a Gulf-based bank with a branch in London. The society didn't know much about the bank, nor about the business of Islamic finance, but we desperately needed the money to survive and they fitted the profile of a perfect sponsor. So we gave them a platform and they came, complete with exhibition-stand banners and cameras.

I wasn't a finance or economics major and I didn't understand a word they said. They spoke about *musharaka*, *mudaraba* and *murabaha*, but it might as well have been Serbo-Croat. I noticed a smartly dressed woman in the front row of the audience taking notes in a leather-bound Filofax. What was she doing here? She looked more town than gown, yet she seemed to be getting what they were saying, nodding her head and scribbling furiously. What were they saying? I had no idea and, to be honest, it didn't seem very important. Other than the City banker in the front row, the audience didn't connect with them – they seemed to have nothing relevant to say to us. It should have been a recruitment opportunity for them – just as HSBC's Iqbal Khan would do much more successfully a few years later – but they seemed content to regurgitate the abstruse definitions of Islamic commercial contracts without any apparent depth of understanding. If only they had engaged us with questions such as: what did these bankers do that was different? What effect does doing business in an Islamic way have on society, on humanity? Why should we consider this subject important? Nothing. Just technical jargon and corporate blandness.

At the time, home financing was a particularly pressing need for the Muslim community, though the products that came to market were confusingly similar to their interest-bearing equivalents and considerably more expensive. Since tax authorities allow interest payments to be tax deductible, thus rendering interest-bearing debt a cheaper form of financing than equity shares, one Islamic bank resorted to using the very word 'interest' instead of 'profit' or 'rate of return'. Opining on this apparent breach of Sharia, a prominent group of scholars was moved to issue a *fatwa* acknowledging the benefits that the

British tax system gave to interest paid and received at a bank, stating:

> Despite the fact that interest, as conventionally used in banking transactions, coincides precisely with *Riba*, which is forbidden in Sharia to pay or receive, and regardless of whether the underlying transaction is a consumption or production loan, we have found that there is no objection to the use of the term 'interest' in the cases related to those dealings with Al-Baraka Bank, London, aiming to benefit from the financial advantages given to interest in various cases of deposits and financing. In this regard, it is imperative to ensure that the term 'interest' in the sense described above is used only in the forms required by entities other than the bank, e.g. tax declaration forms for depositors, or special forms used in various financing cases. However, if the intention is to change the nature of the transaction to make it an interest-bearing loan, then such transaction will be fundamentally impermissible.[4]

But this would not wash with the majority of the Muslim community, many of whom would not have been aware of highbrow scholarly discussions behind locked doors, or the existence of the *fatwa*. All they saw was a piece of paper with the word 'interest' appearing regularly. And at other times, where a mortgage provider used the word 'profit', the financing agreement often looked like an amended version of a conventional loan agreement. More often than not, potential buyers of these mortgage products simply turned to their brand-name high-street bank instead, angry at the apparent fraud perpetrated on them by Islamic banks. The early entrants of the 1990s had simply left a bad taste in the mouth and spoilt the market for everyone.

Might Islamic banks have entered the market differently? Advocates of home financing via mutual cooperatives point out that such a model remains true to Islamic principles of equity participation. The members of the cooperative are the funding base, taking true real estate risk, both the upside and the downside.

Ansar Finance Group in the city of Manchester in northwest England is a rare example of this model. Billing itself as 'the most Sharia compliant home finance model in the UK and beyond',[5] it approached the issue of Islamic home financing by first considering the spirit of the Sharia, not just its letter. Other Islamic mortgage providers had adopted models such as the sale and leaseback transaction, in which the bank buys the property and leases it back to the customer. The customer repurchases the bank's share of the property over time with principal repayments alongside their rent – much like principal and interest repayments in a conventional mortgage, although of course the form is very different. Alternatively, and more heinously, Islamic mortgage providers would offer the commodity *murabaha*.

Let's leave aside the commodity *murabaha* structure as evidently dubious, since to many observers including the conservative Sheikh Hussain Hamed Hassan it looks like a loan, smells like a loan and acts like a loan. Let's instead focus on the sale and leaseback, otherwise known as an '*ijara* plus diminishing *musharaka*', a structure that has come to be accepted by much of the industry as Sharia credible since it involves the transfer of title deed of the property to the bank.

In one such structure used by a UK-based bank as well as the majority of home financing institutions in the Gulf, the bank purchases the customer's property, registering it under its own name. A partnership contract between the bank and its customer (the end buyer of the house) splits a beneficial interest in the property in proportion to the principal amounts advanced by each party for the original purchase from the vendor. For example, the bank may finance half of the value of the property, the customer the other half, and the partnership agreement will reflect this initial split in ownership. As the bank has legal title to the property, the customer – the end buyer financing the home – becomes the tenant under the lease, paying periodic rental amounts to the bank. At each rental repayment date, the customer also makes a principal repayment in order to buy the bank's beneficial interest in the partnership until such a point that the customer has acquired the full interest in the partnership, hence a diminishing *musharaka* or partnership. In our example, the bank would start with 50 per cent ownership and end with zero ownership by the maturity of the agreement. Instead of a borrower in a conventional mortgage paying principal plus interest to the bank, in this case the home buyer has paid the bank to repurchase ownership 'units' in the property plus a rental payment for the portion of the property that he or she doesn't own. The economics of the two types of transaction may be the same, but in the Sharia-compliant version the bank has taken a real asset on its books.

Of particular note is the fact that the purchase by the customer of units in the investment partnership is made at a price that has been set at the beginning of the financing period. In other words, if the house costs $100,000 to purchase and each unit is $1,000, then the customer would repurchase every unit from the bank at a cost of exactly $1,000, irrespective of which direction house prices are moving. This has come in for criticism from some scholars in a discussion similar to the debate on whether a purchase undertaking in a *sukuk* transaction to buy back the *sukuk* at its maturity should be at par value (set at the same price as the original *sukuk* amount) or at market value at the time of repurchase.[6]

What if the customer was required to purchase units in the partnership at a price determined by the market at the time of purchase? Thus, if the value of the property rises, then the tenant would be required to purchase beneficial interest in the partnership at a higher value than the original purchase price by the bank. In our example above, if house prices move 10 per cent upwards a year after purchase of the property, then the next set of units to be repurchased by the customer from the bank would cost the customer $1,100 each. Conversely, if the value of the property falls, then a valuation would lead to a reduced unit price in the partnership. No Sharia scholar to date has objected to such a structure, and indeed that is the model used by Ansar Finance Group.

In line with Sharia requirements for correct apportionment of asset risk, and in contrast to some lease-based home financing products, the Ansar product requires maintenance and insurance costs to be shared between the customer and Ansar pro rata to their ownership in the partnership. In addition, so that customers are not heavily disadvantaged against conventional mortgage products if the real estate market is rising, capital gains may be biased in favour of the customer, though naturally the full gain will not accrue to the customer. Hence, in a rising market, the conventional high-street mortgage will always be commercially more attractive. The compensation for this cap on the upside is that the customer is able to purchase units in the partnership at a reduced cost in a falling market, since the losses are also shared in proportion to the ownership. In the economic climate of 2007 onwards, this may have been a significant attraction of the product.

A true profit-and-loss-sharing home financing product, then. According to the scholar who approved the product, 'the scheme adopts a unique system of joint ownership that fulfils the aims and objectives of Islamic finance. I urge both Muslims and non-Muslims to study it objectively and thoroughly in order to realise how true Islamic finance deals fairly with all parties to a transaction, both the weaker and the stronger. . .I would like to encourage Muslims and non-Muslims who dream of building a fair society, free from oppression by debt and its detrimental consequences, to try their best to ensure that schemes such as this are successful.'[7]

And yet, human nature being what it is, homebuyers typically feel optimistic when buying a property, and expect their asset to rise in value over time. Faced with the option of keeping the upside to themselves through conventional products (or through diminishing *musharaka* products with a repurchase price fixed in advance), take-up of this equity-like financing product has not been as strong as hoped for by some in the industry. Alas, leverage is a hard habit to break.

Had a sufficient mass of buyers opted for such a model at a time when Islamic products did not exist in the UK, and Islamic banks were making tentative forays into that market, might the Muslim community in the UK have turned into a poster child for the global Islamic finance industry? The few isolated attempts to turn a community home-financing need into a viable business fell flat in the 1990s, perhaps because such a model disturbed the comfortable holding pattern that the traditional Islamic banks were accustomed to. Perhaps without the industry's help, the community of Muslim professionals – doctors, high-street lawyers, owners of small businesses – who proposed these initiatives found themselves unable to lobby the right legislative bodies with any credibility, or to muster the right infrastructure. It wasn't their fault that initiatives such as Ansar were poorly marketed – they had patients and clients to attend to, small businesses to run. Nor were they demographically significant enough to lobby the big institutions effectively.

So if the Islamic banks are playing water polo in football gear, should Muslims be looking to the conventional banks instead? Can they offer a wider array of products at more competitive terms and with greater adherence to Sharia standards? Despite the turmoil of the credit crisis, global investment banks remain Petri dishes of innovation, deploying vast armies of intellectually capable product specialists to develop ever mutating financial instruments. Their sales tentacles stretch across all markets, burrowing into every corner of the investor universe. Give them a set of parameters and, if the opportunity is lucrative enough, they will develop a product to satisfy those parameters. They build a machine around that product to mechanize its delivery, enabling it to flow out of the door.

In recent years, scholars began to recognize the merit of fast-tracking the development of Islamic products in partnership with these technically proficient flow monsters. Where once Islamic institutions had developed the industry at their own pace, they now had a fierce competition on their hands. The game was changing – its new entrants were stronger, faster and more ruthless. Their water cooler conversations were peppered with 'market share', 'run rates', 'wallet size' and 'value at risk'. They touched down on runways shimmering in the desert heat, strolley in one hand and bulging laptop bag slung over the shoulder, sprinting to the front of immigration queues, their British and European passports meriting no more than a perfunctory glance.

Islamic finance was an intellectual curiosity for them. Once upon a time, they structured tax-efficient investment products domiciled in Luxembourg for the benefit of Belgian dentists, that archetypal high-income European retail buyer of financial product. Now their target was richer – the ultra high net worth Gulf prince – and the parameters within which they operated even more inscrutable. They lived to create and sell product as fast as possible, as if it were manufactured on a factory conveyor belt. Standardization initiatives and product 'platforms' – generic programmes to industrialize the production of vast quantities of financial products, especially high-value derivatives – were their obsession. The local and regional banks didn't stand a chance.

Perhaps the old man at the conference was right to be suspicious. If he believed that the big conventional firms intended to suck the life out of Islamic finance, he might have found plenty of supporting evidence. That said, if he looked hard enough, he might have found as much evidence among the Islamic banks themselves. In private, bankers and lawyers were willing to talk freely about the sharp practices they were witness to, not just by conventional international institutions but also by regional Islamic ones.

One Samadi lawyer described a client of his, a Middle Eastern Islamic bank, buying a real estate loan portfolio, a conventional portfolio with conventional leverage. The Western-trained management of the bank instructed the lawyer to change the transaction documents to replace the word 'interest' with 'profit'. They would buy the loan portfolio regardless and put it on the bank's books for the benefit of the bank's own balance sheet, otherwise known as the prop trading desk. The Sharia board needn't be involved, and if any future acquisitions of assets under that loan book were to be flagged in the Sharia certification process, the deals would be disguised to look compliant. In short, the bankers were defrauding their scholars and their shareholders.

Another Samadi lawyer reserved his contempt for the conventional institutions for whom he set up offshore fund and *sukuk* vehicles. 'Conventional banks have no love for Islamic finance', he said. 'How can you possibly assume they want to develop *true* Islamic finance? That would remove them from the equation. Islamic finance would destroy them, so for example they create bond-like structures and call them *sukuk*. Even Islamic banks now accept this debt-like instrument, and *sukuk* is killing Islamic finance.'

A quarter-to-quarter focus on turnover hasn't helped the banking industry's cause in winning the hearts and minds of the Islamic investor community. Appointing conventionally trained managers to develop Islamic business, or setting strategies in this marketplace without understanding the mind of the Muslim customer, have proven to be their downfall.

At the Masjid Al-Samad in Dubai's executive expatriate heartland, a group of British-born Samadiites have been keeping a close eye on the British Islamic banking industry. Although they haven't yet forsaken their chosen vocation, unlike their fellow worshipper Sulaiman, they nevertheless have deep reservations. Until 2011, not one of the UK's five FSA-registered Islamic banks had yet appointed a Muslim to the position of CEO, and all five banks had barely moved out of the comfort zone of the commodity *murabaha*.

'You need cultural affinity', says one Samadi banker. 'It isn't enough to be merely a solid banker.'

Another concurs, though his focus is on Islamic windows at conventional banks:

> A non-insider is suddenly thrust into the limelight to develop the Islamic business of a conventional bank or a key division of an Islamic bank. He fronts their activities at conferences and sets their product strategy. His loyalties are firstly to his bonus and secondly to his shareholders. But the products he understands are conventional ones and he just wants to replicate them. He doesn't get the whole 'Sharia compliant' versus 'Sharia based' debate. Muslims do. But the moment they start to openly question the ethics of their profession, they're out of a job. Meanwhile the secular, politically astute operator with a background in conventional banking continues to run the industry.

Perhaps as long as the Islamic finance industry continues to borrow both resources and ideas from the conventional industry, and is forced by legislation, regulation and tax authorities to operate as a moneylender and not a merchant, then the debate around 'Sharia compliant' versus 'Sharia based' will remain biased in favour of the former. In other words, Islamic financial products will remain reverse engineered from their conventional equivalents – like the commodity *murabaha* home mortgage – instead of based on a purer structure – like

Ansar's profit-and-loss-sharing mortgage. And in perpetuating Sharia-compliant instead of Sharia-based products, the holistic approach demanded by the Sharia in regulating one's worldly affairs is lost. Considerations about the environment, labour practices or societal improvement are put to one side as otherwise conventional corporations use Islamic instruments such as *sukuk* as a means to chase shareholder return.

And whilst the immediate effect of appointing technically proficient executives is a ramping up of research and development, leading to a rapid increase in product innovation, innovation can soon turn sour. Initially, new markets are created and customer brand loyalties cemented. No clearer example of this can be found than in the case of Deutsche Bank. It burst onto the Islamic scene with previously unimagined transactions such as the Safa Tower and the PCFC *sukuk*, and singlehandedly invented the Islamic derivatives industry.

With its commitment to innovation and quality, Deutsche Bank turned itself into the *de facto* industry leader. But did it care for the industry and its customer base? If the economic tide turned, would it and its international competitors tough it out with their customers or would they row back out to sea? How far would these conventional banks go to close profitable transactions? Would they be willing to uphold the Sharia, come what may, or would they find ways to bypass the constraints and obligations expected by their customer base and scholars?

Men like Sheikh Nizam Yaquby had recognized the benefits to the development of the industry of bringing in the global banking behemoths, embracing their entry into the market. But, of late, he and his fellow scholars had gradually started to pull back on the special permissions they had once granted in the early days 'for the good of the growth of the industry'. Having been given this kick-start, the industry was now thriving and financial legislation was now more inclusive. Commodity *murabaha* was gradually becoming a structure acceptable only when no alternatives were available – when, for example, tax authorities might penalize an alternative structure. And, even then, its usage could not be justified as a precedent for future similar deals. Sheikh Hussain, too, would watch his *wa'd* creation like a hawk, realizing that the barbarian hordes had been unleashed from the gates of the flow monsters. Without inherent checks and balances, this nascent industry would die before adolescence unless the standard bearers stood up to dubious structures.

As we saw in earlier chapters, Deutsche Bank courted controversy over the *wa'd* structure, and its Islamic structuring team began a painful process of disbanding as the post-2007 economic downturn played out. Within the team, disagreement surfaced over the use of the *wa'd* to replicate non-compliant trading strategies. With a factory now in existence to issue Islamic structured products, most of the dedicated Sharia structuring input was no longer required, and even dedicated Islamic sales staff were caught in the redundancy crosshairs, leaving their conventional colleagues to manage relationships with Islamic banks. Why retain Islamic specialists when conventional bankers can do the same job and won't have the same moral objections? By early 2011, as markets debated whether the world would enter a double dip recession, not a single dedicated Islamic structurer or salesperson remained at Deutsche. Islamic finance had become 'a luxury the bank can't afford'.[8]

Where once Islamic finance had been viewed as a strategic project, as the economic climate deteriorated global investment banks changed tack and opted to sell Islamic product opportunistically. A holistic approach was no longer required: product platforms had been set up in the boom years and the banks could simply churn out product off the back of those platforms. *Fatwas* from several years ago would simply be reused for new products. Islamic finance had turned into a curiosity, an intellectual game, and its star players had no love for it.

Investment banks were not alone in their attitudes towards the industry. Private equity firms briefly flirted with Sharia-compliant funds in the hope of diversifying away from their traditional investor base. But, by and large, they too merely mirrored the conventional banks' opportunism. The head of one of the Middle East's leading private equity firms, when asked why he had pursued only one Sharia-compliant fund and then subsequently reverted to launching conventional funds, replied: 'I made my *niyya* [voiced my intention to God], performed *wudu* [ritual ablution before prayer], prayed, but God did not answer.' Having sold a substantial portion of units in his Islamic fund to conventional investors such as large US pension funds and Asian banks, he felt that the additional effort to attract Islamic Gulf and Malaysian money had not been worth it.

In February 2011, the governor of Qatar Central Bank suddenly and unexpectedly instructed conventional lenders to close down their Islamic operations in the country by the end of the year.[9] Only two months earlier, he had been inaugurating the Doha branch of HSBC Amanah, HSBC's Islamic banking arm. At first bankers assumed some awful scandal had been perpetrated, prompting this draconian demand, yet none was uncovered. The more cynical fell back on the conspiracy theory, suggesting that leading figures in the Qatari financial community had taken stock positions in the country's Islamic banks with prior knowledge of the announcement. Yet although shares in Doha's Islamic banks jumped as much as 10 per cent following the announcement, and conventional lenders fell commensurately, there was no hard evidence to substantiate this.

One Qatari columnist for the newspaper *Al Sharq* was moved to launch a scathing attack on the QCB by suggesting it should learn from the experiences of foreign regulators in monitoring the activities of banks with 'mixed operations'.[10] 'It's a harsh and imprudent measure to take', he wrote, suggesting a reform of wrongdoing banks rather than a complete closure of their activities. 'The QCB move threatens to undermine the development of the Islamic banking industry in Qatar. It would lead to a monopoly of the full-fledged Islamic banks and they would not be bothered about improving their services. They wouldn't be taking their customers seriously.'

The QCB countered by stating that alternative capital adequacy rules were in the pipeline for Islamic institutions, and that conventional institutions would not be able to follow both sets of rules simultaneously.[11] It also suggested that it was too difficult to supervise and monitor both Islamic and conventional operations of commercial banks, since depositor funds would get 'mixed up'. It acknowledged that the basic financing methods used by Islamic institutions were inherently equity-like and therefore more risky: the Islamic institution deploying products based on *mudaraba*, *musharaka*, *istisna* and *ijara* contracts was acting as a merchant, not a lender. 'It is difficult to fully protect the rights of depositors.' So the QCB was acknowledging the inherently unbalanced playing field in which Islamic institutions were operating, and was attempting to level that field.

Bankers were furious, claiming that the decision had been unilateral, unfair and irrational – that competition would be reduced and the consumer would suffer. Product innovation would be paralysed and customer choice would dry up. There would be no incentive on Islamic institutions to improve.

And yet some in the industry – just a handful, mind – felt that this was perhaps a move the industry needed. First to level the playing field and, second, to restore credibility. Unknown to most, regulators and scholars had been having closed door discussions in the lead up to the ban. The scholars were wising up to structured product platforms that gave the investor no legally enforceable security interest in the Islamic assets; or that allowed for the bank to reuse those assets for its own purposes without permission of the investor; or commodity *murabaha* transactions to finance real estate assets because the credit risk management departments of conventional banks couldn't envisage any financing that didn't look like, smell like and act like an interest-bearing loan; or products that engaged in non-compliant hedges on the other side of the trade, because the Islamic investor couldn't see the hedge; or, at its most basic, the simple co-mingling of Islamic depositors' funds in centralized pools of money where returns were smeared into one homogeneous whole.

Around about the same time, another much larger scandal was brewing on Wall Street. One of the world's largest brokerage firms, MF Global, suffered a spectacular implosion as a result of an improper transfer of over $891 million from apparently segregated customer accounts to one of MF Global's own broker-dealer accounts to cover trading losses at the firm.

The outspoken trends forecaster and publisher of the *Trends Journal*, Gerald Celente, did not see this one coming. Despite his much publicized earlier predictions of global turmoil and open criticism of Wall Street excesses, he was caught napping and lost what he claimed were his life savings in the collapse of MF Global.[12] A well-known 'gold bull', Celente had built up a position in gold by buying coins, bullion and gold futures through brokers on commodities futures exchanges. On these exchanges, he would buy a 'future' position on gold, by paying now and taking physical delivery on a pre-specified future date.

On 30 October 2011, a unit of MF Global reported to the Chicago Mercantile Exchange and the Commodities Futures Trading Commission that there was a material shortfall of hundreds of millions of dollars in segregated customer funds. MF had been using customer funds to 'meet liquidity issues' in the days prior to its bankruptcy. It had mixed customer funds and used them for its own account, transferring them out of the US. When these apparently intraday loans were not returned by the end of the day, panic ensued, and the loans from customer accounts just got bigger. Customer accounts were frozen and the following day, the company filed for bankruptcy.

Celente was furious, demanding to know why MF Global's CEO, Jon Corzine, a former CEO of Goldman Sachs, Governor of New Jersey and a US Senator, would not be going to jail over this.

'I found out they took all my money – all my money – out of my account and put it in the hands of a trustee. . .I said you mean Meyer Lansky and Al Capone decided to take my money. . .?' ranted Celente, referring to two of the most infamous names in organized crime.[13]

He had a point. His New York mannerisms and language were a little more colourful than most of MF's customers, and perhaps his reputation as an unrepentant eschatologist and economic doom-monger did his cause few favours, but many co-investors might have agreed when he suggested that the 'M' in MF should stand for Mother and the 'F' should. . .well, you get the picture.[14]

'This guy's sitting at the casino, making bets, 36 to 1!' he yelled at a news anchor, referring to Corzine and his firm's usage of customer funds for allegedly making leveraged bets on European government bonds.[15] 'He's cleaned out and ruined a lot of people!'

The lack of separation between customer funds and a firm's own money had caused the largest Wall Street meltdown since Lehman Brothers in September 2008. It was no leap of logic to see that the conventional financial services industry continued to risk the health of the world's economy by allowing invest-ment bankers to play with money that didn't belong to them.

Will Islamic finance head the same way? Will it, too, replicate the conventional industry to such an extent that it, too, may mingle depositors' funds with the institution's own funds? Or will it recognize the real economy role that money must have – attachment to real assets and segregation of ownership?

Perhaps, rather than being the kneejerk reaction of a hysterical regulator, the Qatar Central Bank had instead taken a bold leap forward in protecting the interests of Islamic depositors. Perhaps it was in fact reclaiming the ethical values of the Islamic finance industry.

11

Arbitraging Islam: The Great Vampire Squid Arrives

The whole thing is a joke. And the joke is on us.

Gerald Celente[1]

It is important to note that the structured finance methods of Sharia arbitrage – which were copied from Western regulatory arbitrage methods aiming to reduce tax burdens on high net worth individuals – have already had a chequered history. Indeed, American regulators and accountants were slow to uncover some of the abuses of those structures, which later featured prominently in corporate scandals, such as Enron's. In this regard, regulators and enforcement officials in the countries wherein Islamic finance has thrived are clearly less sophisticated than their Western counterparts, and hence less likely to uncover devious intentions underneath complicated financial structures. Given the industry's young age and fragility, it would be wise to move to simpler and more transparent modes of operation, to minimize the risks of abuse by criminal elements.[2]

Strong words, and not those of an outsider or a layman, but a respected expert, Mahmoud El-Gamal, Professor of Economics and Statistics at Rice University in the United States. An out-spoken critic of an industry he views as a sham, Professor El-Gamal has a problem with Sharia arbitrage. Although financial arbitrage is generally the practice of exploiting profitable discrepancies between markets – usually by buying a financial product in one market and selling it at a higher price in another – Sharia arbitrage is a form of regulatory arbitrage – that is, the act of restructuring a financial product that is available in one market in order to make it tradeable in another. And El-Gamal believes that the practice of Sharia arbitrage is the reason why Islamic finance is merely mimicking the culture of an investment banking industry rocked by a failure to manage risk adequately.

In a conference room in Paris, global desk heads at a large French bank are gathering to contemplate their entry into the Islamic finance space. The backdrop is grim. In late 2011, angry crowds are gathering in Wall Street, and in other cities around the world, to protest the injustice of a capitalist system that rewards those who take excessive risks with others' money, then watch smugly as taxpayers bail out their indiscretions. The Greeks are about to go to a shock referendum on austerity measures, threatening the collapse of the Eurozone. Liquidity is drying up around the world and the threat of financial Armageddon seems to be ever present. Can these French bankers afford the luxury of considering an entirely new line of products, so alien to their core business, at a time when shareholders are demand-ing immediate solutions to increase the bank's liquidity and boost the bottom line?

Just three years earlier, at rival bank Société Générale, trader Jérôme Kerviel was accused of losing the bank €4.9 billion in unauthorized trades, apparently arbitraging discrepancies in the pricing between equities and their derivatives. Only two months earlier, in September 2011, UBS trader Kweku Adoboli lost the Swiss bank $2.3 billion as a result of unauthorized trades by speculating on stock indices. The resultant investigation claimed the jobs of the UBS CEO, two co-heads of the equities division (one of them the charismatic Swiss Algerian, Yassine Bouhara, Deutsche's former Godfather of the Middle East), and eight suspended members of staff.

In a climate of fear and mistrust, the desk heads in the conference room want to know more about Sharia risk. What legal, financial and reputational impact would the risk of entering into Sharia-compliant contracts have for them? How could they work that arbitrage to their advantage without tripping over it?

Some in the room can barely hide their disdain for mixing business with religion, a curious French aversion to allowing religion to intrude in matters of daily life, as if a connection to morality and ethics should only be of relevance once a week in Church. Others are concerned that trading with Islamic financial institutions might somehow taint their own reputation, as if those institutions must by definition have a greater degree of exposure to laundered terrorist money.

It is a new era of Sharia scrutiny by scholars, punctuated by declarations from leading figures such as Mufti Taqi Usmani who, at a stroke, can radically alter the landscape of the industry. There is money to be made, but there are risks in doing so, and the French bank is about to embark on a Rumsfeldian journey of 'unknown unknowns'.

But while our French friends are taking the time to understand the nuances of Islamic finance before dipping their toes, the same cannot be said for Goldman Sachs, the institution famously described as 'a great vampire squid, wrapped around the face of humanity, relentlessly jamming their blood funnel into anything that smells like money'.[3] In the search for liquidity, the vampire squid has discovered that Islamic institutions are sitting on piles of cash, waiting to deploy them on blue chip investments. The time has come to tap this liquidity. The time has come for Goldman Sachs, the hedonistic poster boy of the boom years of investment banking, to find God.

The smell of money led Goldman Sachs to my door in the summer of 2011 to discuss a *sukuk* issuance. 'We're looking at a commodity *murabaha* for a conventional financial institution', they told me. Could they not consider an alternative structure? There were plenty of options out there, we would undoubtedly find something that works, I suggested. Best not to make it look overtly like an interest-bearing bond and attach Arabic words to it. It doesn't look good.

'But how is that any different from the use of the commodity *murabaha* as an inter-bank financing instrument?' they asked. After all, Islamic banks today fund their day-to-day activities in the inter-bank market by 'borrowing' privately through the use of this instrument.

It was a perfectly fair point – if they can do it, why can't we? Why should a publicly listed instrument that works in the same way be considered any different? What they were effectively doing was creating a giant machine for inter-bank liquidity, 'programmizing' what was already in existence. This was the flow monsters at work in all their industrial glory.

'Also, the institution wants to use the money however it sees fit,' they said.

'So let me get this straight', I said. 'You want to raise a public bond underpinned by the simultaneous buying and selling of metal warrants on an exchange, and you want a *fatwa* to certify this as compliant with Sharia? Then you want the institution to use the money raised from Islamic investors to fund its conventional activities – like lending with interest, trading of debt and intangible contracts, shorting of stock?'

We parted ways and Goldman Sachs found themselves an advisory firm willing to take on the deal. It seemed the mighty Goldman Sachs had learnt little from the debacle of the sub-prime mortgage disaster and consequent economic tsunami, as has been well documented in numerous books and journals.[4] Though publicly sensitive to criticism of its role – and that of its alumni – in the global financial crisis, its institutional thick skin remained apparently impenetrable to reputational considerations.

Although I did not know it at the time, Goldman Sachs had been talking about raising money for itself. Its $2 billion *sukuk* programme was doomed to failure the moment it was launched. In theory, this new debt issuance would squirt a refreshingly different type of liquidity into a balance sheet still rebounding from the depths of the financial crisis. Islamic investors, offering their hard-earned, clean, socially responsible cash, would be the new saviours.

But in practice it was a compromised solution, created for a bank more used to closing deals fast and furiously. The alternative was too participative, too real economy, too Islamic, too far removed from the reality of modern conventional finance. The deal team did not have the time or the inclination to learn how to do business in a way that met the spirit and letter of the law. What they needed was a Sharia advisory firm who would give them a solution that looked like their day-to-day money-market transactions, and that all important *fatwa*. Ironically, an industry predicated on ethical, real economy solutions was excluding the ethical advisors.

And although the programme had not yet been launched, the French bankers gathering in a Parisian boardroom to contemplate their entry into the Islamic world were sitting up and taking notice. 'How is it possible that a conventional financial institution like Goldman can fund itself with Islamic money?' asks one of the desk heads around the conference table.

It is an excellent question. How indeed? The answer is that Goldman Sachs was playing the Sharia arbitrage card. Whether Islamic investors would in fact buy the paper would be another matter.

In Saudi Arabia, an unknown former journalist and student of Islamic finance by the name of Mohammed Khnifer was preparing to answer the question. As the debate over Goldman's *sukuk* gathered momentum in private circles, the young Saudi pored over the *sukuk* prospectus and was disturbed by what he found. In a blog that quickly became viral among the Islamic finance community,[5] Khnifer claimed that Goldman's debt issuance desk had opted for the *tawarruq*, the simultaneous purchase and resale of commodities on a metals exchange, the modern incarnation of El Diwany's derided medieval construct, the *contractum trinius*. In order to get their credit traders, risk management committee, legal team and compliance department onside, the Goldman bankers had followed the path of least resistance – a product they could instantly compare to an interest-bearing bond.

But this was not the only thing bothering Khnifer. The monies raised were not specified for any ostensibly 'Islamic' purpose: no funding of a separate Islamic 'window' that served only customers wishing to buy Sharia-compliant products, no financing of Sharia-compliant trading activities or assets.[6] No mention of socially responsible investing, or ethical business. Just the good old day-to-day ordinary business activities of the Goldman Sachs that the media loves to hate, the giant vampire squid. If that money raised from Islamic investors was used to facilitate the shorting of the subprime mortgage market, there was nothing in the legal documentation preventing the bank from doing so.

And finally, there was the question of tradeability. This was a security listed on the Irish Stock Exchange. Although the official prospectus advised investors that the instrument could not be considered Sharia compliant if it were traded at any value other than its par (face) value,[7] there was nothing to stop traders on the exchange trading it at a value set by the market. In other words, it represented the trading of a debt or a cash flow – impermissible in Islam – and not the exchange of a debt at its face value, which would be considered acceptable.

It wasn't just the purists frothing at the mouth. In an unguarded moment over an informal coffee, one head of bond markets at a rival European institution described the deal as 'a pile of shit'. Although a non-Muslim, he felt the target market had been cheated. In playing the Sharia arbitrage card, Goldman Sachs had tripped up on Sharia risk: the risk that one man's Sharia compliant was another man's pile of shit.

As the Goldman *sukuk* controversy raged in the blogosphere and at coffee houses in Dubai, I arrived at the World Islamic Banking Conference in Bahrain to moderate a panel on Sharia. In advance of the session, I asked the panellists – all active participants in the Islamic finance industry – if they would mind discussing the *sukuk*. The answer was unanimous: they would mind, and can we talk about something else please. Not a single one of the five panellists was willing to go on the record to analyse the Sharia issues. Taking on one of the world's most powerful banks in public at the WIBC was not a risk worth taking.

One of the panellists had been involved in the Sharia board review of the Goldman Sachs *sukuk*. In private, he described a scene of tension to me. At the Sharia review meeting, only a few of the eight named scholars were able to attend the meeting in person. The commercial pressures were enormous. One of the great banking institutions was turning to Islamic finance, a milestone achievement for the industry. To turn down this structure would be to destroy several months of work, hamper the opportunity for the industry to leverage its future off the best and brightest minds, and ruin carefully cultivated relationships.

The group of jurists was divided. One specified the proviso that the money raised would only be used for Sharia-compliant purposes, in the same way that Islamic banks are bound to do in their inter-bank funding instruments. This would have at least made the instrument acceptable to a portion of the market, but this proviso had not been relayed to investors or made public.

The very fact that the deal was public and listed on an exchange – rather than a private bilateral funding – meant, according to that scholar, that it should be held up to higher standards. Another scholar had not seen the legal documents underpinning the *sukuk* but was willing to sign on the basis of the bankers' oral communications with him.

At the WIBC, another attendee in the audience that day had been named in the prospectus as one of the eight members of the Sharia board of the advisory firm who had procured the *fatwa* for the product. And yet he had not attended that final review meeting. In classic legalese, the *sukuk* prospectus had hinted that a *fatwa* would be procured but did not specify when, and which of the named scholars would actually sign the *fatwa*.[8] When I asked him in a private moment to clarify his view on the *sukuk*, the scholar denied he was aware of the contents of the *sukuk* documentation, denied that he was still a member of the Sharia board of the advisory firm listed in the prospectus, and denied that he had ever signed any associated *fatwa*. His name had simply been used.

Despite my own attempts to procure the signed document from the scholars who had attended that Sharia board review, no lawyer, banker or scholar was able to offer it to me. The *fatwa* had not been published in the prospectus and appeared to be a protected document. Perhaps it would not have been seemly to publicize a schism in scholarly ranks, but somehow the press had picked up on the tension. *Euroweek*, for example, went as far as describing the scholars as 'surprised and upset to find their names listed' when the prospectus was released.[9]

When the panel session ended, I met up with Khnifer to discuss his publicized articles. With a keen intellect, the advantage of youth and a feeling of invincibility on his side, he had embraced the debate with gusto when he opened it up to public consumption. But now, a few weeks later, he was shifting uncomfortably. Still a freelance consultant looking for a permanent position in the industry, he was worried about the threat of legal action, and the response to his article from all corners of the market.

'They are saying horrible things about me', he told me nervously, his customary broad smile now absent. 'First I started getting emails, then messages on LinkedIn [a social networking site for professionals]. They tell me I will never find work in this industry. '

Through media contacts, Khnifer was hearing the news that his nascent career was in jeopardy. Labelled an 'ignorant industry outsider' with 'crackpot ideas', bankers – both insiders and others – suggested his intention was merely to make a name for himself. *Ad hominem* attacks in online forums and private emails became a daily ritual, most of them focusing on his lack of hands-on experience in the industry, and few were prepared to go on the record to defend his views.

But when an internal memo from Abu Dhabi Islamic Bank was leaked to the market, warning how the *sukuk* was not compliant with its own Sharia board's guidelines,[10] Khnifer started to breathe a little more easily. At last, a prominent market player agreed with him.

'Hopefully this *fatwa* will remove them from my back', he told me. But Khnifer continued to watch his back, afraid that a promising career would end almost before it had started. Had he persisted, it would not have been a fair fight. The ambitious young Saudi dared not take the risk of being swallowed whole. He withdrew quietly from the debate and let others run with it.

Khnifer was not the only one treading carefully. One journalist interviewing a New York-based Goldman Sachs employee after the *sukuk* programme was launched found herself being quizzed about her own credentials to report on the structure.[11]

'"How come the Islamic guys talk to you?"' she described him as asking her, incredulous that a woman should be granted access to a clandestine clique of bearded chauvinists. As she asked him a series of technical questions to clarify the use of the proceeds from the *sukuk*, and the Sharia certification procedure, his composure broke.

"'Look, I don't care about that, honey. I don't give a shit about the little guy",' she relayed. "'I just want to make sure you get the facts straight.'" As far as he was concerned, the press and the blogosphere were misstating the facts, and their over-emphasis on the flow of money – the ethics of the deal – were an unimportant sideshow.

Whether the Middle East was too insignificant for the bond trader from New York to exercise simple manners, or whether he considered Islamic investors dumb enough to be fobbed off without a clear analysis of the matter, the journalist didn't know. But she, too, was learning to tread carefully, and her peers at other news agencies were being asked by their bosses to avoid an open war with the world's most celebrated – or infamous – bank.

To date, no official sale of the *sukuk* has taken place even though the programme has been 'launched', by which is meant that the legal documents underpinning the issuance programme have been published. Rumours abound of financial institutions willing to buy privately placed tranches of the *sukuk*, but no one knows who these institutions are, nor whether in fact a single dollar has been sold. At a time when other financial institutions, including conventional ones, have achieved spectacular oversubscriptions for their own public *sukuk* issuances, investors appear to have sent a clear signal on the subject of Sharia arbitrage.

Commenting generally on the subject of arbitrage, Professor El-Gamal is unequivocal on the subject. For him, layering transactions with a series of complex steps to provide comfort to Islamic investors is merely form over substance: '[The] addition of trading parties as buffers between Islamic financial institutions and transactions deemed to be forbidden (interest-based loans, option and future trading, etc.) must be seen fundamentally as a means of exploiting Sharia arbitrage opportunities.'[12]

Although these comments were published well before the Goldman Sachs *sukuk*, they nevertheless were directly relevant. The obvious red flag – financing of the bank's conventional day-to-day activities – had been ignored in the pursuit of juristic opinions on the individual legs of the transaction. By refusing to buy this paper, finally Islamic investors were starting to push back. It seemed that there simply weren't any takers for the Goldman paper, at any price level. Surely this was a good thing for the Islamic finance industry? On the one hand, the market viewed the investment instrument as contractually dubious and issued by a conventional financial services institution with a reputation for playing fast and loose with the capital markets. The market had sent a clear signal that both spirit and letter of Sharia were important to it. Goldman Sachs's response to criticism had been hostile and lacked empathy. It responded aggressively to vulnerable individuals in private with the intention of quashing debate and had little interest in righting alleged wrongs. It was easy to equate Goldman Sachs with its popular public image. At least that's what I thought until I delved deeper.

Not surprisingly, Goldman Sachs is not the kind of institution willing to go on the record about the structure of *sukuk* and less so the failure of one of its deals. I did speak to someone 'close to the transaction', however, an advisor who had a hand in the structuring.

I met my mystery insider in the Dubai International Financial Centre, the financial zone in the heart of the United Arab Emirates modelled on the City of London's Square Mile, a cluster of futuristic office blocks housing brand-name investment banks, Magic Circle law firms and ancillary service providers. In the shadow of its iconic cubic structure, The Gate – imitating

Paris's Grande Arche in La Défense – we sip *qahwa*, Arabic coffee served with dates.

My contact is intense and passionate about the deal, but unhappy. He is reflecting the sense of frustration that the bankers at Goldman are feeling right now. There is an irony in his dapper dress sense. He sports a tailored suit with a fancy striped lining and a bright pink double-cuff shirt, echoing everything that Dubai stands for: brash, ambitious, confident. But his manifest ebullience is tempered by the frustration felt by deal insiders at the perceived unfair comments from the media, an organized effort he describes as a whispering campaign. Given the context of Goldman Sachs as an apparently unsuitable participant in the Islamic market, I find it initially strange that he quotes a Quranic chapter that reminds the believer to be steadfast and seek refuge in Allah from the power of whispers, 'from the evil of the retreating whisperer who whispers into the hearts of mankind'.[13] This witch hunt against Goldman Sachs was never about the deal itself, he contends. It was about Goldman Sachs. And his client and colleagues on the deal feel hard done by.

In his opinion, this *sukuk* would have been the first step towards 'programmizing' Islamic inter-bank liquidity. It would have moved the industry forward in the same way that Deutsche Bank once moved the game on for Islamic derivatives. As one of the biggest and richest equity trading houses in the world, Goldman Sachs's traders can 'warehouse' massive amounts of equities and sell them to Islamic investors in initial public offerings, 'doing funky things with them' as he put it, like providing financing to holders of the shares, using the shares as collateral. The enormous public offering of Facebook shares could have been a perfect opportunity to set aside a portion of the billions of dollars raised, just for Islamic investors. Imagine that, says my insider. The start of an incredible, gigantic move forwards for Islamic equities activity in the world, which up until now hasn't been realized.

But before they get to that stage, Goldman needs to do the simple stuff: programmizing the inter-bank lending market through commodity *murabaha*, something that happens every day, every minute by Islamic banks. And yet, when done in public by a firm like Goldman, it is met with the most severe whispering campaign designed to kill the idea and the transaction.

The Goldman bankers feel that friends and former colleagues in the industry have deserted them, says my insider. Badmouthed them in public and hung them out to dry. Why did no one discuss the issue directly with them, why a witch hunt through the media? He reels off a list of names of Islamic banks. 'I want them all to look me in the eye and tell me they *don't* do this stuff on a daily basis. They do! So now who's being hypocritical?'

He has a point, I tell myself. After all, the vast majority of Islamic banks fund their Islamic activities with the commodity *murabaha*, a simultaneous buying and selling of metals on an exchange to simulate inter-bank deposits. Perhaps it might be argued in mitigation that the wholly Sharia-compliant institutions have no non-compliant avenues to deploy those funds, and therefore cannot be accused of profiting immorally from Islamic money. However, if the Qatar Central Bank's decision to ban conventional institutions from selling Islamic products is any indicator, then it might be argued that allowing the likes of HSBC and Standard Chartered (both international conventional banks like Goldman Sachs) to profit from Islamic depositors is tantamount to the same thing.

The bankers are palpably frustrated and under pressure. 'They're just waiting for that phone call from HR and their line manager, and get asked to come into a meeting room to discuss the terms of their termination.'

It's another PR mess at a time in the economic cycle when the bank can ill afford bad publicity. Somehow, despite Goldman's many talents, public relations does not seem to be one of them. Even their leased offices in a quiet corner of the DIFC are

denied a simple plaque in the foyer to signify their presence in
the building, as if the key to success is simply to remain low key
even when doing bad stuff, hoping that no one notices.

'They need help. What do they do? They're trying to move
the industry from here [he gestures at one side of the table]
to here [he gestures to the other side]. They want to move
from standardizing liquidity management to creating complex
structures in Sharia-compliant private equity, and that's what
will really turn those guys on. They're Goldman Sachs. I've
seen the other big banks, and I can tell you that these guys are
absolutely the best. Every one of the 440 partners of this firm
is a real equity holder, massively incentivized to be the very best
in the industry. But they need to see genuinely game-changing
P&L – for now, Islamic finance is just the stone in the groove
of the sole of the shoe of the janitor who's ankle deep in water,
cleaning the latrines. We, the Islamic finance industry, are considered insignificant. Unless we can introduce game-changing
concepts, we're never gonna get noticed by these people. Right
now, we're worthless to these guys. We have to make something
happen, otherwise we get moved on. If this industry is gonna
move on, it needs to move on in a revolutionary way.'

Maybe the simple answer is PR, I suggest. It's not a structuring
issue. Those people who invest using the commodity *murabaha*
structure are not the sort to worry too much about Sharia arbitrage. They've already accepted that form over substance is the
nature of the industry, and perhaps they have little interest in
changing the status quo. So, instead, perhaps it's about show-
ing people that Goldman Sachs doesn't kidnap babies, pollute
rivers and torture bunny rabbits. Maybe Goldman should set
up a think tank, which then becomes Goldman's independent
PR agent, a gift to the industry, if you like. It could then begin
moving the industry radically into its next phase of development, just as Deutsche Bank once revolutionized the industry
by leveraging off its own think tank.

The adviser continues. 'The guys that you and I deal with at the regional institutions have no interest in moving the game on – they just want to read the paper, have lunch, socialize with their friends, leave the office at 3 p.m., and do the bare minimum: a couple of commodity *murabaha*s every now and then. I want to revolutionise the industry. I'm not interested in just existing.'

Anyone close to this deal, whether an adviser to the deal or a front office banker, has only a limited amount of time to make an impact, each in a race against the clock, against the patience of Goldman's senior management. Once the traders in New York lose interest in the deal, the Islamic finance industry will have to turn to its next white knight.

In trying to standardize the most basic inter-bank liquidity product, the Goldman bankers ended up alienating their firm from the industry and, in turn, themselves from their beloved firm. And perhaps all because they went public on a structure that some people find dubious, and yet ironically continue to transact in private.

Despite a section of the market's criticism of the structure, the most notable defence came from perhaps one of the industry's most widely respected individuals, Sheikh Hussain Hamed Hassan, a scholar whose rejection of the *tawarruq* transaction is well known:

> We have reviewed the structure and legal documents of the Goldman Sachs one year *Sukuk Al Murabaha* program, and after carefully reviewing the same found them to be in compliance with the AAOIFI standards and the generally accepted Sharia guidelines. I welcome well established conventional industry players such as Goldman Sachs in the Islamic finance world. . .and wish them every success with this product and their future Islamic financial initiatives.[14]

There can be few more solid endorsements in this industry. Technically it was difficult to argue that the *sukuk* held itself out as the outlawed *tawarruq*: that is, it did not require the presence of additional elements such as the immediate sale of commodities to a third party to generate cash (although it did not explicitly preclude this possibility, which prompted Khnifer's suspicions), or Goldman Sachs to sell the commodities back to the original supplier. Nor did the *sukuk* prospectus fail to advise buyers that trading the security above or below par would render it non-compliant (though, of course, it could not prevent this from happening on the stock exchange). So, in some ways, it might be argued that it was a purer *murabaha* transaction than the 'organized *tawarruq*' conducted every day by Islamic institutions in Saudi Arabia to maintain their liquidity.

Even Sheikh Nizam Yaquby, the mysteriously robed Obi-Wan Kenobi whose carefully chosen words had persuaded me to join the industry many years ago, agreed: 'It is a misunderstanding', he said in reference to the media attack on the *sukuk*. 'This *sukuk* was never issued – it was only in the development stage. Goldman Sachs is a very famous institution and it has a proper Sharia board that can guide and advise them.'[15] Well, he was right about it never being issued, but it was only in development limbo because it had not received universal market acceptance.

The backing of industry heavyweights seems more nuanced than the Goldman story being played out in the media, but the clock is ticking. How much longer will the partners at Goldman indulge the concept of Islamic finance? For them, this *sukuk* has been an exploding nail bomb of scholar disputes and market whisperings. A rumour circulates the market that one of the named scholars has refused to sign the *fatwa* because of a dispute over his fee. Another attached a proviso to the *fatwa*, which has not been publicized. Another two say they have nothing to do with the Sharia board any more.[16] One says he is on the board but never saw the documents.[17]

The lawyers to the deal and Goldman's capital markets bankers have allowed the use of vague references to Sharia in the documentation and, not surprisingly, these have been highlighted by a suspicious market as opaque and obfuscatory. Perhaps the mismanaged Sharia certification process had not been given the importance it deserved. Or perhaps, given the reputation that preceded the bank, it was impossible for Goldman Sachs to play in the ethical space at all.

For the Sharia advisory firm that advised Goldman Sachs, it would turn out to be their last major deal. They folded a year after the programme was launched.[18] Market rumours suggested that their reputation had been destroyed by just one deal, though market rumours were wrong in this case. The firm had always struggled to make money in a market where advice was not valued, and the firm's management had always been in conflict with a closed group of shareholders. For shareholders, perhaps this latest episode was the last straw. The chief executive officer was not happy. His extraordinary ability to visualize the abstract and cut through the most complex problems had not been enough to save his job at his former employer, Deutsche Bank, who had shut down his beloved Islamic finance team. The firm was former Deutsche subsidiary, Dar Al Istithmar. The chief executive? Belgian rocket scientist, Geert Bossuyt.

12

The Future of Islamic Finance

They are all suffering from cognitive dissonance.

Professor Mahmoud El-Gamal
(referring to the industry's scholars)

As 2012 came to a close, copies of the Goldman Sachs *sukuk* prospectus were gathering dust on the shelves of the bank's anonymous offices in DIFC. By December, almost exactly one year after the launch of the programme, one of the Arab world's leading newspapers declared the *sukuk* dead.[1]

At the likes of Barclays, Deutsche, Credit Suisse, UBS, Credit Agricole, and many other global institutions, Islamic finance had morphed from 'strategic' to 'opportunistic' as the global financial crisis unfolded. All had either lost key personnel or formally shut down their Islamic finance teams. In public they made assurances that the Islamic market remained important to them,[2] but in private they conceded they no longer had the expertise to transact.

And then came the big one: HSBC. Iqbal Khan, the founder of Amanah – HSBC's Islamic subsidiary – had already fallen on his sword a few years earlier following the arrival of the unsympathetic Michael Geoghegan. Without their charismatic and connected leader to defend them, Amanah was cruelly culled in late 2012, ostensibly because Islamic finance was no longer an economically viable business for the global banking giant. In HSBC's own words:

'[HSBC] allocate[s] capital to markets and businesses with clear growth potential. . .we [therefore] no longer offer Shari'ah compliant products in some markets.'[3]

Some insiders took a very different view to the official line. HSBC was in the throes of an unpleasant investigation by the Securities and Exchange Commission into breaches of anti-money laundering rules. Four of the institutions named by the US authorities in whose names accounts had been opened at HSBC included institutions with alleged links to terrorist financing.[4] One was a Saudi Arabian bank that had categorically denounced terrorism and denied all links to it.[5] Al-Qaida sympathizers may well hold bank accounts at high-street banks in London, argued Amanah insiders. You could probably follow the flow of money back from any bank in the world to some criminal activity and find yourself in breach of anti-money laundering rules. Why single out Al Rajhi over any other bank? To some, the allegations felt like the immediate aftermath of 9/11 when international banks profiled their Middle Eastern account holders in scrupulous detail, prompting an exodus of clean money back to the Gulf region, precipitating a regional boom in bank assets, stock markets and property.

The same insiders contended that HSBC had struck a deal with the SEC. A plea bargain: we'll close down our Islamic banking arm in six countries if you reduce the sentence. One of the handful of remaining senior bankers at Amanah was there at its inception in the 1990s, and he concurred with this view. It wasn't about the economics, he told me. Amanah had attracted significant deposits: 'We were making good money but they had to show something was being done about financing of terrorists. Decisions were made without consultation.'

And so, said the Amanah banker, they conflated unsubstantiated allegations of links to Al-Qaida and killed their support for Islamic markets. It was tantamount to equating Sharia-compliant finance to terrorist finance, as one populist British daily newspaper was fond of doing in hysteria-laden opinion pieces.[6] Sharia had become a convenient bogeyman for HSBC.

The view that the decision wasn't commercial wasn't just held by Amanah insiders with an axe to grind. One *Financial Times* journalist had been called by the marketing team at HSBC a year earlier in 2011, asking for all references to HSBC to be removed from the *FT*'s annual Islamic finance supplement. It seemed a little odd given HSBC's immense standing in the industry (and their historical support for the supplement) but the journalist complied. 'There was apparently some internal tension about Islamic finance', she told me. 'They didn't want to be too forward in their support for the industry.' How odd, when they were riding so high.

Now the senior Amanah banker, the former protégé of Iqbal Khan, contemplates his future. He's looking into the restaurant business and thinks maybe the banking game is over for him. Eighteen years of hard-won experience at the coal face of international Islamic capital markets will be coming to an end.

He is not alone. UBS's talented Hussein Hassan – the ex-Deutsche banker who wrote the White Paper (and not the scholar, Sheikh Hussain Hamed Hassan) – ponders life as a farmer in his native Kenya as UBS, too, exits the business. A short while later he enters through the revolving door at JP Morgan, which continues to blow hot and cold on Islamic finance. This week, it's back in fashion.

Deutsche's innovator Geert Bossuyt departed in a shutdown of Deutsche's Islamic activities some years ago but opted to stay in the game by acting as a consultant to the banks. His ill-fated advisory firm took on the Goldman Sachs mandate, and folded a year later. Despite the setback, he is quietly confident that the industry desperately needs his brand of highbrow technical advice. At the same coffee shop in Dubai where the advisor on the Goldman transaction had earlier pleaded his case, Bossuyt tells me he recognizes that a bank is not an Islamic concept, forcing bankers like him to squeeze a square peg into a round hole. And though his industry reputation is that of a conventional super-banker getting the toughest deals done by any means necessary – 'conservative products for conservative investors and aggressive products for aggressive investors' – on this occasion he says he advised Goldman to ensure that the use of the fund raised by the *sukuk* issuance should be Sharia compliant. His client and its legal team ignored him.

Amanah founder Iqbal Khan has turned his attention away from banking to private equity, perhaps reasoning that equity-like products are closer to the spirit of Islamic finance. If the regional banks are to take up the slack where HSBC and others left off, they will have a smaller base of experienced and talented executives to choose from. And yet, somehow Iqbal Khan remains optimistic. We spend a few minutes together in a conference ante-room before a panel session is due to start. Isn't he sad to see his legacy being ripped apart?

'Sad? No, not at all. This decision must have been made with the best interests of HSBC at heart', he tells me, diplomatically skirting the nasty business of corporate politics. 'The whole banking industry has suffered in this crisis and Islamic finance is no exception. It is no doubt a very rational decision and we need to be less emotional about such things. I was immensely privileged to work with my colleagues at HSBC and proud of what they have become. They've gone on to do great things.'

That's his legacy as far as he's concerned, not the bank itself. I sense he is quite emotional about his staff, moulded in his own image to disseminate a philosophy of ethical banking, and there's no doubt in my mind that his pride in his legacy is sincere. His staff were like his children, mentored and protected by him. Now grown up and flown the nest, they are dispersed throughout the world to spread the good Gospel.

Away from the banking industry, Iqbal's private equity firm is concerned primarily with taking risk by buying and selling assets – real trade, perhaps what a 'merchant' bank should be doing. This is a departure from his former life as a provider of banking products to bank customers. Maybe Iqbal Khan has discovered he is more comfortable dealing in equity – risk-sharing – than debt, where risk is firmly passed on to the borrower. In his Amanah days he had not been an advocate of the burgeoning Islamic derivatives industry, focusing instead on the simple day-to-day products that retail customers wanted. Maybe, like Iqbal, there is a critical mass of industry specialists – many of them Amanah alumni – becoming increasingly uncomfortable with 'reverse-engineering' financial products so that conventional products can be deemed Sharia compliant with the mere addition of a 'wrapper'.

On the subject of the fate of the Islamic finance industry, especially in the light of the setback to his beloved alma mater, Iqbal takes a typically philosophical – or, if you like, Islamic – view. 'Allah the Glorified and Exalted[7] has a plan', he reassures me with the utmost confidence. 'He hasn't surrendered the remote control of the world to Mr Obama or anyone else. From a historical perspective, the first Islamic finance transactions [of the modern era] were *musharaka* in nature – sharing in profits and losses of ventures, real economy. But the universal banking model took over as people searched for debt-like products. Private equity is inherently suited to Islamic finance. And it will come back. The institutional sector will open up – the leverage model is dead. Asset managers will look to the real economy and share in its returns.'

The man who replaced Iqbal Khan as the head of Amanah

has also stepped down. He had read the writing on the wall six months earlier, as global markets bounced along the bottom of the curve, and big banks looked for scapegoats and easy fixes to allay shareholder concerns. Back then, he approached HSBC's arch rival, Standard Chartered, to open his own personal bank account, reasoning that only they could offer the same level of retail service as HSBC globally and on an Islamic basis. With a wry smile on his face reflecting the irony of a bank's CEO opening a checking account with his greatest rival, he says he will remain a StanChart customer 'until such time as they take a similar decision'.

So is that it, then, for the Islamic finance industry? The withdrawal of the flow monsters, the creative innovators with big balance sheets and legions of sales personnel marching across the world?

'The industry should rejoice', he says when I ask him if he is sad about HSBC's withdrawal. The little guys are the ones who suffer from HSBC's presence. If it stays in the industry for ever, it would 'mop them up', he says.[8] 'There can be local institutions who can step into our shoes and lead [the industry].'

But the smaller wholly Islamic institutions are hamstrung. Operating under the same rules as conventional institutions, they are forced to offer debt-like products so that they set aside the same proportion of their balance sheet to cope with potential shocks, as their regulators require them to. The moment they begin operating as a manager of deposits, a 'merchant' trading inventory rather than lending money, they cease to be a bank and their funding costs become prohibitively expensive.

And so they find themselves forced to revert to their default product: a commodity *murabaha* loan, without which they do not exist. Even the sale and leaseback structure – the *ijara* – as used in the majority of *sukuk* transactions, has been criticized by some, despite its attachment to a real asset. A minority of detractors deem it to conform to the industry's need to seek abnormal rents by leveraging assets and thus gearing up investor returns. For these detractors, including Professor El-Gamal, the focus on slavishly replicating the debt model of conventional finance gives Islamic finance no unique or ethical character. According to him, there is nothing uniquely 'Islamic' about it:

> if Islamic financial providers were to focus on the substance of Islamic jurisprudence instead of its forms, they can explain to customers that some – but not all – forms of debt are harmful, and some – but not all – forms of interest are harmful.[9]. . .In the area of Islamic finance, one could argue that the unique power of religious injunctions (especially against *riba* and *gharar* [uncertainty]) is that they protect individuals from temporary greed-driven heightening of their appetites for risk. Alas, by shunning mutuality and adopting some of the most transparent forms of Sharia arbitrage, the regulatory substance of the Sharia has been squandered, while adherence to its forms has continued tragically in the shallowest way.[10]

Ouch. Perhaps he might concur, then, with both the Vatican and also a former Achbishop of Canterbury, the head of the Church of England and the symbolic head of the worldwide Anglican Community. Archbishop Rowan Williams wrote to the *Financial Times* in November 2011, a few days after the Vatican had published a bold forty-one-page statement calling for the establishment of a 'global public authority' and a 'central world bank'.[11] Protesters with no specific agenda other than a rage against what they saw as the disastrous effects of global capitalism had camped out on Wall Street and outside London's St Paul's Cathedral. The Archbishop marvelled at how the Church of England could still be used by British society as a stage 'on which to conduct by proxy the arguments that society itself does not know how to handle'.[12]

'The Church of England and the Church Universal have a proper interest in the ethics of the financial world and in the question of whether our financial practices serve those who need to be served – or have simply become idols that themselves demand uncritical service.'[13]

Condemning the 'idolatory of the market' and 'neo-liberal thinking', the Vatican called on the world to examine the principles and the moral values at the basis of social coexistence. It warned that society would head towards an abyss of growing hostility and violence, ultimately undermining 'the very foundations of democratic institutions, even the ones considered most solid'. It was, in short, suggesting the end of civilization as we know it unless solutions were found to 'injustice'. At a press conference, the Cardinal responsible for the document questioned whether those on Wall Street '[are] actually serving the interests of humanity and the common good'.[14]

These fine sentiments were spectacularly overshadowed by an own goal two years later from Williams's successor, the Rt Revd Justin Welby, a former oil industry executive and a member of the Parliamentary Commission on Banking Standards. Wading into the public debate over high-street 'payday' lenders charging vulnerable borrowers usurious rates – 5,853 per cent annually being a typical and scarcely believable example[15] – Welby vowed to put payday lenders out of business by using the Church to build up Britain's network of credit unions. Welby told the *Financial Times* that he would compete against Wonga – one of the UK's leading payday lenders – and put it out of existence. A day later, the *Financial Times* discovered that the Church of England had itself indirectly invested in Wonga[16] and the Archbishop declared himself 'embarrassed' and 'irritated' to have discovered the holding.[17]

Despite the Church taking an active role in the debate over ethical banking recently, its message on usury had been undermined. Keeping track of the Church's pension fund investments would have been no easy task, with holdings across 'a diversified portfolio including equities, real estate and alternative investment strategies'. That latter asset class – alternative investments – gives me some cause for concern. These include, after all, hedge funds, many of whom aggressively leverage their holdings with debt, and engage in ruthless trading strategies that maximize the pursuit of profit above all else. Leverage, shorting, event arbitrage, credit default swaps, complex derivatives – these are all instruments and techniques used by hedge fund managers to generate absolute returns. And though the Church publicly declares its commitment to manage its assets in a way that reflects the Church's teachings and values, as well as being a signatory to the UN Principles for Responsible Investment, it might not have found itself in this embarrassing predicament had it – ironically – asked a Sharia -compliant asset manager to invest and monitor its holdings.

And quite what Jesus would have made of Welby's stated intent to open his network of 15,000 church premises to existing credit unions and offering volunteers to help run them – in an attempt to compete Wonga out of business – God only knows. Perhaps the only recorded instance of Jesus striking down with great vengeance and furious anger[18] took place against the money changers in Herod's Temple – and today the Church of England is inviting the moneylenders back in.

Pointing the finger of blame at individuals, however, is not constructive and is plainly wrong. The Archbishop can hardly be personally responsible for monitoring the billions of dollars his fund managers oversee. The Church's lively engagement with the banking industry over the past few years has seen valuable contributions such as that of the Church Commissioners' fund, an endowment worth £5.5 billion, taking part in the 'Shareholder Spring' of 2012 to express concern over executive pay, complaining to 200 of the UK's largest companies, and seeking assurances from Barclays – one of the most prominent transgressors in recent banking scandals – that it was making a 'determined and successful effort to effect a fundamental turnaround in culture'.[19] The fund even sold off shares in News Corporation as a result of failing to allay the Church's concerns over corporate governance, the kind of action of which the Sharia board of an Islamic bank might approve. There are, despite the recent controversy, strong similarities in values between the Church and Islam when it comes to finance.

And though Christianity and Islam seem to have a common sense of morality and justice in matters of wealth, one does not have to be religious to recognize the shortcomings of modern financial markets. The founder of the annual World Economic Forum – where Mufti Taqi Usmani had delivered his lecture on reformation of the economic system only a couple of years earlier – acknowledged 'a general morality gap'.

'We are in an era of profound change that urgently requires new ways of thinking instead of more business-as-usual', said Klaus Schwab. 'Capitalism in its current form has no place in the world around us.'[20]

But what new ways of thinking are required and, just as importantly, how to implement these reforms? For the Vatican, the practical solution pivoted on minimizing the damage of certain practices rather than a radical rethink of the nature of money itself. Among some of the bolder rhetoric on establishing a global authority, it also suggested pragmatic incremental changes. Routine banking business should be clearly separated from speculative transactions – in other words, the separation of the high-street retail banks from the more risky investment banks. Banks should be recapitalized by public money and in return should be obliged to help reinvigorate the real economy. And, finally, the financial transaction tax, more popularly known as the 'Robin Hood Tax' – a 0.05 per cent tax levied on all share, bond, currency and derivative transactions – should be imposed on financial institutions with the resulting funds designated for investment in the real economy.

Is this enough? Do these tweaks to the financial regulatory system address the moral agenda of the protesters at St Paul's? Is Islamic finance's risk-sharing model a more far-reaching solution?

And do Muslims – and indeed non-Muslims looking for ethical ways to invest and finance themselves – really want a true risk-sharing model? Because if they don't, then those like Tarek El Diwany, the cult figure fighting a one-man crusade against *riba*, must give up. If no one wants to buy what he is selling, then he too must turn to opening a restaurant or running a farm.

I catch up with Tarek in the City of London shortly after HSBC's shock announcement. Despite the freezing conditions, he wears a short-sleeved shirt and light-brown sports jacket, making me feel very self-conscious in my distinctly City attire. He bounds up to me, apologizing profusely for the lateness of his train into Liverpool Street Station, and extends a hearty handshake full of his trademark energy and enthusiasm.

We discuss home financing using real profit-and-loss sharing, and the prevalence of debt-like structures at Islamic institutions in Britain. We concur they have been a failure: a failure to engage the Muslim community, a failure to differentiate themselves from conventional banks. We agree that Islamic finance should have been about bringing something wholesome and beneficial to everyone, irrespective of creed.

Over the years, he has found himself fighting the views of scholars, the standard bearers of Sharia. So much so, that some refused to be on the same panel as him at conferences, refusing even to engage. 'They didn't have an answer, and the best way to appear not to be wrong is not to engage in the first place', he says. He found himself relegated to the final afternoon slot on the second day of conferences, talking to an empty room. Eventually, conference organizers didn't invite him at all.

As if the frothing-at-the-mouth opinion pieces in British tabloid newspapers hadn't already twisted the lay public's perception of Sharia or Islamic finance through the peddling of deliberate misinformation, Tarek feels that his own people are unwilling to change the status quo.

We look across the table at each other, depressed. Even I'm having my own existential crisis. In the course of my work in the industry, I've structured and sold everything. Every product, every asset class, every structural variation. Ultimately my clients (investors) and my employers (banks) want the same thing – leverage and capital guarantees. The former fuels the greed of customers, the latter requires clever contractual manipulation to arbitrage Sharia opinions.

Should we just give up? Tarek is adamant and earnest in his response. No, absolutely no. We have to keep fighting, he advises. We just need to be smarter about it. There are other guys out there, other Sulaimans and Tareks with phenomenal product knowledge and energy, sincerely looking to change things for the better. One day, that group of sincere and credible individuals will find their own critical mass, and create something unique. It will need a patron with deep pockets willing to change the face of the industry – deep enough that he doesn't need the infrastructure and resources of a Deutsche Bank or an HSBC to back his deals. Someone who views his investment as a *sadaqa* – a charitable act. A ticket to Paradise.

I visit Iqbal Khan to discuss a transaction with his private equity firm and before long our conversation digresses. As we analyse the specific technicalities of the transaction, he pauses and then springs a question.

'Harris, are you happy?' he asks, more than a little tangentially. For a moment, I am not quite sure how to respond.

I fumble my way through a nebulous answer and immediately wish I had been more honest. The truth is, not really. How can I be? Something inside is not quite right. For years I've peddled the idea that Islam offers a unique view of trade and commerce, and yet my working day revolves around replicating what conventional banks do. Sometimes, as in the case of the sale and leaseback *sukuk*, there is some justification for rent-seeking legal devices that use a real asset as an underlying. Though not all will agree, at least it beats the simultaneous buying and selling of copper on the London Metal Exchange to synthesize a loan.

If conventional capitalism – fuelled by the fractional reserve banking model – has spawned the private cartel that is the global finance industry – the cartel that President Thomas Jefferson warned us about – then the modern Islamic finance industry seems little different to outside observers. Surely adopting it in its current form as an economic model would only lead to the same slavishness to debt, cyclical uncertainty and wealth disparity that the world experiences under conventional finance.

Is the Islamic finance industry to be blamed for its own weaknesses? Perhaps not. Commercial pressures have forced the industry into a corner: without conventional banks to offer macroeconomic hedges and inter-bank funding, the Islamic institutions struggle to survive. Credit traders at powerful conventional institutions who transact with Islamic institutions want to see risk packaged in a certain way. Their credit committees don't believe in the cult of equity, only debt. They are banks, after all.

Regulators force Islamic banks to allocate capital to investment structures they lend on (like the profit-sharing *musharaka*) in a proportion that is many multiples of regulatory capital allocated to commodity *murabaha* structures. Tax authorities allow interest expenses to be deducted from taxable profits, unlike dividends on equity-like structures. And though their skill base is critical to the industry, non-Muslim conventional bankers dominate the industry, and they care little for the essence of Sharia. The more the industry grows, the more it does so by an increasing compromise of its once core principles.

'You must remain sincere and committed', Iqbal tells me. He advises me to continue to say no to deals I don't like from a

Sharia perspective, the deals that quite obviously flout the spirit of the law, and remove ethics from consideration. Don't let the industry dictate its terms. Let God dictate. 'In the end, your *rizq* is written.' Your providence, your wealth. God has already decided whether you'll die a rich man or poor, so you may as well do the right thing.

Something is dawning on me, though it's taken me most of my career to realize and articulate it. Like most of my fellow Samadiites, commercial realities have tended to dictate the manner in which we conduct our business. Any hint to our employers that one's life ought to be dedicated to the pursuit of truth and justice – to God, no less – would remove the veneer of acquiescence that ensures we keep our jobs. In our private lives, we tell ourselves that our providence from Allah is already written and that therefore pursuit of a permissible – *halal* – income is a righteous act, its converse a sin. The corporation, on the other hand, demands absolute submission from its employees; a faceless entity that forces us to consider money a morality so imperative that anthropologist David Graeber concludes all others moralities seem frivolous in comparison.[21] The structure of the corporation eliminates imperatives other than profit, encouraging executives to give little thought to '[firing] lifelong employees a week before retirement, or [dumping] carcinogenic waste next to schools. . .because they are mere employees whose only responsibility is to provide the maximum return on investment for the company's stockholders'.[22]

It's only when I have the chance to meet Professor El-Gamal in Houston that I am explicitly confronted with my problem. Driving through the Rice University campus, I am struck by how quiet and charming it is in the world of academia – how far removed from the bustling ant colonies of Wall Street and the City of London. It is an environment where a keen mind perhaps can better see the wood despite the trees. Nestled within these genteel green avenues is the Baker Institute for Public

Policy, where El-Gamal teaches economics, statistics, finance
and management.

I find the institute across from a large fountain, still incongru-
ously noisy and active in a deserted campus that has shut down
for the Christmas holidays. Inside, El-Gamal's office is lined with
volumes of classical texts on jurisprudence in Arabic from the
likes of Ibn Rushd, their colourful spines spelling out the titles
in calligraphy, letter by letter, across each individual volume.
They are oddly juxtaposed with books about Bayesian networks,
signifying the professor's wider teaching responsibilities.

He greets me warmly and I am immediately struck by his
easy manner. Dressed as one might expect an American college
lecturer to be – black polo shirt, slacks, a short grey beard and
neatly groomed hair – I find him exceptionally thoughtful,
introspective, and willing to exchange radical ideas without fear
of censure.

Indeed, in the opening exchange of words, he immediately
suggests to me that my chosen vocation is the result of incoher-
ent pietism. 'You're suffering from cognitive dissonance. So are
the scholars. They're all suffering from cognitive dissonance.'
Both blunt and likeable at the same time, El-Gamal does not
sugar-coat his views.

Though his manner is undiplomatic, his argument is right-
brained – nuanced and reflective. '[You're] not satisfied to admit
that the emperor has no clothes, never has, and never will. [You]
continue to refer to some mythical moral standard that a "true"
Islamic finance, whatever that may be, can offer to humanity –
not recognizing that there is nothing distinctively "Islamic" in
any of these prohibitions and financial views expressed by Taqi
Usmani or others.'

Wait a minute. Did he just diss Justice Mufti Muhammad
Taqi Usmani, one of the most respected Sharia scholars in the
world? And me as well, to my face! I am not sure whether it
would be expedient for me to feign offence, and robustly defend

myself, though in fact I am curious and looking forward to some refreshingly alternative views. What does he mean, I have cognitive dissonance? What conflicting views do I hold that make me feel guilt or frustration or anxiety? How does he even know that I am feeling this way?

For El-Gamal, Islamic finance is primarily about religious identity and has arisen from the writings of Islamist intellectuals of the mid-twentieth century, seeking to rid their societies of Western banking practices introduced during colonial periods. For these intellectuals, Islamic finance was a Utopian dream to rid the world of interest, explicitly prohibited by Islamic scripture. The solution for these intellectuals was to build all financial intermediation services on the basis of equity-based profit sharing, and the Mit Ghamr experiment was one of the first of its type.

But the dream of economic development and poverty alleviation was not to last. Islamic financiers began to approach the discipline from a practical rather than ideological standpoint: the use of legal devices – Sharia arbitrage – became rampant, and special purpose vehicles became the wrapping paper to restructure interest-bearing debt into rent or price mark-ups. For El-Gamal, these sale and rent contracts were spurious attempts to rename interest as profit or rent, for an additional cost that Muslims were only too eager to pay.

'In the ancient world, arbitraging *fatwas* was very difficult', he explains. You had to travel vast distances to meet prominent scholars and procure their opinions. 'Today you can arbitrage this ancient law written in the twelfth century and that's easy – you can run rings around it. [In fact] Islamic jurisprudence was written for society to shun risk, to shun excessive risk.' In other words, today we use Islamic jurisprudence to replicate what the modern financial system provides to everyone else, rather than to protect the weak and restrain our natural tendency for greed.

And yet, here we run into a paradox. If the proselytizing

faith of Islam is to remain alive and healthy, it needs to hold its own in an increasingly sophisticated and polarized world. 'You have no choice but to keep up', says El-Gamal. 'If the other side produces better weapons than you, then it would be lunacy to let others have a competitive advantage over you.' So he is suggesting that replicating 'their' financial products is necessary. Perhaps it's not even a necessary 'evil' – it's just progress. And it need not be approved by the faith, because it doesn't need to be. It's just finance. So do it, but do it ethically – according to the spirit of the Sharia. Reject these nonsensical modern versions of *contractum trinius* and *retrovenditio* to justify the existence of an industry that need not exist. 'There are many ways to sell your soul to the devil and using religion is the lowest of the low. For years, I tried to give the scholars the benefit of the doubt but not any more. A small sin becomes a large sin if it becomes habitual', he says.

For a few uncomfortable moments I'm anxious that I'm being exposed as a charlatan. He's right, I tell myself. Every inter-bank liquidity trade is a compromise. Every attempt to share in the risk of an asset that a customer wishes to finance is watered down by credit risk departments and regulators, until eventually the transaction that remains is one that the conventional bank across the high street can simply do more cheaply. No wonder the conventional banks entered this market in their droves when the market was booming – economies of scale and willing customers meant easy money for them.

I spend a few minutes trying to justify my motivations to the professor. All the arguments that Iqbal Khan and Tarek El Diwany have outlined to me: the daily *jihad* – the striving – that people like us undertake in our day-to-day lives, to uphold what is good. Without people like me, I reason, the industry would be filled with those who seek to milk it for personal gain, and ultimately will destroy it. So what, I shrug, the whole industry is a work in progress – even the cynical participants recognize that. We're working towards an ideal, an equity-based economic system, and – God willing – we'll achieve it one day. Perhaps the end justifies the means.

I don't feel I'm even convincing myself. I've had this conversation before, with Tarek and others. And though I refused to admit it to myself, I always left those conversations in that confused state of mind between the satisfaction that I'm doing something morally upright and noble, and the guilt that perhaps I'm trying to fool myself and my customers. I am experiencing cognitive dissonance. El-Gamal has heard the argument before as well. And though I know he's not convinced, he softens a little.

'Cognitive dissonance is very useful', he responds. 'It helps you to get out of bed in the morning and believe that you can do something useful.' He suggests that if I want to stay in the industry I should hold on to it. I'm not sure how to take that, but he seems so well meaning, I don't think he's mocking me. It sounds like sincere advice.

As for himself, he severed ties with his friends in the industry long ago. Not out of choice – it's just that they couldn't handle his outspoken views. The only scholar who has dared to agree publicly with his point of view is Sheikh Hussain, the octogenarian chairman of Dubai Islamic Bank's Sharia board. Perhaps it was the common Egyptian heritage that the two men share. Certainly both are close participants and observers of the Arab Spring – El-Gamal having just come away from a daily news briefing he provides for Bloomberg News on the current Egyptian constitutional crisis. The father of the modern Islamic finance movement, Sheikh Hussain, meanwhile, has been drafting Egypt's new constitution, culminating in an appearance on live national television to read the constitution article by article.

Perhaps these ties of kinship have helped El-Gamal to feel a greater degree of respect for Sheikh Hussain than perhaps for any other scholar in the industry. But despite this, El-Gamal thinks that even the good doctor demonstrates a little cognitive dissonance. Dubai Islamic Bank, for example, is the oldest existing Islamic financial institution in the Middle East, set up by the guiding hand of the venerable scholar in the 1970s and still to this day certified for Sharia compliance by the Sharia board that he chairs. And yet, El-Gamal feels that the bank continues to engage in the subterfuge that is modern Islamic finance. They were the guys, after all, who sold Deutsche's hedge fund-backed double-*wa'd* structured product to their customers.

Other scholars get shorter shrift. Even the most highly respected names are not close enough to the world of complex modern financial instruments to opine on the subject, claims El-Gamal. When it comes to the Islamic finance industry, it's not so much debt or even interest that El-Gamal has a primary problem with. It is the scholars themselves. 'Some Sharia scholars are cynical, but others have been picked for their compliance', he says, lamenting the dominance of a small number of individuals who define the industry by approving its products.

What upsets El-Gamal most of all is the fact that Islamic product manufacturers and their scholars pretend that what they offer is even required by the religion. He is right, of course, about debt. Debt itself is not prohibited, though some champions of equity-based financing might tell you otherwise. Indeed there are examples of the Prophet and his companions being indebted to others, though, it must be said, without the additional burden of interest on their loans.

'Islamic finance specialists are like gun manufacturers', he explains. Most people don't really need a gun, but if they do purchase one, their intent determines how harmful it could be. 'If Geert Bossuyt walks in through the door, I'm afraid', says El-Gamal. To him, the ex-Deutsche Bank ex-Dar Al Istithmar boss is the gunrunner to tribal warlords and drug dealers, like Nicolas Cage in the film *Lord of War*, selling loaded automatic assault rifles to the psychopathic and mentally unstable. Bossuyt, on the other hand, will argue that he is simply providing a service that people want.

Some will want to use that product in ways that may seem unethical, like the banker who wants to use the double-*wa'd* structure to buy a credit default swap – an insurance policy – on the default of a nation, even when his own institution has no intrinsic interest or exposure to that country. But men like Bossuyt will argue, so what? Who is he to judge to whom he should sell and to whom he shouldn't, as long as it's within the law of the land? If a man wants to buy a fire insurance policy on his neighbour's house, it's not his place to refuse.

But the law of the land was changing. As the European Union pushed ahead with its regulatory crackdown on trading of sovereign debt-related derivatives at the heart of the Eurozone crisis, politicians in the European Parliament were almost unanimously in agreement on the subject of ensuring market stability. Concerned about 'naked' short selling of shares and sovereign debt – that is where the seller has made no prior arrangement to borrow the security he intends to sell (even though he doesn't actually own it) – the politicians voted 507 to 25 in favour of restricting the practice.[23]

'Parliament has successfully fought for very strict conditions for short selling to contain destructive speculation', said one German politician,[24] little realizing how similar to classical Islamic jurisprudence were the restrictions against greed voted on by his parliamentary colleagues.

And so I leave my interview with El-Gamal both enlightened and confused. He may have the best of intentions but his increasing isolation from his peer group and the industry he was once part of means that his views have become marginalized and almost forgotten. It is a shame, as he has so much to offer; he remains right-brained in a world where the left-brained are honoured and rewarded. In choosing to take the path of academia over Wall Street, he implicitly accepted that his providence from

God had already been written. Today he tells his PhD students, 'I'm only going to teach you if you go into the regulatory side, so the system doesn't collapse. Don't envy the guys across the table, and don't demonize them.'

Islamic bankers and lawyers feel the same conflict inside, but generally internalize those feelings.

At a symposium arranged by a Magic Circle law firm, one of the world's leading Islamic finance lawyers gathered a group of scholars together for a day-long session on current deal trends. The workshop was intended to help the scholars understand the detailed commercial issues in real-life case studies, so that they would be better prepared in future to opine on their Sharia compliance. At the close of the day, the lawyer related, the scholars gathered their thoughts in a final session. One scholar hinted at the dissonance inside him, and set off a wave of agreement among his peers. It seemed that every scholar in the room was living with his own internal conflict, each human enough to have felt pressured into approving loan-like structures. With every new transaction, they would suggest an equity-based structure, like *musharaka* – the investment partnership – and find themselves gravitating towards either a series of additional contracts to mitigate the equity basis of the transaction, or instead avoid the complex legal device altogether and employ a simple commodity *murabaha*. The resultant structure would be debt-like and help their clients meet their regulatory requirements.

Each scholar was prepared to admit that he was participating in an industry that valued form over substance. Could they not resist? Would strength of numbers not give them the momentum to say no, and move away from reverse engineering? Apparently not. The banks were simply too strong and refusal to cooperate would quickly remove oneself from the game. As El-Gamal had said, scholars would be picked for their acquiescence, and those who wished not to participate would find their voice in academia, teaching students to be gamekeepers, not poachers.

So is the industry perhaps in a state of stagnation? The standard bearers want to move it in a direction that their forebears, the post-colonial intellectuals of the Islamic world, once envisaged. The banks and their regulators will not let them. I am reminded of a question that Iqbal Khan asks me before we part company. 'If you could be anything you wanted to be, do anything you wanted, what would it be?'

I wasn't ready for the question. In fact my answer was embarrassingly dumb and childish. I told Iqbal Khan – perhaps the most popular and respected Islamic banker in the world – that I would revive my stalled career as a racing driver; I stood up, shook hands and thanked him for his time. What a cretinous response. My pre-teen children could have answered the question better.

When I got back home, I thought about the question more carefully. The industry lacks a megabank with state backing. Oh sure, the Islamic Development Bank exists – a multilateral institution owned by dozens of Islamic nations – but it is a bank in the traditional sense. The megabank's premise would be mutuality and an equity basis, a sort of gigantic private equity firm with enough liquidity to provide counterparties with access to macroeconomic hedging and other non-debt financial services. On a mutual basis, like a cooperative insurance company, not using the derivatives we see today, just as Sulaiman had suggested earlier. It wouldn't be predicated on reverse engineering the conventional industry with Sharia wrappers. Its client base would be small and medium-sized enterprises, retail customers, the man in the street – not multinationals building luxury hotels for oligarchs on reclaimed islands in the sea.

As the first of its kind, it might even have limited commercial success. But it might also spawn a new generation of Islamic institution. One that will allay the fears and guilt of bankers, lawyers and scholars seeking God's pleasure.

And, just as Deutsche Bank had once established a think

tank with the aim of conducting industry-leading research
into Islamic finance, the megabank could sponsor just such a
think tank, drawing together the world's leading scholars from
Malaysia's central bank Sharia board to AAOIFI in Bahrain. But
rather than focus on setting guidelines and standards for the
industry – as AAOIFI and others already do – it would be run
by front office bankers and lawyers, not academics and scholars.
Its purpose would be to push the envelope on product design,
seeking better ways to deliver financial products without the
commercial constraints of quarterly budgets or balance-sheet
risk.

A Utopian dream for an incurable idealist, maybe. But doable?
Perhaps. In fact, perhaps the Islamic Development Bank itself
may move in that direction. Shortly after the Goldman Sachs
controversy, young Mohammed Khnifer accepted an offer
from the IDB to take him on as a product structurer, a sort of
free-thinking scientist given the tools to smash atoms at each
other in the name of fundamental research.

In the meantime, until such time as the concept of mutuality
moves out of the narrow world of Islamic insurance to the wider
world of Islamic banking – the next step in its evolution – the
existing industry can find ways to mitigate its guilt. Trade finance,
for example, is a perfect asset class to explore. Commodities
traders – companies that buy and sell agricultural produce, oil,
gas, copper, ethanol, all manner of raw materials – need short-
term financing in order to fund their inventories. Not being cash
rich, they typically approach conventional banks to lend them
money for, say, sixty days, during which time they buy the stock
from source suppliers and sell it on for a profit to end users.
Islamic banks can play a critical role in a vital economic activity
– they can finance inventory through a 'true' *murabaha*, where
the bank owns the produce and on-sells it to the trader for a
price mark-up. A real economy, merchant activity. Merchant
capitalism at its best, in the manner in which twelfth-century

Muslim traders introduced dynamic entrepreneurship to a primitive Europe. And an asset class that would solve the persistent 'gap risk' – the mismatch in tenors between a bank's assets and liabilities – that Islamic banks are prone to.

What about taking up the mantle on ethical finance? Instead of financing the purchase of English Premier League football clubs – complete with pork pie stalls and bars serving alcohol,[25] cleverly 'structured' out of the deal via a wrapper – perhaps Islamic institutions should take a greater role in championing employee rights and environmental concerns in the deals they finance – 'Sharia based' not just 'Sharia compliant'. Perhaps the types of assets they should be looking to finance should be the lifeblood of a real economy, the small and medium enterprises, rather than trophy assets for the personal enjoyment of ultra-high net worth princes.

I find myself reluctant to point the finger of blame at the scholars. The vast majority I have worked with have shown admirable personal characteristics and recognize the deficiencies in the industry they serve. They have shown remarkable restraint in the manner in which they have responded to criticism. Sheikh Yusuf DeLorenzo, for example, was the recipient of open criticism from Professor El-Gamal for his role in the creation of Shariah Capital's long/short hedge fund,[26] who described the marketing of the fund as 'near-fraudulent'. Sheikh Yusuf's response was calm and measured, scholarly you might say: 'Mahmoud El-Gamal has said some awful things, but what he is doing is important. Not only do I support his right to do it, but I believe what he is doing is important for the industry.' He goes on to emphasize the dangers faced by the industry in allowing the cynical and the acquiescent to dominate it, a view deeply held by El-Gamal: 'I am worried about the deviousness of some in this industry, and how this filters down to the retail level which leaves everyone open to participating in *riba* without realizing it.'

Despite the manifest shortcomings of the modern Islamic finance industry, there remains within it something wholesome in its participants' willingness to introspect. This introspection is a form of self-regulation, providing hope to people like me and my customers that it will evolve for the better. And though I find myself often questioning whether I and my fellow bankers and lawyers should simply give up and devote our energies else-where, something tells me that we'll get there in the end.

In an age in which Sharia is increasingly demonized, Islamic finance has the power to unite people of divergent beliefs. Of course, every now and then we read an opinion piece that Sharia law is insidiously creeping into civilized Western society and that right-thinking people need to take a stand or see their hard won freedoms dissolved. Or we may see politicians suggesting that Islamic finance is incompatible with Western standards of fair play, equality and liberty, as did one Australian senator who described Sharia as incompatible with Australia's Western values, and opposed the introduction of any form of Islamic finance into Australia.[27]

Perhaps that same senator thought that excessive leverage, the infamous 'liar loans' of the subprime mortgage debacle, collater-alized debt obligations backed by worthless pieces of paper, and that other 'socially useless' banking instruments were entirely compatible with Australia's Western values.[28] Perhaps he would also have been horrified to hear that the UK government had banned short selling of bank shares during the depths of the financial crisis.[29] As the softly spoken ex-Magic Circle lawyer, Sulaiman, had said when we met to discuss his disillusionment with the industry, 'Can you imagine a *Daily Mail* headline say-ing "UK regulator implements Sharia law to prevent financial meltdown?"' We wonder what the Australian politician would have made of that.

If there is something insidious, it is not the poison of a foreign law come to rob us of our freedoms, to enslave our women, bludgeon our arts and throttle our sciences. It is the belief that Sharia is incompatible with the mores of a civilized society. Was there a higher seat of learning than Baghdad's *Bayt al-Hikma* – the House of Wisdom – or a greater model of tolerance than the Muslim city of Cordoba during Europe's Dark Ages?

Just as there may be a witch hunt against Islam and all it represents, is there also an inferiority complex among Muslims, caused by a wider feeling of impotence against a sense of neocolonialism, a deep-rooted sense that the Muslim is no longer master of his own house? Some observers might argue that militant Islam is a by-product of colonial empire building, whereas the preceding 1,350 years witnessed Islam of a different kind, often gentler and almost always with a sense of justice unmatched in neighbouring societies.

Former human rights barrister Sadakat Kadri documents his personal journey of discovery of Sharia law in his excellent book *Heaven on Earth*.[30] And though not all Muslims might agree with his views on (for example) literalism in Islam, he reminds us that Western ways of handling criminal justice and war have many deficiencies of their own. He also concludes that 'no interpretation of the Sharia has ever been timeless, and Islam has never been doomed to insist otherwise. . .Islamic jurisprudence has not spent the fourteen hundred years opposed to change; it has been defined by it.'

For Kadri, an austere interpretation of Islam that has caused panic among some in the West is a recent phenomenon, one that runs counter to a history of transformation and inclusiveness. Over the last forty years, governments looking to instil an Islamic identity have favoured a literalist approach obsessed with punishment and cruelty, ignoring a millennium of legal development framed by the middle path and context. Islam's innate capacity to borrow and learn from other cultures once imbued Sharia with an organic and fluid vitality that adapted to the demands of a changing world. It was this inclusiveness and vitality that encouraged its early scholars to focus on those aspects of the Prophet's life that might have been summed up by his famous saying: 'Beware of going to extremes in religion, for those before you were only destroyed through excessiveness'.[31] In seeking to avoid extremism, the classical scholars looked to Greek, Persian, Byzantine and Indian civilizations for inspiration, taking what was beneficial and rejecting what the Prophet had rejected in his life. The most obvious beneficiaries of this approach were the natural sciences and law. And although, for example, strict punishments could be meted out to those who committed heinous crimes, early Islam had often focused on leaving the door open for repentance, forgiveness and mercy. Despite this, post-colonial Islamic movements seem to have ignored a historical tendency for a gentler form of Islam, one more in harmony with neighbouring cultures. Perhaps the modern-day Muslim leader, faced with an existential threat, looks to fetter the freedoms that once gave his people their greatest strength, and now views the West in the same monolithic way he may be viewed by them?

Perhaps Islamic finance is one of the ways in which to bridge that gap, to bring empowerment and wealth distribution at all levels of society, irrespective of belief. But the continuing demonization of Islam and Sharia means that the Islamic finance industry must engage in a public relations offensive. It must divest itself of the perception that it is somehow linked to militancy, that it is incompatible with Western values. It must rebrand itself as ethical, prudent, safe, reliable and as a contributor to the real economy – a creator of jobs and real wealth, distributed across society.

As the protesters gather on Wall Street and outside St Paul's Cathedral, and the world fights a double-dip global recession, perhaps now is the second chance for Islamic finance to prove itself. No more spurious industry awards and vacuous back slapping at conferences. No more replication of credit default swaps on conventional corporate bonds, no more Sharia wrappers, no more voodoo magic.

Perhaps even non-Muslims might concede that Islam can bring something to the world that the world can embrace with open arms, just as the world once embraced its contribution to astronomy, medicine, mathematics and the arts. The Middle Ages witnessed dramatic scientific, cultural and economic innovations in the West; not in the European West, but in the Islamic West as it would have been viewed from the perspective of regions such as India or China. Christendom and its primitive principalities slumbered whilst Islamic lands prospered. The translations by Muslim scholars of great Greek philosophers catalysed and melded with the revealed religious traditions of the Abrahamic faiths to advance scientific rationalism and merchant capitalism, concepts that have survived and are championed in the West today as its own invention.

Like Cordoba or Baghdad several centuries before, Islamic finance must now find its own centre for the pursuit of excellence, its own House of Wisdom. Perhaps Dubai is that very centre, and the bankers and lawyers of Masjid Al-Samad its heart.

Acknowledgements

Without Ehsan Masood's wealth of experience, I might never have got this project off the ground. His generous advice throughout the writing of this book nudged me in directions I had not previously given thought to, and I am immensely grateful for his time and efforts. Ehsan also introduced me to my agent Peter Tallack, whose invaluable assistance helped to make a first-time author presentable to my publisher. *Heaven's Bankers* is a reality thanks to the patience of the team at Constable & Robinson, and in particular Andreas Campomar and Elizabeth Stone.

I am indebted to the grandfather of the modern Islamic finance industry, Sheikh Hussain Hamed Hassan, who has patiently endured my questions over the last decade. His exceptional mind and force of personality have been a beacon for the industry, and he remains pre-eminent among his peers. Along with my fellow industry colleagues, I pray for his health and to continue to receive his guidance.

Three other individuals have helped to shape my thinking: Iqbal Khan as the inspirational leader who introduced me to Islamic finance, Tarek El Diwany for being the voice of my inner conscience, and Mahmoud El-Gamal for helping me to recognize my dissonance. Islamic finance is not an easy discipline. It is technically involved and politically fraught. When we enter the industry, we may be trying to hark back to the ideals of merchant capitalism from a bygone era, but instead find ourselves in conflict with modern notions of a greedy, self-centred, debt-obsessed, survival-of-the-fittest financial jungle. Sometimes we give up trying, and manage farms and restaurants instead. Sometimes we are forced to drop out of the system and comment on it from afar. And sometimes we acquiesce. Iqbal reminds me of a supplication whilst struggling against something difficult: 'Oh Allah, nothing is easy except what You have made easy. If You wish, You can make what is difficult easy.'

A number of people interviewed for the book declined to be named but were of critical importance to the narrative. They ranged across professions, from journalism to banking, law and Islamic jurisprudence. I thank them all for their generous time and unique insights. One in particular had the courage to speak out when he felt it mattered most, Mohammed Khnifer. Were it not for his youthful energy and fortitude – and of those like him – we might never encourage financial institutions to mend their ways.

My wife Sadia Irfan and brother Nabil Irfan diligently read and reread the manuscript, offering helpful suggestions and constructive criticism. Whilst Sadia was the voice of common sense and a long-suffering support during the book's gestation, Nabil's love of reading and finance – often at the same time – meant I had the perfect target reader. If this book is vaguely readable, then they must share the credit. Nick Phipps, too, was helpful and supportive in ensuring the final polish was applied the right way.

The Samadiites were a part of my life for eleven years, and it is Tamir Mohammed who brought us together, building a community without parallel, our own *Bayt al-Hikma*. A man of *hayya*, Tamir reminded me of a prayer reported to have been offered originally by the first Caliph, Abu Bakr as-Siddiq: 'I ask Allah to make me better than the people think of me, and for Him to forgive me for what they do not know about me, and do not take me to account for what they say.'

Glossary

Bold type indicates a cross-reference to another Glossary item

AAA (pronounced 'triple A')

The highest grade of credit rating – an evaluation of the credit-worthiness of a debtor. Typically, a credit rating is assigned by an entity known as a credit rating agency to any borrower on the basis of that borrower's ability to repay a loan. The agency takes into account various quantitative and qualitative data in order to assign a grade. The highest grade is often referred to as AAA, pronounced 'triple A', and describes a borrower with the lowest expectation of default.

AAOIFI

Accounting and Auditing Organization for Islamic Financial Institutions. A Bahrain-based not-for-profit organization established to maintain and promote Sharia standards for the Islamic finance industry. Its stated aim is to prepare accounting, auditing, governance, ethics and Sharia standards for Islamic financial institutions, central banks and other participants in the industry. It is supported by 200 institutional members from 40 countries, and is widely viewed as an authoritative body whose pronouncements on the acceptability or otherwise of contractual structures in relation to Islamic financial instruments are to be viewed in the same vein as regulatory edicts.

Absolute return

An investment return that is uncorrelated with the wider market, and able to extract profit perhaps even when markets may generally be in decline. They are so called because they tend to **hedge** their positions to movements in markets, for example by 'going long' (or buying) certain stocks, whilst simultaneously 'going short' (or selling, see **short sale**) other stocks. This natural balancing act means that they may find positive returns in markets whether those markets are bullish (rising) or bearish (falling).

Arbun

A commercial purchase contract that allows a downpayment by a buyer towards the purchase of an item from a seller, akin to a modern financial call **option**: if the buyer opts to complete the sale, the *arbun* counts towards the total purchase price; if the buyer does not complete, he forfeits his deposit. The *arbun* downpayment is part of the total price of the item being purchased. It is considered controversial in classical jurisprudence, and only one orthodox school of Islamic law (*madhab*), the Hanbali school, accepts it as a valid contract. However, modern Islamic finance has tended to adopt this view.

Asset-backed

In conventional finance, an asset-backed **security** is one that derives its income from a specified pool of underlying assets (such as rental income from real estate). These assets are therefore described as 'backing' the instrument as collateral for investors, and are therefore 'collateralized obligations'. The asset-backed securities may be sold to general investors in a process known as securitization, and each security represents a fraction of the total value of the underlying pool of assets. In the event of a default in repayment by the securities to the investors, investors typically have recourse to the underlying pool of assets, hence 'asset-backed'. Similarly in the context of Islamic finance, a *sukuk* may be described as asset-backed on the basis that income from the *sukuk* is directly attributed to an underlying pool of assets. In the event that the *sukuk* fails to repay according to an expected schedule of repayments, investors may have recourse to the underlying assets. See also **asset-based**.

Asset-based

Typically, a *sukuk*, or Islamic bond, may not have direct owner-ship or legal title to the underlying pool of assets from which it derives its income. In the absence of direct ownership, there exists instead a contractual link between the financing and the underlying asset. The originator of the *sukuk* – in other words the company raising the financing – is the ultimate guarantor of the **bond**. The company guarantees the repayment of this **bond** through a commitment to repay at the maturity of the *sukuk*. As a result, the credit rating of the *sukuk* is in fact the credit of the originator (the company raising money), and not that of the specific assets that underpin the *sukuk* (such as real estate owned by the company). See, by way of contrast, **asset-backed**.

Asset class

A group of financial instruments, or **securities**, that have similar characteristics. An asset class may, for example, tend to exhibit similar risk and return properties, and be governed by similar laws and regulations. Examples of asset classes include **equities** (stocks or shares), **bonds, exchange traded funds**, real estate and **hedge funds**.

Bay al-ina

A sale and buyback agreement employed by some financial insti-tutions as a purported **Sharia**-compliant method of financing, although widely condemned by both classical and contemporary jurists. The sale and buyback is intended to produce the effect of an interest-bearing loan by employing two separate contracts, each individually compliant with the **Sharia**: the lender buys from the borrower goods for cash and then sells those goods back to him for a higher price on credit, the difference in price being the interest charged. The concept of combining two sales within one is universally prohibited and supported by various recorded sayings of the Prophet in the **Hadith**. See also *retrovenditio*.

Bayt al-Hikma
The House of Wisdom, a library and research institution established in the Abbasid period of the caliphate in Baghdad. It was considered to have been the leading intellectual hub during a period of scientific and cultural advancement of the Islamic world during the Middle Ages. From the ninth to the thirteenth century, its scholars translated books from other civilizations into Arabic and contributed to the study of mathematics, astronomy, medicine, chemistry, zoology and cartography. Often referred to as 'Dar Al-Hikma' (also translated as House of Wisdom), this second name was used to refer to the House of Wisdom in its later years, although since there is another Dar Al-Hikma founded by the Fatimid caliphate in Cairo in the eleventh century, for the avoidance of doubt this book refers to Bayt al-Hikma throughout.

Bayt al-Maal
The House of Wealth, a State-run financial institution established by the early Islamic caliphate for the administration of taxes, including the distribution of *zakat*. It acted as a conduit for the welfare state and introduced the concept of social security to the Islamic world. Its innovations included the introduction of unemployment insurance, retirement and invalidity pensions, provision for widows and orphans, public trusteeship, charitable trusts (see *waqf*), and food coupons.

Bond
A tradeable debt **security**, representing a loan divided into tiny pieces to be traded like a stock. The borrower is also known as an issuer, since it issues the bond on the public markets. The investor who buys the bond is the lender and is also known as the bond holder. The bond holder earns a stream of interest payments from the issuer, each of which is known as a **coupon**. Periodic repayments to the bond holder may or may not include repayments of the principal amount of the bond in addition to the interest **coupon**. Where a periodic payment does not include the principal, principal is typically repaid in full at maturity of the bond. In the event of a bankruptcy of the issuer, bond holders are typically repaid before **equity** (share) holders.

Bulge bracket
A generic term applied to the world's largest international **investment banks**. Since there are no precise criteria to define such a list, conventionally it is assumed that those banks occupying, say, a position in the global top 10 in multiple disciplines simultaneously – typically **equity** and debt **security** arranging, **corporate finance** (**M&A**) advice, and trading activities in various **asset classes** – would merit inclusion in such a list.

Burqa
A long outer garment, usually in black, worn by women in many Islamic countries, and often covering the face (but usually not the eyes). Generally not considered compulsory in Islamic law. See also *hijab*.

Caliph
The head of state and title of the ruler of the Islamic *ummah* (the global Islamic community). In the early years following the death of Prophet Muhammad, four men held the title of Caliph: Abu Bakr as-Siddiq, Umar ibn al-Khattab, Uthman ibn Affan,

and 'Ali ibn Abi Talib. These four are known by the majority **Sunni** sect as the Rightly Guided Caliphs. The minority **Shia** sect recognize only 'Ali ibn Abi Talib as the rightful successor to Prophet Muhammad. After the Rightly Guided Caliphs, caliphates were ruled by dynasties: the Ummayad, Abbasid, Fatimid and finally the Ottoman Dynasty that ended in the early twentieth century.

CDO / collateralized debt obligation

A type of **asset-backed security** that pools together income-generating assets into discrete packages – or **tranches** – that can be sold to investors as a tradeable debt **security**. The underlying assets of a CDO are typically debt obligations such as mortgages or loans that act as collateral for the CDO. **Tranching** of a CDO allows assets of a similar risk profile to be grouped together: thus **senior** tranches represent the least risky portion with a higher credit rating (see **AAA**) and lower **coupons**, whereas **junior** tranches represent more risky portions with lower credit rating and higher **coupons** to compensate for the greater risk of default.

CDS / credit default swap

A type of **derivative** contract that pays out like an insurance policy in the event that the underlying entity – a nation or a corporation – defaults on its debt obligations. Like an insurance policy, the cost of purchasing a credit default swap is a function of the likelihood of default by the underlying entity. The more risky the entity, the higher the cost of the CDS.

Commercial banking (also known as **wholesale banking**)

The provision of banking services such as accepting corporate deposits, lending to corporations, and offering basic investment products. In contrast, **retail banking** offers such services to individual members of the public. Not to be confused with investment banking, which is generally associated with activities related to sales and trading in the capital markets, and **corporate finance** advice.

Commodity *murabaha*

A variant of the *murabaha* contract in Islamic commercial law through which the subject of the *murabaha* contract is a **liquid**, tradeable commodity, such as copper. This form of the *murabaha* is typically used by banks to simultaneously purchase and resale a known quantity and quality of commodities to give effect to a cash flow that closely mimics a conventional loan contract. Where a commodity *murabaha* gives rise to such an effect, it is known as a *tawarruq* transaction and is considered controversial by many scholars due to its construal as a *hilah*, or legal trick, intended to circumvent the ban on usury.

Contractum trinius

A legal device employed by bankers in early Christian nations to circumvent the Church's ban on usury. Bankers entered into three contracts with borrowers: an investment, a sale of profit and an insurance contract. Each individual contract was permissible under Church law, but in combination the three contracts produced an interest-bearing loan, a transaction explicitly outlawed by the Church.

Convertible bond

A type of **bond** issued by a company that converts into a predetermined amount of the **equity** shares of that company at maturity in order to repay the **bond**. Sometimes, the conversion into shares may take place at specified points during the **bond**'s life. Where a **bond** converts into the shares of a company other than the issuer of the **bond**, it is known as an exchangeable bond since the **bond** exchanges into the shares of a different company.

Corporate finance

A generic term that may have a number of different interpretations, but generally considered the area of finance related to sources of funding and the capital structure of corporations. More specifically in the field of investment banking, the corporate finance division of an investment bank provides advice to its clients – corporations or governments – on raising new capital (such as the issuance of **equity** shares or **bonds**), acquiring or merging with new companies (including advice related to defending a company against the takeover by another company), and restructuring of a company's existing balance sheet. See also **M&A**.

Coupon

The periodic interest payment on a **bond**, or periodic profit payment on a *sukuk*.

Credit derivative

A type of **derivative** contract whose value is derived from an underlying debt instrument, such as a loan or a **bond**. Credit derivatives are typically privately held negotiable bilateral contracts and are often used to manage the holder's exposure to various credit risks. For example, a **CDS** is a type of credit derivative that may insure the holder against default by an entity to which the holder is already commercially exposed.

Derivative

A financial contract that derives its value from the performance of an underlying asset or mathematical formula. Simple derivatives include **equity** call **options**, which give the buyer of the **option** the right to buy a specified share at a predetermined price at some point in the future. More complex derivatives include **hedging** products and **structured products**. Derivatives allow counterparties in the derivative agreement to benefit from a pay-off in the future according to the outcome of future events, without necessarily having to invest directly in the underlying assets. Thus for example, an **equity** call **option** allows the investor in the **option** to participate in the upside of a stock without having to buy that stock.

Equity

A generic term that may have many different applications but in essence describes ownership in an asset after all debts associated with asset are repaid. Shares (also known as stock) in a company are a form of equity because they represent partial ownership of that company.

ETF / exchange traded fund

A **security** that is tradeable on an exchange like an **equity** stock and whose value is calculated as a function of a specified group of assets. For example an ETF may track an index like the FTSE 100 Index whose value is a weighted average of the largest 100 companies listed on the London Stock Exchange. Thus, as the market capitalization of the top 100 companies goes up, so too will the value of an ETF linked to the FTSE 100 Index. ETFs are popular with investors due to the convenience of trading in a market without having to trade each underlying share or security individually, leading to lower overall trading costs and tax efficiency.

Fatwa

A judicial pronouncement or legal opinion on a matter of **Sharia**. In the Islamic finance industry, a *fatwa* is typically a short document announcing that a qualified scholar has reviewed the legal and commercial aspects of a transaction and found them to be in compliance with **Sharia**.

Fiqh
Islamic jurisprudence. *Fiqh* is a detailed codification of the **Sharia** and is based on the **Quran**, *Sunnah* (actions and sayings) of the Prophet as recorded in the books of **Hadith**. Scholars then derive additional legislation by logical deduction, then by analogous deduction, then finally by relying on the social customs of the time.

Fractional reserve banking (reserve ratio)
The practice by banks of retaining reserve funds in an amount equal to a portion of customer deposits to satisfy future demand for customer withdrawals, such a ratio being known as the reserve ratio. The unreserved portion of funds is used to make loans to other customers or invest elsewhere. A 'run on the bank' occurs if a large proportion of depositors demand their money back at the same time. In such a circumstance, the bank may seek protection from a state-run central bank, that acts as a 'lender of last resort'.

Fund manager
Also known as an asset manager. The person or financial institution responsible for managing investors' funds according to a pre-specified investment strategy, for example stocks in companies operating in the emerging markets. See also **mutual fund**, **hedge fund** and **ETF**.

Funduq
A trading exchange prevalent in the major cities of the Middle East during the Middle Ages. Originally functioning as lodgings for pilgrims and travelling merchants, *funduqs* evolved into storage facilities and then into trading centres for rulers and leading merchant families in the region. The evolution of *funduqs* into commodity exchanges and warehouses enabled merchant families to finance state projects and operate an early form of

banking institution, taking in deposits and advancing credit to customers.

GCC
Gulf Cooperation Council, comprising Saudi Arabia, the UAE, Bahrain, Kuwait, Qatar and Oman.

Gharar
Uncertainty in a contract under Islamic commercial law, prohibited by the **Sharia**. Uncertainty is defined as lack of knowledge of the subject matter, such as the failure to identify the subject matter of the contract or the failure to determine the contract; lack of knowledge of the price of the subject matter, or the quantity, or the deferred period of delivery if there is one; lack of knowledge of the existence or the impossibility of its acquisition, including hindrances to its delivery; and lack of knowledge of its sound or continued existence. Uncertainty must be excessive in order to invalidate a contract. It is a condition of a sale contract that the seller must own the subject of the sale prior to selling, and that the seller has no right to sell something he does not own. Therefore, almost all **short** selling as conventionally practised in the financial markets is not valid in the **Sharia**.

Hadith
The books that document the *Sunnah* (actions and sayings of the Prophet) through a chain of scholarly authority. Hadith is often translated as 'tradition' but also means report, account or narrative. The life of the Prophet was recorded by his companions and passed through individuals according to a recorded chain of narration, before being compiled into large collections of books during the eighth and ninth centuries. The Hadith are relied upon as precedent in the codification of the **Sharia** into *fiqh*, or jurisprudence.

Hajj
The annual pilgrimage to **Makkah**. Considered an obligatory religious duty to be fulfilled by every able-bodied Muslim who can afford to do so at least once in his or her lifetime. Although the Hajj is associated with Prophet Muhammad, Muslims consider the origins of the pilgrimage to date back to the time of Prophet Abraham, and some of the religious rituals that comprise parts of the pilgrimage relate to events from the life of Abraham. See also *ihram* and **Makkah**.

Halal
Acceptable or religiously permissible.

Haram
Forbidden or religiously impermissible.

Hawala
A network of money transfer agencies established in the early Middle Ages in Middle Eastern cities to facilitate cross-border trade. This network would influence the development of the agency concept in common and civil laws throughout Europe.

Hedge / hedging
An investment position intended to offset potential losses or gains that may be incurred by a related investment. A financial hedge may be effected through a **derivative** contract. Examples of hedging include interest rate swaps that may allow (for example) a home buyer to fix his mortgage repayments at one rate of interest for a number of years before the loan reverts to a 'floating' interest rate basis (whereby it may typically track a central bank base rate instead). Another example would be a currency forward, enabling a company to fix its rate of exchange between two currencies at some point in the future. A hedge is not always effected through a **derivative**. For example, if oil prices are rising

and one owns a gas-guzzling SUV, one may decide to hedge one's exposure to fuel price rises by buying shares in a major petroleum company. This would be a form of 'natural' hedge.

Hedge fund
A fund that invests in a manner that generates an **absolute return** (a return that is uncorrelated with the wider market). Hedge funds employ trading strategies that may enable them to extract profit even when markets are generally in decline. They are so called because they tend to **hedge** their positions to movements in markets, for example by 'going long' (or buying) certain stocks, whilst simultaneously 'going **short**' (or selling) others. This natural balancing act means that they may find positive returns in markets whether those markets are bullish (rising) or bearish (falling). In recent years, hedge funds have courted controversy over their deployment of aggressive trading strategies that may sometimes help to rapidly bring down the stock price of a company, or over their excessive use of debt to buy investments.

Hijab
Headscarf worn by Muslim women, considered an obligatory item of clothing after the age of puberty, and to be worn in the presence of men who are not closely related. Covers the hair but not the face. See also *burqa*.

Hilah
Legal trick or ruse used in a commercial transaction to circumvent a **Sharia** prohibition.

HNWI / high net worth individual
A person with a high net worth. Typically, banks tend to view an individual as a HNWI if he or she has investable assets worth at least $1 million. Some banks further categorize individuals

as 'very high net worth' or 'ultra high net worth' according to parameters that may vary from institution to institution. Typically someone with investable assets between \$5 million and \$50 million would be considered very high net worth, and above this range would be considered ultra high net worth.

Ihram
The two pieces of unstitched white cloth worn by a male pilgrim during the **Hajj**. Its simplicity is intended to signify equality before Allah, irrespective of one's material wealth. *Ihram* also means the state of purity into which a Muslim must enter before performing the **Hajj**. See also **Hajj**.

Ijara
A lease contract. The *ijara* is often combined with one or more other contracts to give effect to a more complex transaction. For example an *ijara* with a diminishing *musharaka* allows a home buyer to finance the purchase of a house by sharing in the ownership of a property with the bank under a *musharaka* (partnership) agreement, whilst simultaneously paying rent to the bank under the *ijara* contract for the portion of the house that the home buyer does not own.

Ijtihad
Literally an 'exertion' or 'effort', describing the act of a scholar to expend effort in examining textual evidences in order to reach a religious ruling, or *fatwa*. Such rulings constitute the body of knowledge known as *fiqh*, or jurisprudence. Scholars are required to have a classical training in theology, law and Arabic (to be able to understand the primary texts); a comprehensive grasp of the **Quran** and **Hadith**, including the context in which each Quranic verse was revealed (and abrogations of such verses as appropriate) or the context in which each legal rite and pronouncement of the Prophet was applied; a sound understanding

of the derivation of Islamic legal theory, general legal maxims, and the objectives of the **Sharia**.

Imam

The leader of the congregational prayer in a mosque, or alternatively a title assigned to a prominent jurist. In the **Shia** sect of Islam, imam is a specific title accorded to certain individuals among the descendants of Prophet Muhammad who are believed to possess special spiritual and political authority over the *ummah* (community). See also **Shia**.

Investment banking

The provision of financial services generally associated with activities related to sales and trading in the capital markets, and **corporate finance** advice, including **M&A**. Investment banks tend to have expertise across **asset classes**, including stocks, **bonds**, **derivatives**, currencies, commodities, and alternative investment products like **hedge funds**. Investment banks may also trade for their own book. In contrast, **commercial** or wholesale banking is the provision of loans to corporate and government clients, and the taking of deposits from such clients as well as the provision of simple investment products; **retail banking** offers such services to individual members of the public. Investment banking may also be known as merchant banking, although merchant banks are conventionally smaller, more traditional institutions than international investment banks, with a more focused range of services. See also **bulge bracket**.

IPO / initial public offering

The sale of a company's stock for the first time to the public. An IPO typically takes place when a company seeks to grow its capital base without constraining itself with additional debt, and existing shareholders are willing to dilute their ownership of the company. The company – also known as an issuer – is generally advised by an investment bank and law firm throughout the offering process. The company's shares are typically listed on a stock exchange.

ISDA / International Swaps and Derivatives Association

A global trade association comprising over 800 member institutions in 60 countries with the objective of '[building] robust, stable financial markets and a strong financial regulatory framework' in the area of **derivatives**. ISDA is responsible for developing the ISDA Master Agreement, a legal document designed to make the execution of bilateral derivative contracts standardized and more efficient. See also *Tahawwut*.

Istisna

A contract of exchange with deferred delivery, typically used in the forward purchase of manufactured goods over time. Related to the *salam* contract, the *istisna* allows the buyer of pre-specified goods to pay either in a lump sum on delivery of those goods, or in instalments as the goods are delivered over time. The *istisna* is suitable for construction contracts whereby a bank may make payments to a building contractor in order to fund construction over a period of time. See also *salam*.

Jihad

Literally a 'striving' or 'effort' in the way of Allah. Scholars commonly refer to an inner spiritual struggle and an outer physical struggle. The non-violent inner struggle is considered the greater jihad by a believer to fulfil his or her religious duties. The concept of jihad also encapsulates a lesser jihad which is a physical struggle against persecution and oppression in both violent and non-violent forms. This physical struggle has come to characterize the contemporary view of jihad as a violent struggle against the enemies of Islam.

Junior debt
Also known as subordinated debt. A type of debt that is either unsecured against an asset as collateral or has a lower priority of repayment than another debt claim against a given asset in the event of the borrower's default. Since the junior portion of debt against an asset has a lower probability of being repaid in the event of bankruptcy or other credit default event, junior debt has a higher interest rate than **senior debt**.

Kaaba
The cubic structure draped in black cloth that Muslims believe has been in existence since the time of the Prophet Abraham, towards which Muslims turn five times a day to offer their daily prayers. Situated in the city of **Makkah**, every able-bodied Muslim with means is obliged to make a pilgrimage (the **Hajj**) once in his or her life. The Kaaba is the most sacred site in Islam and is the focal point of a ritual associated with the **Hajj** that requires pilgrims to circumambulate a fixed number of times. See also **Hajj** and **Makkah**.

LIBOR / London inter-bank offered rate
The rate at which banks borrow money from other banks in the London inter-bank market. The value of LIBOR is fixed on a daily basis by the British Bankers' Association and is the most widely used benchmark for short-term interest rates.

Liquidity / liquid
Liquidity is the ability to readily convert an asset into cash. The easier the ability to convert, the more liquid is the asset. Liquidity also describes the ease with which an asset is traded in the market without affecting the asset's market price – the easier an asset can be traded (for example the more shares of a company are in existence and are tradeable by the public), the greater its liquidity. Conversely, an illiquid asset is one that cannot easily be traded or converted into cash.

M&A / mergers and acquisitions

A specialism within **corporate finance** concerned with buying, selling, merging and dividing of different companies. See also **corporate finance**.

Madhab or school of jurisprudence

Sunni Muslims tend to belong to one of four schools of *fiqh* – or jurisprudence – all generally acknowledged to be of equal orthodoxy and ranking. Amongst **Sunnis**, there are generally considered to be four eminent jurists of Islam (**imams**), each of whom is responsible for an eponymous school of jurisprudence: Imam Abu Hanifa, Imam Malik ibn Anas, Imam Muhammad ibn Idris al-Shafii and Imam Ahmad ibn Hanbal who respectively give us the Hanafi, Maliki, Shafii and Hanbali schools. The juristic works of Imam Jafar as-Sadiq represent the school for the majority of the **Shia** community.

Madina

The city located in modern Saudi Arabia to which the Prophet migrated with his followers from **Makkah** in the year AD 622. That year became the first year of the Islamic calendar. Madina is Islam's second holiest city after **Makkah** and is the burial place of Muhammad.

Magic Circle

A term applied to the five leading law firms in the United Kingdom. There are no precise criteria to define the list of Magic Circle firms although they are generally considered the most prestigious and profitable British law firms. They include: Allen & Overy, Clifford Chance, Freshfields Bruckhaus Deringer, Linklaters and Slaughter & May. The five leading London-based barristers' chambers also constitute the Bar's Magic Circle.

Makkah
Islam's holiest city and the birthplace of Prophet Muhammad in what is modern-day Saudi Arabia. Makkah contains the **Masjid Al-Haram** and the **Kaaba,** and is the destination of the annual **Hajj** pilgrimage.

Masjid Al-Haram
The Sacred Mosque or the Grand Mosque. Located in the city of **Makkah**, it is the largest mosque in the world at the centre of which is the cubic structure, the **Kaaba**, towards which all Muslims turn to pray five times a day. The Mosque is also the main site of the annual **Hajj** pilgrimage.

Mezzanine
A type of debt financing that sits between **senior** debt and **equity** in priority of repayment. It is therefore not as risky as **equity**, but more risky than **senior** debt. It may or may not be secured by collateral and tends to have an interest rate that is in between **senior** debt and equity of that asset. Sometimes, mezzanine debt may convert into **equity** shares either as an intended form of repayment at maturity, or in circumstances where the borrower is unable to repay the capital and must offer shares in payment instead.

Mudaraba
An investment partnership whereby investors place money with a manager who invests or manages that capital on their behalf to produce a return. Similar to a *musharaka* except that in a *musharaka*, there may not necessarily be one individual assigned to manage the capital in the partnership agreement. Profits are split between the manager and the investors according to a pre-agreed formula, and losses are borne in relation to the amount of capital invested by each investor. See also *musharaka* and *wakala*.

Mufti
Honorific title given to a scholar who is qualified to provide legal opinions (*fatwas*) on matters of *fiqh* (jurisprudence).

Murabaha
A type of contract of exchange in Islamic law, primarily intended as a method of financing goods on a 'cost-plus' basis. Under a *murabaha,* a financier or merchant buys a product in the market at cost and sells it on to a buyer at a cost plus mark-up. See also **commodity** *murabaha* and *tawarruq.*

Musharaka
An investment partnership whereby investors pool their money into a venture to generate a return. Similar in concept to modern venture capital. Profits are split between investors according to a pre-agreed formula, and losses are borne in relation to the amount of capital invested by each investor. Similar to a *mudaraba* except that unlike a *mudaraba*, there is no single party assigned to manage the venture without contribution of capital. See also *mudaraba* and *wakala.*

Mutual fund
A professionally managed investment vehicle usually made up of a pool of cash from multiple investors. The mutual fund is managed by a **fund manager** who invests according to investment objectives pre-agreed with investors. For example those objectives might specify that the fund invests in European equities in the real estate sector. The fund may have further objectives such as defining to what extent the target investments generate either ongoing income or long-term growth. See also **fund manager**.

Option
A type of **derivative** contract that gives the buyer (or 'holder') of an option the right – but not the obligation – to buy or sell

an underlying asset. A 'call' option gives the holder the right to buy, say, a share in Microsoft at a specified price at a specified point in the future. Therefore, if the investor believes Microsoft shares will rise in value, he purchases the option for a fraction of the cost of the underlying share and redeems the option at maturity, recouping as his profit the difference between the market value of the Microsoft share at the maturity date, and the cost of the option plus the 'strike price' – the agreed-upon price of the share at which the option is exercised. If, for example, the option costs 10 cents and the strike price for the underlying Microsoft share is 100 cents, then if the Microsoft share rises to 120 cents by the maturity date, the investor would exercise his option and recoup 10 cents in profit (120-100-10). Thus for only a 10 cents outlay, he has made 10 cents in profit, a 100 per cent return. This is an example of gearing (since the underlying share rose in price by only 20 per cent). If the Microsoft share value were to fall (or rise to no more than 110 cents), then the investor would forfeit the option premium already paid since there is no point in exercising the option. In contrast, a 'put' option gives the holder the right to sell a **security** at a specified price at a specified point in the future. An investor would typically buy a put option where he feels that the price of the underlying will fall in the future.

Ponzi

Named after Charles Ponzi, an Italian immigrant to North America in the early twentieth century who defrauded investors out of their savings in an elaborate scheme. A Ponzi scheme is a fraudulent investment operation that pays investors from existing capital or from fresh capital paid into the scheme by new investors, rather than generating profits by investing in a defined business or venture. The scheme is sustained as long as it offers high rates of return to new investors who continue to pump in fresh money. A Ponzi scheme may sometimes begin operations as a legitimate investment vehicle, such as a **hedge fund**. However, if the vehicle unexpectedly loses money and an unscrupulous **fund manager** fails to inform investors, but instead decides to report fabricated returns, he may decide to continue paying high returns to investors by passing on newly injected funds from new investors. Ponzi schemes generally unravel when the promoter vanishes with his gains, or new entrants fail to materialize, or there is a systemic crisis such as a sharp decline in the economy causing investors to redeem en masse.

Prime broker

A brokerage service provided by **investment banks** to the **hedge fund** industry. The service typically allows the **hedge fund** manager to trade **securities**, and most significantly to **short** securities.

Private banking

The provision of banking services to **high net worth individuals**. In contrast, **retail banking** services are for the mass market. Private banking services are usually delivered through personal relationship managers – known as wealth managers or private bankers – and may include tailored advice to clients on wealth portfolios, personal loans, sophisticated investment and savings products, and treasury management facilities (such as foreign exchange).

Private equity

Equity in assets whose shares are not publicly traded on a stock exchange. Private equity firms typically trade the shares of illiquid privately held companies (see **liquidity**). Since these shares are difficult to acquire or sell (being closely held by a small number of private investors), private equity firms typically work more closely with the management of the companies to restructure them and/or enhance their value than is the case for

fund managers of **mutual funds** or other similar public stock funds. Private equity firms are sometimes referred to as buy-out firms because they may 'buy out' the publicly listed shares of a company, thus 'delisting' the stock and bringing the company into a closely held private ownership. Such an ownership forces a closer relationship between shareholders and management, and allows shareholders greater influence and control over the company. Private equity investments typically demand a financial commitment over a longer time horizon to realize value than is the case for publicly listed stock (for example, to restructure a company in a distressed situation).

Proprietary trading / prop trading
Trading by an **investment bank** using its own money for its own gain, and not using clients' money for the benefit of the bank's clients. Prop trading is not to be confused with the operations of a bank's **treasury department** which is responsible for prudently managing a bank's exposures to macroeconomic fluctuations (for example, currencies or interest rates).

Prospectus
The legal document issued to prospective investors in a public or private **security** by the **investment bank** arranging the offering of the **security**. Sometimes referred to as an information memorandum, offering memorandum or placement memorandum, the prospectus details the salient features of the financial instrument being offered to prospective investors. For example, a *sukuk* prospectus may include a description of the transaction legal structure, a description of the sponsor or issuing company, a set of financial statements for that company, the purpose of the money raised from the *sukuk* offering, the sources from which repayments of **coupons** and principal will be made to investors, detailed terms and conditions of the offering, and a summary of legal, regulatory and **Sharia** risks related to the offering.

Purchase undertaking

An undertaking given by the issuer of a *sukuk* that units in the underlying asset will be bought back at maturity by the issuing company at a pre-determined value, usually the value at which the *sukuk* was originally issued. For example, in a *sukuk* based on the *musharaka* (partnership) arrangement, the 'obligor' (the sponsoring company) would promise to repurchase the units of the *musharaka* partnership on redemption of the *sukuk*. This undertaking gives comfort to investors that their bond will be repaid by the obligor in full at maturity. The purchase undertaking has attracted controversy in the Islamic finance industry for its resemblance to a full and unconditional repayment of a conventional **bond** (an interest-bearing guaranteed fixed-income product) and hence a possible contravention of **Sharia** prohibitions on interest and guarantees.

Qiyas

A legal analogy. One of the tools used by scholars to derive *fiqh* rulings (*fatwas*).

Quantitative easing / QE

A monetary policy used by central banks to stimulate an economy when other tools of monetary policy have become ineffective. Generally, central banks tend to buy or sell government **bonds** in order to maintain inter-bank lending interest rates at a given target value. In contrast, QE involves the central bank buying specified amounts of long-term financial instruments from **commercial** and **investment banks** in order to increase the money supply in the economy, thus increasing the price of those financial instruments and therefore lowering their yield. QE is typically deployed when interest rates are near zero, when a large number of loans have defaulted or are non-performing thus preventing further lending by banks, and when there is a risk of recession or depression.

Quran
The central religious text of Islam, believed by Muslims to
be the literal word of God (Allah), and to have been relayed
by God to Prophet Muhammad through the Angel Gabriel.
Muslims believe the Quran to be a perfect document that has
been unchanged since its revelation to the Prophet. The Quran
governs the principles by which a Muslim lives and gives rise to
Sharia law in conjunction with the books of **Hadith**.

Repo / repurchase agreement
A type of financial instrument used in **treasury** management. A
repo is a form of short-term borrowing for a financial institution through which it borrows money from another party and
simultaneously sells that counterparty a security, promising to
repurchase the security at maturity of the borrowing. A repo is
therefore effectively a collateralized short-term loan.

Retail banking
The provision of banking services to the general public, usually
through brand name high-street banks. Services include, but are
not limited to, deposit taking, payment services, personal loans,
loans against assets (particularly home and car financing) and
simple investment or savings products. See also **private banking**, **commercial banking** and **investment banking**.

Retrovenditio
Literally 'selling back'. A legal device used by Christian financiers in the Middle Ages to circumvent the ban on usury. Similar
to *bay al-ina*.

Riba
Literally meaning 'excess' or 'increase' but commonly translated
as interest or usury.

Rizq

Sustenance or providence from God, believed to be pre-ordained. Commonly considered to refer to one's material wealth.

Sakk

Early form of cheque. Singular of *sukuk*, now more commonly referring to a note traded as a **security**.

Salam (not to be confused with the greeting of peace, 'salaam') A type of purchase contract enabling the forward sale of a commodity. In early Islamic times, farmers awaiting the harvest of crops would sell a pre-specified quantity and quality of crop at a price agreed today to be delivered at a specified point in the future. This would enable the farmer to lock in a price and receive money up-front. See also *istisna*.

Security

A tradeable asset. May be classified as, for example, a debt or **equity** security. A **bond** or *sukuk* are examples of debt securities. A share in a corporation is an example of an **equity** security. Securities are typically tradeable on an exchange.

Senior debt

A type of debt that has the highest priority of repayment in the event of the borrower's default, and is typically secured by the borrower's collateral. Since the senior portion of debt secured against an asset has a higher probability of being repaid in the event of bankruptcy or other credit default event of the borrower, senior debt has a lower interest rate than **junior debt**.

Shadow banking

The provision of banking services, especially lending, either by financial institutions that are not overseen by regulators (such as **hedge funds**) or by regulated institutions conducting unregulated activities (such as the trading of **credit default swaps**).

Shalwar kameez

Traditional South Asian dress worn by both men and women consisting of a long tunic and loose trousers.

Sharia

Islamic law, derived primarily from the **Quran** and **Hadith**. The Sharia is considered to be the infallible law of God (Allah), in contrast to *fiqh* (jurisprudence) which is considered human interpretation of the Sharia.

Sheikh

Honorific title applied to religious scholars and male rulers or male members of a ruling family.

Shia

Literally 'partisan' or 'faction'. The second largest denomination of Islam and followers of Prophet Muhammad's son-in-law and cousin, Ali ibn Abi Talib, who was appointed the fourth **caliph** after the Prophet's death. Shias believe that Ali was Muhammad's true successor as leader to the Muslim *ummah* and should have been appointed the first **caliph**. The Shia community considers certain individuals among the descendants of the Prophet – known as the **Imams** – to have special spiritual and political authority over the *ummah*. See also **Sunni**.

Short sale

Also known as 'shorting'. The sale of a **security** that one does not own, although this is usually only performed when the seller has already borrowed that **security**. Short selling is motivated by the expectation on the part of the seller that the price of a **security** will fall enabling it to be bought back at a lower price in order to make a profit. In contrast, 'going long' is the practice of buying **securities** in the expectation of a price rise. Where a seller has neither first borrowed the **security** nor ensured that it can be borrowed before it is due to be delivered to the buyer, this is known as 'naked shorting' and is considered a risky and controversial practice. Following the high profile collapse of various financial institutions in 2008, central banks and regulatory authorities in a number of jurisdictions enacted new rulings banning the practice of naked short selling, thus mitigating the possibility of market participants driving down the price of a company's stock during the global financial crisis.

SPV / special purpose vehicle
A shell company set up specifically for a narrowly defined purpose, often to take ownership of specified assets from which investors in that SPV will earn a return, a practice known as 'ring-fencing'. *Sukuk* holders typically make their investment in, and earn their **coupon** from, a special purpose vehicle.

Structured product
A type of complex **derivative** investment product, for which there is such a variety that there is no simple uniform definition. Like any **derivative**, a structured product derives its value from an underlying asset. Unlike simple **derivatives** such as **options**, a structured product typically allows the investor to earn a return on the initial investment which may be linked to a pre-defined strategy or 'basket' of **securities** or combination of different **asset classes**. Structured products may typically be defined through a mathematical formula that links the return (either an ongoing income or a capital gain at maturity of the product) to a benchmark or index. Examples of such indices may include the FTSE 100 index or even the weather. In contrast to an **ETF**, a structured product is typically not traded on an exchange but instead may be issued through a bilateral agreement from the

product provider (such as an **investment bank**) to the customer (such as a **HNWI**).

Subprime
A type of borrower with a poor credit history or one who has elected not to supply the lender with credit data. As a result, a subprime borrower pays a high rate of interest.

Suftaja
A letter of credit or bill of exchange used by merchants in the Middle Ages to facilitate trade along major trade routes without the need to carry large sums of gold or silver.

Sukuk
A fixed income investment product (that is one that pays a fixed running yield throughout its life), similar in economic profile to a conventional **bond**, but whose underlying contractual structure is **Sharia** compliant. As a result, *sukuk* are typically **asset-based** or **asset-backed**. Like **bonds**, *sukuk* are often listed on public exchanges and may be owned by and traded amongst thousands of investors in which case they would generally be **liquid** instruments – ones that may be converted into cash quickly and easily with a relatively stable price on an open market.

Sunnah
The actions and sayings of Prophet Muhammad that are recorded in the **Hadith**.

Sunni
The largest denomination of Islam and sometimes referred to (by Sunnis themselves) as orthodox Islam. Unlike the **Shia** community, Sunnis believe that Abu Bakr as-Siddiq was rightfully appointed the first **caliph** after the Prophet's death. See also **Shia**.

Swap
A type of **derivative** contract in which one party exchanges the cash flows of its financial asset(s) for the cash flows of another party's financial asset(s). For example, a swap contract that allows a manufacturing company to convert its dollar income into euros on an ongoing basis would be a currency swap. A swap that allows a home buyer to fix an interest rate for several years (instead of paying a rate typically benchmarked to a central bank rate on a floating basis) would be an interest rate swap. In both examples, a bank would normally sit on the other side of the trade as a counterparty. Swaps may be used for **hedging** or speculation.

Tahawwut
A template master agreement for **Sharia**-compliant **hedging** contracts developed by **ISDA** and the International Islamic Finance Market.

Takaful
Sharia-compliant mutual insurance.

Tawarruq
See **commodity** *murabaha*.

Thawb
Traditional ankle-length Arabic dress worn by men. Often coloured white with long sleeves. Also known as *dishdasha* or *kandura*.

Total return swap
A **derivative** contract that **swaps** the risks of underlying assets between two counterparties. As a result of this type of **swap**, each counterparty is effectively exposed to the full cash flows, credit and market risk of the other's asset without having to own that asset.

Tranche
A portion or slice of a financing, usually one that has collated the debt obligations of **securities** with similar characteristics, especially their credit risk. In a 'multi-tranche' financing, a borrower may have multiple loans of differing risk profiles. For example, a **senior debt** tranche will be higher in the priority of repayment to the lender and may have greater collateral assigned to it; a **junior debt** tranche will be lower in priority and may have little or no collateral. Tranching of a **CDO** allows assets of a similar risk profile to be grouped together: thus **senior** tranches represent the least risky portion with a higher credit rating (see **AAA**) and lower **coupons**, whereas **junior** tranches represent more risky portions with lower credit rating and higher **coupons** to compensate for the greater risk of default.

Treasury department
The division of a bank responsible for managing the bank's exposure to macroeconomic fluctuations, including currencies, interest rates or commodity prices. The purpose of a treasury department is not the pursuit of outsize profits, but to ensure the bank has sufficient **liquidity** to meet its obligations to customers, that it has mitigated its operational, financial and reputational risk and that its overall position in markets is prudently managed. Not to be confused with a bank's **proprietary trading** desk.

Ummah
Literally 'nation' or 'community'. Refers to the global community of Muslims.

Usufruct
A right of enjoyment, allowing the holder to benefit from an asset that may be legally titled to another party. From the Latin, *usus et fructus*, meaning usage and enjoyment.

Wa'd
Literally 'undertaking' or 'promise'. Used as the basis of Islamic **derivative** contracts, particularly in **option**-like contracts.

Wakala
An agency contract whereby the agent, or *wakeel*, invests capital provided by an investor according to pre-agreed parameters. The *wakala* is often used by Islamic banks as a mode of deploying customer deposits to generate a return for depositors.

Waqf
Charitable trust system developed during the early evolution of *fiqh* (jurisprudence). This legal form of social collective ownership gave rise to the trust law in later European legal systems.

Yield
Income on an investment, usually expressed as a percentage of the value of the underlying asset. Yield is earned on a **security** in the form of dividends (if the asset is an **equity security**) or in the form of **coupons** (if the asset is a **bond**). Yield is earned on a real estate asset in the form of rental payments.

Zakat
An obligatory charitable tax on a person's wealth intended to purify one's wealth, and one of the five pillars of Islam. Simplistically it is generally calculated as 2.5 per cent on the gross value of one's assets and is payable on an annual basis (per the lunar calendar, which makes it a slightly higher rate when calculated against a solar calendar). However, the more complex one's financial affairs, the more complex is the *zakat* calculation. For example, there are different rates for different types of asset (such as agricultural land on which *zakat* is due at either 5 or 10 per cent depending on whether the land is irrigated). One's intentions in relation to the asset may determine how

much *zakat* is due: if an investor keeps a property for rental purposes, then *zakat* is generally considered to be payable on the rental income; if the investor holds that property for capital gain, then *zakat* is generally considered payable on the market value of the property, since it is being treated as inventory for trading purposes.

Notes

Prologue

1 An optimistic view, but one that may have merit. Source: Rushdi Siddiqui, Thomson Reuters; at the Dubai International Financial Centre MENASA Forum, 24 May 2010. 'Islamic finance set to be a $2 trillion industry globally within five years': http://www.ameinfo.com/233491.html. By late 2013, Ernst & Young claimed that Islamic banking assets had crossed US$1.7 trillion (World Islamic Banking Competitiveness Report 2013–14, Ernst & Young).

2 The Kuala Lumpur-based Islamic Financial Services Board believes the Islamic finance industry's assets may quadruple to $2.8 trillion by 2015 from approximately $700 billion in 2005 ('Sharia compliant finance faces hurdle, lacks expertise, U.K. body says', Bloomberg, 26 April 2010: http://www.bloomberg.com/news/2010-04-06/islamic-finance-assets-may-surge-five-fold-to-5-trillion-moody-s-says.html).

3 'France's burqa ban: women are "effectively under house arrest"', *Guardian*, 19 September 2011.

4 'Enough is enough: ban the Koran', Geert Wilder's Weblog, 10 August 2007.

5 'Swiss minaret ban condemned by Vatican', *Daily Telegraph*, 30 November 2009.

6 Though this ban was blocked in November 2010 by a federal judge who ruled the law to be unconstitutional. See, for example, 'Judge blocks Oklahoma's ban on using shariah law in court', the *New York Times*, 29 November 2010.

7   Summary of 'Sharia Law and American State Courts: An Assessment of State Appellate Court Cases', Center for Security Policy, published on their website shariahinamericancourts.com, 21 June 2011.

8   'In Islamic law, Gingrich sees a mortal threat to U.S.', the *New York Times*, 21 December 2011.

9   Goldman Sachs as described by Matt Taibbi in 'The great American bubble machine', *Rolling Stone* magazine, 9 July 2009.

Chapter 1

1   Not his real name.

2   HSBC press releases and website, October 2012. See for example http://www.hsbc.ae/1/2/common/amanah-faq

3   'the industry has been growing at a compounded annual growth rate of 23.5% from 2006 to 2010', Razi Fakih, CEO of HSBC Amanah, 'The Growth of Islamic Finance', Chartered Institute of Management Accountants (undated).

4   For more information, refer to Michael Morgan, *Lost History: The Enduring Legacy of Muslim Scientists, Thinkers and Artists* (National Geographic Society, 2008); Salim Al-Hassani, *1001 Inventions: Muslim Heritage in Our World* (Foundation for Science, Technology & Civilisation, 2006); Ehsan Masood, *Science and Islam* (Icon Books, 2009).

5   Hereinafter, I omit the term of reverence 'peace be upon him', a rough approximation of the traditional Arabic phrase *salla Allahu 'alayhi wa sallam* – or the blessings of Allah and peace be upon him – when referring to the Prophet. This is merely intended to facilitate a little more fluidity of prose for non-Muslim readers in keeping with the style and theme of the book, though of course I (and Muslim readers) would voice this phrase whenever the Prophet is mentioned.

6   A consensus arrived at by various data providers, including Moody's, Ernst & Young and McKinsey & Company. See Prologue, note 1.

7   'The World Islamic Banking Competitiveness Report, In Search of New Opportunities', McKinsey & Company, 2010–11.

Chapter 2

1 Justice Mufti Muhammad Taqi Usmani, 'Post-crisis Reforms: Some Points to Ponder' (January 2010).
2 'Davos 2010 ends with bankers on the defensive', BBC News, 31 January 2010. http://news.bbc.co.uk/2/hi/8489946.stm
3 Quran, 5:3.
4 The Farewell Sermon, as documented in Saheeh Al-Bukhari from Abi Bakrah Nufayi bin Al-Harith as-safha ar-raqm 7447 and also Hadith numbers 1739, 1740, 1741; Saheeh Al-Muslim, Book 7, Hadith 2803; Imam Al-Tirmidhi, from Amro bin Al-Ahwas as-safha ar-raqm 3087; Musnad of Imam Ahmed ibn Hanbal, Hadith 19774; and others.
5 Ibid.
6 Ibid.
7 See, for example, *Abu Hanifa: The Quintessence of Islamic Law* (Harris-Greenwell, date uncertain); or Muhammad Abu Zahra, *The Four Imams* (Dar Al Taqwa, 2010), p. 123.
8 Muhammad Abu Zahra, *The Four Imams* (Dar Al Taqwa, 2010), p. 128.
9 Ibid., p. 170.
10 See for example Chapter 20, P. Sevket, 'Finance in the Ottoman Empire, 1453–1854', *Handbook of Key Financial Markets, Institutions and Infrastructure* (Elsevier, 2013); or P. Sevket, 'The evolution of financial institutions in the Ottoman Empire', *Financial History Review*, Vol. 11, Issue 01 (Cambridge University Press, 2004), pp. 7–32.
11 *Loans and Credit in Early 17th Century Ottoman Judicial Records, Journal of the Economic and Social History of the Orient*, XVI (1973), pp. 168–216, as referenced in P. Sevket, *Finance in the Ottoman Empire*.
12 'Most sukuk not "Islamic", body claims', Reuters (22 November 2007). http://www.arabianbusiness.com/most-sukuk-not-islamic-body-claims-197156.html
13 Al-Ghazali, *Ihya'ul-uloom*, v.4, (1997), p. 348, as quoted in Usmani.
14 See, for example, David Graeber, *Debt: The First 5,000 Years* (Melville House, 2012), p. 38.

15   Ibid., pp. 64–5.
16   See, for example, Nehemiah, 5:1–13.
17   John, 2:13–16.
18   Matthew, 21:13.
19   Tarek El Diwany, *The Problem With Interest* (Kreatoc, 2003), pp. 22–4.
20   Ibid., p. 23.
21   Ibid., p. 25.
22   Al-Ghazali, *Ihya'ul-uloom*, through Qal'awi, *Al-Masarif-al-Islamiyyah* (Dar al-Maktabi 1998), p. 52, as quoted in Usmani.
23   Tirmidhi, *Buyu'*, Book 12, Chapter 19, Hadith 1232.
24   Saheeh Al-Bukhari, *Buyu'*, Book 34, Chapter 55, Hadith 2136.
25   Tirmidhi, Book 12, Chapter 19, Hadith 1234.
26   Tarek El Diwany, *The Problem With Interest*, pp. 22–4.
27   Correspondence with Mohammed Amin in response to a review of El Diwany, *Islamic Banking and Finance: What It Is and What It Could Be* (1st Ethical Charitable Trust, 2010). http://www.mohammedamin.com/Reviews/Islamic-Banking-and-Finance-Editor-TEl-Diwany.html
28   Heinrich Böll, *Anekdote zur Senkung der Arbeitsmoral*, Norddeutscher Rundfunk, 1963.

Chapter 3

1   *The Four Imams*, Muhammad Abu Zahra (Dar Al Taqwa, 2010), p. 139.
2   Ibid., p. 148.
3   Ibid.: see for example pp. 149–50.
4   Quran, 2:275–9.
5   'The Text of the Historic Judgement on *Riba*', 23 December 1999, The Supreme Court of Pakistan, as written by Justice Muhammad Taqi Usmani.
6   See for example Saheeh Al-Muslim, Book 10, Hadith 3854.
7   'The Text of the Historic Judgement on *Riba*', 23 December 1999, The Supreme Court of Pakistan, paragraph 194.
8   Ibid., paragraph 195.
9   Ibid., paragraphs 11–35.
10   El Diwany, *The Problem With Interest*, p. 27.

11   Quran, 3:130.
12   'The Text of the Historic Judgement on *Riba*', 23 December 1999, The Supreme Court of Pakistan, paragraphs 90–106.
13   Ibid., paragraphs 116–69.
14   Ibid., paragraphs 43–54 and paragraphs 107–12.
15   Ibn Rushd, *Bidayat Al-Mujtahid*, The Book of Buyu', 24.2.5.
16   Mahmoud A. El-Gamal, *Islamic Finance: Law, Economics and Practice* (Cambridge University Press, 2007), p. 58.
17   Ibid., p. 59.
18   Safdar Mandviwala, *The Amanah Files* (unpublished, date uncertain), p. 4.
19   Based on interviews with a former senior staff member.
20   Safdar Mandviwala, *The Amanah Files*, p. 13.
21   Ibid., p. 15.
22   Based on interviews with a former senior staff member.
23   Archbishop Rowan Williams, 'Civil and religious law in England: a religious perspective', *Guardian*, 7 February 2008. http://www.guardian.co.uk/uk/2008/feb/07/religion.world2.
24   'Sharia law in UK is "unavoidable"', BBC News, 7 February 2008. http://news.bbc.co.uk/1/hi/7232661.stm.
25   Based on interviews.

Chapter 4

1   'Top scholar hails boom in Islamic finance', *Financial Times*, 1 June 2006.
2   'Family fortunes: the obscure origins of a crisis at a Saudi conglomerate', *The Economist*, 18 June 2009. http://www.economist.com/node/13876724.
3   Nassim Nicholas Taleb, *Fooled by Randomness: The Hidden Role of Chance in Life and the Markets* (London: Texere, 2001) and *The Black Swan: The Impact of the Highly Improbable* (New York: Random House, 2007).
4   Letter to shareholders, Warren E. Buffett, Berkshire Hathaway, 21 February 2003, p. 15.
5   Tarek El Diwany, 'Questions for the scholars', September 2007, http://www.islamic-finance.com/item146_f.htm
6   'PCFC Development FZCO Preliminary Offering Circular',

30 December 2005, condition 4.1 of the Terms and Conditions of the Certificates, p. 33.

7   Ibid., see for example Risk Factors: Acquisition, p. 21.

8   Surprise, surprise, it's the same head of MENA sales! Based on internal conversations at Deutsche Bank, *c.* late 2008.

Chapter 5

1   *Financial Times* Islamic Finance Supplement, 1 June 2006.

2   Declan Lawn, 'Comic Relief money invested in arms and tobacco shares', BBC News, 10 December 2013.

3   Ibid.

4   Ibid.

5   'Church of England invests in Wonga backer', *Financial Times*, 25 July 2013.

6   Euromoney: http://www.euromoney.com/Article/2762000/ Islamic-finance-awards-Deal-of-the-year-and-best-sukuk-deal. html, and Islamic Finance News: http://www.islamicfinance-news.com/pdf/doty10_results.pdf.

7   'The Day of the Locusts', *Time*, 15 May 2005. http://www.time. com/time/magazine/article/0,9171,1061439,00.html

8   Sheikh Yusuf Talal DeLorenzo, *A Compendium of Legal Opinions on the Operations of Islamic Banks*, English translation with Arabic text (London: Institute of Islamic Banking and Insurance, Vol. I 1997, Vol. II 2000, Vol. III 2004).

9   'When Hedge Funds Meet Islamic Finance', *The Wall Street Journal*, 9 August 2007.

10   Ibid.

11   *Journal of the Islamic Fiqh Academy*, 1993, vol. 1, no. 8, p. 641.

12   'The Shariah-Compliant Arboon Short Sale', Shariah Capital, 2008, slides 16–20, http://www.shariahcap.com/pubs/shariah/ arboon_explained.pdf.

13   Sheikh Yusuf Talal DeLorenzo, 'The Arboon Sale: A Shariah Compliant Alternative to Selling Short with Borrowed Securities' (2008), p. 6, http://www.shariacap.com/staging/pubs/sharia/ the_arboon_sale_english.

14   'Madoff Jailed after Admitting Epic Scam', *The Wall Street Journal*, 13 March 2009. http://online.wsj.com/article/ SB123685693449906551.html?mod=djemalertNEWS

Chapter 6

1 Tarek El Diwany, *Islamic Banking and Finance: What It Is and What It Could Be.*
2 Quran, 2:275.
3 Muhammad Taqi Usmani, *An Introduction to Islamic Finance* (Idaratul Ma'arif, 1999), p. 105.
4 See for example Ibn Rushd, *Bidayat al-Mujtahid*, The Book of Buyu', 24.2.3.1.
5 'The Text of the Historic Judgement on *Riba*', 23 December 1999, The Supreme Court of Pakistan, paragraph 227.
6 'Islamic bonds recruited for purchase of 007's favourite car', *Financial Times*, 17 March 2007.
7 *Islamic Alternative Investments: a guide to managing and investing Shari'a compliant private equity, real estate and hedge funds*, PEI Media Limited, 2008, p. 68.
8 'Pioneering Innovative Sharia Compliant Solutions' (Deutsche Bank, 2007), p. 9.
9 Ibid., p. 22.
10 This merits a fuller discussion, which is outside the scope of this book.
11 'DIB launches 5 year capital protected notes linked to DB-GSAM ALPS Hedge Fund Index', press release, 12 June 2007. http://www.ameinfo.com/123279.html.
12 'Questioning "Shariah Conversion Technology"', *Dinar Standard*, 26 January 2008.
13 Yusuf Talal DeLorenzo, 'The Total Returns Swap and the "Shariah Conversion Technology" Stratagem', in C. Beard, *Conventional? The Relationship between Islamic Finance and the Financial Mainstream* (Arab Financial Forum, 2008).
14 Ibid.
15 'Don't fear the riba', *Arabian Business*, 24 January 2008. http://www.arabianbusiness.com/don-t-fear-riba-122012.html.
16 DeLorenzo, 'The Total Returns Swap'.
17 Ibid.
18 Ibid.
19 'Don't fear the riba', *Arabian Business*, 24 January 2008. http://www.arabianbusiness.com/don-t-fear-riba-122012.html.

20 Confirmed following a reading of the Al Miyar platform docu-
    ments by a former Deutsche Bank in-house counsel who was
    directly responsible for the legal drafting of these documents.
21 Ibid. This is known as rehypothecation, where a bank or broker-
    dealer reuses collateral pledged by its clients as collateral for its
    own borrowings.

Chapter 7

1 Adair Turner (former chairman of the UK Financial Services
   Authority) interviewed by *Prospect* magazine, 'How to Tame
   Global Finance', 27 August 2009.
2 'Why Wasn't AIG Hedged?' *Forbes*, 28 September 2008. http://
   www.forbes.com/2008/09/28/croesus-aig-credit-biz-cx_
   rl_0928croesus.html.
3 'Mastering Sharia', *Risk* magazine, 30 March 2010. http://www.
   risk.net/risk-magazine/feature/1598877/mastering-sharia.
4 In fact, in the case of the *Tahawwut*, the Islamic contract used is a
   musawama, which is similar to a *murabaha*.
5 These can be found on ISDA's website, at the following url:
   http://www.isda.org/docproj/stat_of_net_opin.html.

Chapter 8

1 Variously ascribed to him in a letter to John Taylor in 1816, or in
   a letter to James Monroe in 1815, or in a letter to Secretary of the
   Treasury Albert Gallatin in 1802, and/or later published in *The
   Debate Over the Recharter of the Bank Bill* in 1809. There is some
   debate among historians as to whether Thomas Jefferson did in
   fact say these very words. It is certainly true that he expressed
   disdain and mistrust of banks and paper currency, but as to these
   specific quotations there is no absolutely definitive proof he
   has been quoted verbatim, since the earliest known references
   appeared some time after his death.
2 See for example Michael Lewis, *The Big Short* (W. W. Norton &
   Company, 2010), or Gillian Tett, *Fool's Gold* (Little, Brown, 2009).
3 'BNP Paribas Investment Partners temporarily suspends the
   calculation of net asset value of the following funds: Parvest

Dynamic ABS, BNP Paribas ABS EURIBOR and BNP Paribas ABS EONIA', press release, 9 August 2007.

4 Oliver Wyman, 'State of the Financial Services Industry 2011'.

5 Justice Mufti Muhammad Taqi Usmani, Post-crisis reforms: some points to ponder, (www.muftitaqiusmani.com January 2010).

6 'GMO Quarterly Letter', Fall 2008, Part I.

7 This example can be found in El Diwany, *Islamic Banking and Finance: What It Is and What It Could Be*, and Diwany, *The Problem With Interest*, p. 44.

8 El Diwany, *Islamic Banking and Finance: What It Is and What It Could Be*.

9 Variously also quoted as 'on the continent their Fathers occupied'.

10 See note 1, this chapter.

11 See for example Antony C. Sutton, *The Federal Reserve Conspiracy* (CPA, 1995).

12 *Richardson's Messages* quoting Andrew Jackson addressing the American people, 4 March 1837, volume 4, p. 1523.

13 Quoted in Sutton, *The Federal Reserve Conspiracy*, p. 21.

14 For a comprehensive discussion on present value and the opportunity cost of capital, see, for example, Richard A. Brealey and Stewart C. Myers, *Principles of Corporate Finance* (McGraw-Hill, 2010), Part One.

15 El Diwany, *The Problem With Interest*, pp. 13–16, based on an idea from Michael Lipton, University of Sussex, 1992.

Chapter 9

1 EFG-Hermes report, quoted in *Arabian Business*, AME Info, Bloomberg and other media, September 2008.

2 'Dubai property prices "will never decline"', *Emirates* 24/7, 20 October 2008. http://www.emirates247.com/2.277/construction/ dubai-property-prices-will-never-decline-2008-10-20-1.57497.

3 Also translated as 'ask Allah copiously' or 'make beautiful your plea [to Allah]'.

4 *Abu Naeem in Al-Hulya*, narrated from Abu Umama, 10/27.

5 'Dubai government statements on Nakheel, $5 billion bond', Bloomberg, 25 November 2009. http://www.bloomberg.com/ apps/news?pid=newsarchive&sid=auMhyjedmkps.

6 Ibid.

7 'Dubai index slumps to july low as Nakheel repayment date nears', Bloomberg, 8 December 2009. http://www.bloomberg.com/ apps/news?pid=newsarchive&sid=aGgRls83DqUc.

8 'Dubai recovery hopes hit by debt "standstill" call', *Daily Telegraph*, 25 November 2009. http://www.telegraph.co.uk/ finance/globalbusiness/6655687/Dubai-recovery-hopes-hit-by-debt-standstill-call.html.

9 Ibid.

10 'Nakheel Development Limited Offering Circular', 13 December 2006, p. 10.

11 From Nakheel's own literature. See their website www.waterfront. ae.

12 Maples Finance Limited, an independent provider of specialized fiduciary and fund services domiciled in the Cayman Islands.

13 Dubai Islamic Bank PJSC, see 'Nakheel Development Limited Offering Circular', 13 December 2006, p. 59.

14 See 'What can Nakheel sukuk holders expect in a default?', Blake Goud, Sharing Risk dot Org, 30 November 2009; and 'Dubai Debt Crisis: a Legal Analysis of the Nakheel Sukuk', Omar Salah, TISCO Working Paper Series on Banking, Finance and Services, No. 05/2010.

15 'Nakheel Development Limited Offering Circular', 13 December 2006, p. 36.

16 Sheikh Nizam Yaquby at the Euromoney 9th Annual Islamic Finance Summit, London, 23 February 2010.

17 'Property Law in Jordan, Kingdom of Saudi Arabia, Qatar and United Arab Emirates', Al Tamimi & Company (2009), p. 3. http://www.tamimi.com/files/Legal%20Brochures/property-law(1).pdf .

18 'Nakheel Development Limited Offering Circular', 13 December 2006, p. 46.

19 Ibid., p. 50.

20 Ibid., p. 46.

21 *Deals of the Year 2006 Handbook*, Islamic Finance News (RedMoney Group, 2006), p. 6.

22 '$10 billion deal agreed to help pay off Dubai World debt', *Arabian Business*, 14 December 2009. http://www.arabianbusiness

.com/-10bn-deal-agreed-help-pay-off-dubai-world-debt-10058. html.

23 'Dubai renames world's tallest tower Burj Khalifa – after ruler that bailed out emirate', *The Times*, 4 January 2010.

24 See note 4 above, this chapter.

25 Quran, 16:71.

26 'Saudi donates billions to charity', *Al Jazeera*, 15 May 2011. http://english.aljazeera.net/video/middleeast/2011/ 05/201151522136786875.html.

27 Translation of various articles in the Arabic language press. See, for example, http://forums.islamicawakening.com/f9/arabic-news-corner-46619/

28 See note 26, this chapter.

29 Forbes on Warren Buffett, 10 March 2005. http:// www.forbes.com/2005/03/10/cx_bill05_homeslide_2. html?thisSpeed=6000000000.

30 Warren Buffett, 'My philanthropic pledge', *CNN Money*, 26 June 2010.

Chapter 10

1 Not his real name.

2 *Hayya* is not easily translated into English, but shyness and modesty are a close approximation. *Hayya* is considered a highly desirable quality in a Muslim, though – not surprisingly – is of little import in the modern business environment.

3 St Cyprian, *De Lapsis*, trans. Reverend Patrick Cleary, *The Church and Usury* ([written *c.* 251CE] 1914).

4 'Translation of Selected Fatwas of Al-Baraka Seminars' – Seminar 6, pp. 81–2, Algeria, 2–6 October 1990.

5 From their website, http://www.ansarfinance.com/home-finance/.

6 For a detailed discussion on this, see El Diwany, *Islamic Banking and Finance: What It Is and What It Could Be*, pp. 261–7.

7 *Fatwa* regarding the Ansar Housing Limited scheme, Sheikh Haitham al-Haddad, 8 June 2006. http://iqtisad.blogspot. com/2006/06/fatwa-regarding-ansar-housing-ltd.html

8 See Chapter 4, note 8.

9 'Qatar slaps conventional banks with Islamic units ban', Reuters,

6 February 2011. http://www.reuters.com/article/2011/02/
06/qatar-islamic-idUSLDE71503A20110206.
10 'QCB move on Islamic banks draws flak', *The Peninsula*,
10 February 2011. http://www.thepeninsulaqatar.com/
qatar/142111-qcb-defends-ban-on-islamic-units-of-banks.html.
11 'QCB defends ban on Islamic units of banks', *The Peninsula*,
9 February 2011.
12 *Gerald Celente Hammers MF Global's "MF'ers"'* Capital Account,
RT, 14 November 2011.
13 Gerald Celente interviewed by James Puplava for Financial Sense
Talkradio, 19 November 2011, http://www.financialsense.com/
contributors/2011/12/03/gerald-celente/transcript.
14 See note 12, this chapter.
15 Ibid.

Chapter 11

1 See Chapter 10, note 13.
2 Mahmoud A. El-Gamal, *Islamic Finance: Law, Economics and
Practice* (Cambridge University Press, 2007), p. 177.
3 Goldman Sachs as described by Matt Taibbi in 'The great
American bubble machine', *Rolling Stone* magazine, 9 July 2009.
4 See Chapter 8, note 2.
5 His views have been reported by various media agencies, including Bloomberg, Reuters and the *Financial Times*. For the
full set of papers online, see http://reading.academia.edu/
MohammedKhnifer/Papers.
6 'Base Prospectus of Global Sukuk Company Limited', 18 October
2011, p. 60.
7 Ibid., p. i, p. 12, p. 15, p. 20.
8 Ibid., p. 13.
9 'Scholar row hits Goldman sukuk landmark', *Euroweek*, 6 January
2012.
10 *ADIB Scholars See Goldman Sukuk Non-Islamic, Al-Eqtisadiah
Says*, Bloomberg, 15 February 2012.
11 Based on conversations with the journalist at the WIBC in 2011.
12 Mahmoud A. El-Gamal, *Islamic Finance: Law, Economics and
Practice* (Cambridge University Press, 2007), p. 96.

13 Quran, 114:4–5.
14 Asim Khan, 'Goldman's sukuk: is the criticism fair?', for Reuters, 2 January 2012.
15 'Goldman Sachs Sukuk "all a misunderstanding," says top scholar', *Islamic Business & Finance*, 6 June 2012.
16 'Fake fatwa threatening collapse of instruments' (an approximate translation from the Arabic), *Al Eqtisadiah*, 18 January 2012.
17 See note 9, this chapter.
18 'High-profile Islamic finance firm Dar Al Istithmar closes', Reuters, 29 January 2013.

Chapter 12

1 'Goldman Sachs freezes sukuk due to criticism', *Asharq Al-Awsat*, 25 December 2012. http://www.aawsat.com//details.asp?section=58&issueno=12446&article=710184&feature=1.
2 See, for example: 'Citi, ITFC, Barclays Capital win IFN awards', *Arab News*, 6 March 2011, in which a Barclays Capital spokesman says 'This award clearly reflects our focus on Islamic finance. . .and [we] are committed to continuing to demonstrate our ability to structure innovative, tailor-made financing solutions in Islamic format', a comment apparently made in response to a Reuters report that claimed their Islamic department had been shut down.
3 HSBC press releases and website, October 2012. See for example http://www.hsbc.ae/1/2/common/amanah-faq.
4 'US Vulnerabilities to Money Laundering, Drugs and Terrorist Financing: HSBC Case History', Permanent Subcommittee on Investigations, 17 July 2011.
5 A study by *Forbes Middle East*, 18 June 2012, lists Al Rajhi with assets of $58.94 billion.
6 See, for example: 'Britain's a world-leader in Sharia banking – but we haven't grasped the sinister and dangerous implications', *Daily Mail* (online version), 10 February 2009. http://www.dailymail.co.uk/debate/article-1141087/Britains-world-leader-sharia-banking--havent-grasped-sinister-dangerous-implications.html.
7 A translation of the common Arabic phrase, *subhana wa ta'ala*.
8 Razi Fakih, CEO of HSBC Amanah, interviewed 22 October 2012.

9 El-Gamal, *Islamic Finance: Law, Economics and Practice*, p. 78.
10 Ibid., p. 165.
11 'Towards Reforming the International Financial and Monetary Systems in the Context of Global Public Authority', Pontifical Council for Justice and Peace, The Vatican, 24 October 2011.
12 Rowan Williams, 'Time for us to challenge the idols of high finance', *Financial Times*, 2 November 2011.
13 Ibid.
14 'Vatican calls for global authority on economy', Reuters, 24 October 2011.
15 'Regulator to investigate payday loan industry', *Financial Times*, 27 June 2013.
16 'Church of England invests in Wonga backer', *Financial Times*, 25 July 2013.
17 *Today* programme, BBC Radio 4, 26 July 2013.
18 Okay, so that isn't literally what Ezekiel 25:17 actually says, but you have to admit that Quentin Tarantino does have a way with words. What the Bible actually says is 'And I will execute great vengeance upon them with furious rebukes; and they shall know that I am the Lord, when I shall lay my vengeance upon them.'
19 'Church Commissioners' Fund Annual Report 2012'.
20 'Davos elites to seek reforms of "outdated" capitalism', *AFP*, 18 January 2012.
21 David Graeber, *Debt: The First 5,000 Years* (Melville House, 2012), pp. 319–20.
22 Ibid.
23 'Parliament seals ban on sovereign debt speculation and short selling limitations', *European Parliament News*, 15 November 2011.
24 Markus Feber, interviewed by Reuters, 15 November 2011.
25 Such as the purchase of Leeds United football club by Gulf Finance House, a Sharia-compliant investment house in Bahrain, in November 2012. See for example 'GFH acquires Leeds Utd for £44m', *Financial Times*, 21 November 2012.
26 'Near-fraudulent marketing of 'Islamic Hedge Funds', Islam and Economics, blog by Mahmoud El-Gamal, 26 May 2005, http://elgamal.blogspot.com/2005/05/near-fraudulent-marketing-of-islamic.html.

27 'Sharia or Islamic law is incompatible with Australia's Western values. I want to ensure the Liberal Party is opposed to the government's proposal to introduce any form of sharia-law banking into Australia', said Liberal Senator Cory Bernadi. See 'Lib demands sharia banking is kept out', *The Australian*, 2 November 2010.

28 A comment made by Lord Turner, the chairman of the UK Financial Services Authority, in a 'searing critique of the industry', in 'Financial Services Authority chairman backs tax on "socially useless" banks', *Guardian*, 27 August 2009.

29 'FSA bans short-selling of banks', *Financial Times*, 19 September 2008.

30 A comprehensive description of Sharia law is well outside the scope of this book. For a layman's introduction, see Sadakat Kadri, *Heaven on Earth: A Journey Through Shari'a Law* (Bodley Head, 2011).

31 Sunan An-Nasai, Hadith 3057/Vol.3 Book 24 Hadith 3059 from English translation (Darussalam, 2007) and Sunan ibn Majah 3029.

Index